W9-BMZ-312

Best of Enemies

Best of Enemies

the memoirs of

BASSAM ABU-SHARIF
AND UZI MAHNAIMI

LITTLE, BROWN AND COMPANY
Boston New York Toronto London

FIRST AMERICAN EDITION

ISBN 0-316-00401-4
Library of Congress Catalog Card Number 95-77465

10 9 8 7 6 5 4 3 2 1

MV-NY

Published simultaneously in Canada by Little, Brown & Company (Canada) Limited

Printed in the United States of America

Acknowledgements

Marie Colvin, of the London *Sunday Times*, was generous enough (as usual) to introduce two of her friends: Bassam Abu-Sharif and Uzi Mahnaimi. From this meeting, another friendship developed, which in turn led to the writing of this book.

The writer Shirley Eskapa was the first to encourage the idea of *Tried By Fire*, and put us in touch with our agent, Mark Lucas. In the last year and a half we have learned from Mark that, even without a background in espionage and terrorism, one can still be remarkably persuasive. And through Mark, we met our publisher Alan Samson, from whom we learned that professionalism is the best way to cope with obstacles during the run-up to publication.

And most importantly, we would like to thank William Pearson, without whom this book would not have been written, and also Kate Hayden, for her invaluable editorial help.

Uzi Mahnaimi and Bassam Abu-Sharif
June 1995

PREFACE

 — decorative divider

When I began writing about the Middle East in the mid-1980s, one question kept puzzling me. Why could two peoples as individually warm and talented as Israelis and Palestinians not find a way to end their bitter differences?

In time, I learnt the answer to this puzzle. Men do not make history on a clean slate. They are all in some way the prisoners of the circumstances they inherit from their fathers and grandfathers. In the following pages two exceptional men – bitter enemies in war – tell the story of how they broke out of old patterns of thinking, learnt to understand the problems of the enemy, and eventually became personal friends in the cause of peace.

Uzi Mahnaimi, the son of a general, was a young Israeli soldier when he fought for the first time, in the Yom Kippur war of 1973. In 1982 he was with the spearhead Israeli column that battled its way into Beirut to evict Yasser Arafat's Palestine Liberation Organisation. For many years he worked for military intelligence. His speciality was the shadowy and dangerous game of recruiting Arab spies for Israel.

Bassam Abu-Sharif is one of the most charismatic Palestinian leaders of his generation. He helped to mastermind many terrorist spectaculars, including the multiple hijacking of three airliners to Dawson's Field in Jordan in 1970. He was considered so dangerous by the Mossad, Israel's secret service, that in 1972 it sent a parcel bomb, disguised as a book on Che Guevara, to his office in Beirut. It blew up in his face, removing fingers and an eye. Miraculously, he survived.

But Uzi and Bassam turned out to have two things in common. First, they were patriots, each of whom wanted the best for their own nation. But as they fought they became more and more curious about the other side – and increasingly convinced of the need for an historic compromise between the two peoples. The second thing they had in common was that each was, in his own way, a rebel.

Uzi came from a military family. Yet he quit military intelligence to become a journalist, and he angered many Israelis by going to Tunis to conduct one of the first-ever Israeli interviews with Yasser Arafat and publish the views of the arch-enemy on the front page of his newspaper. As for Bassam, his was one of the first voices within the PLO to call for what once seemed impossible: an agreement to share Palestine between two states, an Israeli and a Palestinian one. For this treason he was denounced by many comrades in the PLO. The Abu Nidal group, one of the deadliest Palestinian factions, threatened to kill him.

By the mid-1990s, relations between Arabs and Israelis had changed beyond recognition. Yitzhak Rabin, Israel's prime minister, has shaken Yasser Arafat's hand on the lawn of the White House. But the story that follows is not a book of theories about diplomacy or the doings of politicians. Uzi and Bassam speak honestly about war, and about how two fighting men in the end conquered personal hatreds and came together to struggle for peace. To this day, the struggle continues.

Peter David
The Economist
June 1995

PROLOGUE
Beirut, 25 July 1972

Bassam Abu-Sharif

I t was very strange. That morning, I behaved in a way that was completely out of character. Usually I got to the offices of *Al–Hadaf*, on West Beirut's Corniche Mazraa, at about eleven. On this day, I awoke at six. I was thinking about Rassan. It was about two weeks since they had killed him. I felt his loss, both as a friend and as a colleague.

My driver was a brave man; he had to be. Like all the other PFLP drivers, he kept the car overnight. The idea was coldly utilitarian: if Mossad had planted a delayed-action bomb in the car, it would most likely explode as he drove across town to pick me up.

At seven-thirty, when I'd finished breakfast, my bodyguard asked if we should wait until the driver came at the normal time of about half-past ten. 'No,' I replied. 'Let's call for a taxi.' Against his advice, I insisted on going to the office at once. It was as if I were being guided to a particular fate.

I was reading through the newspapers, not in my own office but in the post-room next door, when the post arrived. We had an agreement with the Lebanese government that all our mail be put through the explosives detection system at the Central Post Office. When it had been through the detection machine, it was stamped to show that it had been checked and cleared as safe. The postman put a large brown package down on a table. 'Bassam,' he called over to me. 'You've got a present – looks like a book.' I moved slowly across the room, still scanning the newspaper, and glanced down at the parcel. It had my full name clearly written across the outside, in Arabic, in bright green ink. I was astonished to see that it carried my full name: Bassam Towfik Abu-Sharif. Very few people, even among my friends, knew my father's name, Towfik. The parcel was clearly marked with the crucial stamp: 'Inspected for explosives' and the day's date.

I was curious to see what kind of book it was. It was very thick. The flap of the bulky envelope was already open and the book was protruding a little. Reading upside down, I could make out the words, 'Che Guevara'. Now I was really curious. Books about Guevara were extremely rare, and I'd never found more than the odd pamphlet about him. He had been a big hero of mine when I was a teenager and cutting my political teeth. Still standing, holding the newspaper in my right hand, I eased the book out of its packaging. Casually, I began leafing through the pages to see what it was like. The book had a hard cover. Oddly, the first twenty pages or so were uncut. I lifted the uncut section. Underneath, I saw that the book was hollow. There were two explosive charges in this hollow space, wired to go off when the uncut section of the book was lifted.

I had just lifted it.

Best of Enemies

CHAPTER
ONE

Uzi Mahnaimi

M y grandfather's name was 'Peace', to which he might have added: 'Love'. He was born in 1895, with the world shouting change in his ears. All about him was revolution. The first aeroplane shook free of the earth when he was seven; when he was ten, the crew of the Russian battleship *Potemkin* mutinied, murdering most of the officers. Beneath a thin crust of calm, Europe was seething. The Ottoman Empire was unravelling, the Austro-Hungarian Empire was in ferment. The embers of nationalism were everywhere smouldering. The old power-blocks that had kept peace for much of the nineteenth century were beginning to implode – and to explode. It wanted only a touch-paper; in Sarajevo it was shortly to come.

In every way, the new century set its face against the old. Abstraction was born in art, modernism in architecture; women were fighting for – and sometimes winning – the vote.

For a young man like Shalom Kreiner growing up in this environment, standing still wasn't really an option: it was only

1

a question of which way he would jump. In 1912, at the age of seventeen, he made his leap: to Palestine.

Siauliai – 'Shivoli' – where our family lived in northern Lithuania, was inside the Pale of Settlement. The 'Pale' was an area of Russia where Jews were obliged to live by law: they were not allowed to leave it without express permission. Originally a large area stretching from the Baltic coast down into Ukraine, the Pale was large for a ghetto, but it was still a ghetto. As the years went on, the Pale was made smaller and smaller. Jews inside the Pale were subjected to horrible repression under the Tsars. Nineteenth-century Russia had a long history of murdering and assaulting Jews, of stealing their property and wealth, of blackmail and extortion, of random evictions and routine humiliation. Restrictions inside the Pale varied from area to area, but it was almost always impossible for Jews to get any kind of government job, or to have their children educated in a state school. There was a conscription quota for the Imperial Tsarist army, which the Jewish community had to fill in the cruellest possible way: by choosing among their own children. Jews had no political rights; they could not even vote for their local councils. They were forbidden to marry when young; and Jews officially had to use either the Russian or Lithuanian languages.

My grandfather, very exceptionally, went to a Hebrew school in Shivoli. He was the first in our family for centuries to speak the ancient language. His own father, a Rabbi, spoke only Yiddish. Shalom grew up not only speaking, but reading and writing Hebrew, just as Jews had done in the thirteenth century AD, or the third BC.

The seeds of Zionism were being sown.

When Tsar Alexander II was assassinated in 1881, the Jews were blamed. Anti-Jewish violence flared up again. This renewed anti-Semitism, combined with economic hardship and disease, sparked a huge wave of Jewish emigration. By the beginning of the First World War, more than two million Jews had left their Russian Pale for good.

My grandfather was one of them.

Shalom looked around him as he grew up, and liked nothing of what he saw. A glance at his history books told him there would never be peace and security for Jews anywhere, ever, unless they had their own country to live in. He could not hold up his head and be a free man. He had no pride in being Jewish. He rejected his father's religion, and despised those who accepted repression. While the Bolsheviks banished the Tsars, he would cast out the Jew in him. He would become a new model Hebrew. He would build a new country, where there would be no more of the ghetto, where he would find dignity and strength, and live as a normal person, in a nation that was like any other.

Shalom had a dream.

In 1912, Shalom told his parents he was leaving home. It was an act of extreme rebellion, even allowing for the excitement of the age. He had found out about immigration to a new place, where the Jews had ancient historical roots: the Holy Land. Though he rejected their religion he saw no contradiction in looking to the land of Canaan, where the Jews had lived long before the Romans came and drove them out, as his natural and rightful homeland. He was still, when it came right down to it, a Jew.

Shalom called this new place *Eretz Israel* – 'The Land of Israel'. The rest of the world called it Palestine.

As he was still a minor, he needed parental consent to leave home. His father refused absolutely to give it or to help him in any way. But Shalom's mother, my own great-grandmother, understood his drive to live as a free man. By pretending that he was going to visit relatives, she succeeded in wringing permission from the Tsarist authorities for her son to travel outside the Pale.

They went together to have his photograph taken, then to the local police chief who, because he was dealing with Jews, demanded a huge bribe before he would verify the snapshot

3

as a true likeness by signing it on the back. Armed with his primitive Tsarist passport, Shalom set out on one of the greatest adventures in the history of the world. He had no intention of ever coming back.

He travelled by rail through Vilnius and Minsk, then all the way down through Byelorussia and the Ukraine to the Black Sea port of Odessa. There, he took ship for the Holy Land.

The steamer took him first across the Black Sea to Constantinople, then through the Bosphorus into the Sea of Marmara. The weather grew warmer and the ports more exotic, filled with teeming life and the babble of strange tongues. For the first time in his life, Shalom felt truly free on the ship, as free as the sea-birds wheeling across its wake. Down through the Dardanelles he travelled, into the clear blue waters of the Aegean, and out at last into the Mediterranean and his final stopping-place, the port of Jaffa, on the coast of modern-day Israel.

A young boy, clutching the suitcases filled with the warm clothes his mother fondly imagined he would need, he stepped down from the packet-boat into the 38-degree heat of the summer of 1912. Shalom was amazed by what he saw, heard and ate. The heat, noise and dust were overwhelming. The dockside teemed with Arabs, in their distinctive head-dresses called *kaffiyehs* and the flowing robes they called *jellabas*. Fishermen, traders, street-vendors and hawkers of every kind shouted incomprehensible cries. The whole town, apart from the port, seemed to be made up of gloomy, narrow alleys, winding confusingly round a hill. Everything was strange. Even the sun knew no restraint, plunging into the sea so that day turned to night in the twinkling of an eye. Shalom had never seen, let alone eaten, a tomato. An Arab street-vendor offered him one. Biting into it, Shalom was sure its squelchy innards must be rotten; he spat it on the ground, retching in disgust.

After a couple of nights' rest in the Haim Baroch travellers' hostel, Shalom Kreiner joined up with a few other like-minded pioneers. With only the vaguest idea of where they were going,

4

lacking even a map, this motley crew of fresh-faced adventurers set off east on foot into the interior of Palestine. Hope travelled with them.

After several days of backbreaking travel over the roughest of rough country, they arrived in Upper Galilee, a few miles from the border with today's Lebanon. They were utterly unprepared for what they found.

School was the sum of their experience. But they were armed with a supreme determination: where the old Jew fiddled, they would farm; where the old Jew scrabbled for a penny, they would work the honest soil. My grandfather had never touched a hoe in his life: he might not even have seen one. Brought up near the Baltic coast, he knew more about living off the sea than off the land. He was attempting something quite extraordinary, almost impossible – to break the mould of history, to create a new race from the old, in the space of a single generation. The hectic spirit of the new millennium bubbled irrepressibly in his blood. As he went, he burned his bridges behind him. Even his given name, Kreiner, was discarded. In its place he adopted the name of the first acres he tried to farm in Upper Galilee: 'Mahnaim'. This Biblical name, in English, means simply, 'Two Camps'. 'Two Camps' is a pretty strange name, even if you are bent on becoming a new model Hebrew. I carry it to this day.

Mahnaim was a forsaken expanse of mosquito-infested marshland and bitter swamp, in the foothills of the Golan Heights, off the main road between Damascus and the ancient town of Sephat. Here Shalom and his companions pitched their tents.

They were utterly disappointed. In their dream, the river Jordan flowed swift and strong, like the broad Russian rivers of their homelands, through fertile fields of waving yellow corn. The trees sagged with fruit. It was a land of milk and honey. But instead of a great rushing torrent, what they saw from the banks of the biblical river, when they finally reached their Promised Land, was a miserable trickle of brackish green-brown water meandering its way through a bog.

The land had already been abandoned twice, by previous would-be farmers who had found it impossible to work. Though it was harsh and unforgiving, the landscape around was not entirely empty. The odd group of semi-nomadic Arab tribesmen would appear on horseback from time to time, brandish their flintlocks in the direction of the camp, fire off the odd shot, then disappear back into the wilderness. My grandfather had brought some money along, which was as well, for he needed it to survive those first few horrible weeks. The group's attempts at cultivation were a disaster. The whole tiny community clubbed together to buy basic equipment for farming, but the earth was infertile, undrained and intractable. They had to fight for what little drinkable water there was with the local Arab villagers. The weather was appalling: freezing in winter, roasting in summer, when they suffered terribly from sun-stroke. They had no common language with the Arabs. They led a miserable existence.

At the end of the first year, they looked around them and took stock. For every ten pioneers who had landed in Palestine with Shalom, nine had given up, or died. Malaria, typhus and cholera took their toll – as did suicide. Many could take neither the bitter reality of their new lives, nor the prospect of returning home, thus admitting failure to their parents and to themselves. Even death was preferable to that.

My grandfather struggled on, with a handful of dogged survivors. They began to adapt. Mimicking the Arab tribesmen about them, they plucked some savagery from the harsh landscape. They learned to ride the wild Arab ponies, bought themselves rifles, slung long bandoleers stuffed with gleaming cartridges over their Russian-made shirts, protected their skulls from the summer sun with *kaffiyehs*, and themselves from the Arab marauders by shooting at them.

This breed, the ten per cent who stuck it out in Palestine through those dismal early years, were to become the hard core of the future Israel. They would never abandon the dream. As tough and unyielding as the land around them, they were the fittest, and they survived. They took heart for the future from the Balfour Declaration of November 1917, issued by the British government, which 'viewed with favour . . . the establishment in Palestine of a national home for the Jewish people . . .'

By 1917 my grandfather and those who had stuck it out with him had already made it home.

Bassam Abu-Sharif

I have a thousand graves to visit in Jerusalem. And each of those graves has been filled in the wars against Israel.

Until the Zionists came, the Abu-Sharif family had lived in Jerusalem for the better part of 500 years. We traced our line back to the Fatimid dynasty, which descended from the Prophet through his daughter, Fatima. The Fatimids, who were Shi'ites, flourished in the tenth century AD, conquering much of what is now Tunisia, eastern Algeria, Egypt, Morocco and Sicily. Overthrown by the extraordinary Sunni leader Saladin (Salah–al–din al–Ayyoubi) in 1171, the Fatimids dispersed, in the case of my own tribe to Yemen. From that country, in the fifteenth century, a number of the Abu-Sharifs moved to Jerusalem, where they established themselves.

Our traceable history goes back through Sheik Al–Islam Kamal El Deen Abu-Sharif, son of Prince Nasir'ideen Mohammed, son of Abu Bakr, son of our most illustrious ancestor Prince Ali Abu-Sharif al–Magdesi A'Shaafii, who was born in the year 1490 and died in 1562. He was named President of the Salahiya College, the best university of those days, by the Ottoman Sultan of that time. Later, in 1552, he was appointed Grand Mufti of Egypt.

My own great-grandfather, Khalil Abu-Sharif, became head

of what was then the only University of Islamic Studies, in Jerusalem, in 1882. In recognition of his regal Fatimid ancestry, he was awarded the title of Sheik. As head of the Abu-Sharif family, which occupied large areas of land in the villages to the north of Jerusalem, Khalil oversaw the management of the family farming interests. We grew fruit; mainly apples, grapes and dates.

Our family is no exception among Palestinians in regarding the 1917 Balfour Declaration, with its promise of a Jewish homeland in Palestine, as a very serious crime. Balfour's letter gave encouragement to an illegal process.

Because of it, we were to lose everything.

CHAPTER
TWO

Uzi Mahnaimi

Packing up their meagre belongings, Shalom and the other pioneers set out in 1913 to find a better place to farm. To the south-west of the Sea of Galilee, about 50 miles from Mahnaim, they came upon a plug of ancient rock. From the distance, shimmering in the heat, it rose up out of the land like a Crusader castle. It was a natural focus, an impressive feature in this low, otherwise flat, landscape. Upon this new place they bestowed the name 'Merhavia', joining the Hebrew words *Merhav*, 'the space', and *ia*, 'God'.

Here, in their space of God, the tiny band of adventurers began to thrive, and grow in number. Within a few months they had the beginnings of a more successful farming co-operative. The milk and honey still refused to flow, but it was a happier place, which repaid their investment and effort. They had founded the first Hebrew settlement in *Emek Izrael*, 'The valley God will plant'. It was the beginning of modern Israel.

Merhavia was right next to the old Arab village of Solem, itself built on the site of an ancient Muslim fortress. It was

9

not pretty. There were two big problems for the pioneers in their new place: the locals and the Turks. The Arabs – both the nomads and those who lived in the tiny, scrappy villages like Solem – viewed the new arrivals with suspicion and hostility.

The Zionist pioneers believed in freedom – in love, as in all things. They had simply abandoned the conventional institutions of marriage. For them, the codes and mores of a suffocating bourgeois nineteenth-century past were no longer relevant. The local Arab villagers saw that the Zionist women were uncovered: not just bare-headed, but baring their legs and shoulders to the sun as they worked in the fields, quite brazenly. On top of that, they drank alcohol, and were not attached, necessarily, to any one man. They were liberated women, equal in almost every way to their men-folk. This, to the surrounding Palestinians, was disgusting. It was as if an early form of hippie commune had landed suddenly in the middle of their traditional society. They could not accept it. Why should they?

From the first, there were clashes between the two sides. The Arabs excelled as horsemen, and were skilled in the use of guns. Before coming to the Holy Land, my grandfather, like most of his companions, had never touched a gun in his life. But after a few Arab raids, in which things like their stores of hay were looted, they decided to form a self-defence force. Battle was joined.

In the run-up to the First World War, Palestine was still ruled by a type of absolute Turkish monarch known, quaintly enough, as the Sublime Porte. The seat of his authority, crumbling gradually under the weight of the centuries and the attack of the Young Turks movement, was in Constantinople. The local Ottoman governor in Nazareth, about five miles from Merhavia, was firmly against non-Muslim interlopers on his territory and encouraged the Arab attacks. He also refused to let the pioneers put up solid buildings, on the grounds that Merhavia was 'too close to the railway line between Mecca and Damascus'. As the main means of transporting Ottoman troops and supplies, he told them, it had strategic value. On top of that, the railway line was holy to the Turks, as it was to all Muslims. It came from the holiest site in Arabia, the home of the faith: Mecca. The words of the Prophet sang along its tracks.

Then Europe's feudal rulers blundered into war.

The first the Merhavians knew about it was when a large detachment of Turkish soldiers marched into their camp one morning. They commandeered all the community's livestock: horses for the cavalry, donkeys for use as pack animals. Worse, they plundered all the food-stocks.

The Turks came back, again and again. They took everything, they made life hell. The pioneers, clinging on with their broken, grubby fingernails, knew they could not survive. But, just as even Shalom was on the point of giving up, the strangest of all guardian angels stepped in to protect them: the Germans.

One day in the autumn of 1917, a German biplane settled gently on the flat ground below the main group of Zionist cabins. Eight more aircraft alighted in its wake. Shalom looked on in amazement. The Bavarian 304 Squadron of the Königlich Bayerische Fliegertruppen, part of Kaiser Wilhelm's air force, had arrived in Merhavia.

The German squadron came equipped with three Albatros DIII fighter planes and six Rumpler CIV photographic reconnaissance aircraft. Shortly after they had landed, a long column of German airmen marched up from the nearby railhead, laden down with all kinds of equipment. It was obvious they were planning on a long stay: there were tanners and boot-makers, cooks and farriers, coopers and mechanics and engineers, tradesmen of every calling.

With the Turkish star fast on the wane, the Germans had been looking to fill the vacuum. They wanted their 'Place in the Sun'. But at the third battle of Gaza, the British General Allenby's troops finally broke the will and the resistance of the

Turks. The Germans fell back with their allies. The Bavarian 304 Squadron, it so happened, fell back on Merhavia.

On arrival, the Germans kicked all the single men in Merhavia out of their homes. Shalom and the other bachelors were thunderstruck. When they had all been bundled out of their tiny cabins and shacks, the German officers calmly moved in.

With the arrival of some German muscle, the local Turkish governor in Nazareth saw his opportunity to crush the Zionists once and for all. He stepped up his raids on the camp. Turkish infantry came in the middle of the night, smashing their way into the cabins, uprooting tents, ransacking and looting, on the pretext of searching for hidden weapons. Anybody caught with a weapon was put up against a wall and shot. But the Merhavians knew that if they surrendered their weapons, they would be at the mercy of the Arabs. The governor knew this perfectly well, too; Arab attacks always increased in frequency following a Turkish raid.

But then a very strange thing happened – strange, that is, in the light of what would happen in Germany some twenty years later – the Germans stepped in to defend what they'd dubbed *Die Kolonie* – 'the Colony'.

From the first, the German airmen, who were a long way from their native Bavaria, had taken a liking to the pioneers. They discovered that many of the 'Colony', who were white-skinned northern Europeans like themselves, spoke German. Not only that, but there were women in Merhavia – interesting, attractive, liberated women. Contacts, at first frosty, grew slowly warmer.

The squadron's Commanding Officer, Hauptmann Walz, had a particularly good reason for disliking his Arab neighbours. Shortly after arriving in Merhavia, he went for a walk and, breasting a low rise, stumbled straight into a Bedu encampment. Two of the Bedu men leapt on him and beat him to the ground with sticks. They took everything, including his clothes, leaving him bound and naked. He was rescued several hours later by a search party.

Walz told his men to protect the whole of Merhavia, including the pioneers, from Arab attack. After a few exchanges of fire, the raids tailed off.

Next, the Germans took on the Turks. When a squad of Turkish soldiers turned up as usual one bright winter morning in 1917 to conduct yet another 'search' for hidden weapons, Walz and a fellow officer strode up and commanded the Turks to stop. They stopped. And they did not come again. For the Zionists, the German intervention was little short of a miracle.

On 24 December 1917 there had been no flying for several days because of persistent fog and rain. Teaming up with some colony members to form a little theatre company, a few of the Bavarian airmen put on a festive revue satirising the squadron's activities and personalities. My grandfather played his balalaika. A roaring success, this Christmas show brought the two communities even closer together.

Though the Germans had made them physically secure, there was still one problem for the colony: theft. One night Moshe Segalovitch, a friend of Shalom's standing sentry duty, caught a man from the nearby Arab village of Solem in the act of stealing. There was a fight. The Arab took a blow, but got away. Two days later, Segalovitch was shot dead in an ambush. A companion recognised the attacker as the very same thief Segalovitch had caught in the night.

Hauptmann Walz, who liked Segalovitch, was furious when he heard what had happened. The day after the killing, as dawn was breaking, he ordered two of his pilots into the air. At the same time he marched a squad of his men down to Solem. With them, the Germans took a couple of Spandau machine-guns. They spread out and surrounded the Arab village.

Walz called the head men of Solem before him. When they were assembled, he glared at them. 'Bring me the man who ambushed Moshe Segalovitch, or suffer the consequences,' he snapped. The villagers spread their hands. They knew nothing of any murder. 'Bring me the suspect now,' shouted

Walz, 'or I will make you bring him. You have two minutes.'

At the end of the two minutes, they were all still standing there, as if frozen in a tableau. From the pocket of his tunic Walz took out a small signalling mirror. Raising his arm, he tilted the silvered glass until its surface caught the bright rays of the early morning sun.

When he saw the heliograph flash, one of the circling pilots overhead dropped his aircraft's nose. It had a 10-kilogram bomb strapped under a wing, which exploded with a shattering roar at the very edge of the village. The people had never seen or heard anything like this.

Terrified by this awesome display of power, they did not wait for a repeat performance but ran at full speed to a nearby house. In the house was a barrel of flour. Inside that the wanted man was cowering. The villagers dragged him out, screaming and cursing, by the hair. They frog-marched him over to Walz and threw him at the Hauptmann's feet. Two German airmen grabbed hold of the Arab and tied his hands.

It was hard to say whether it was the flour that made the man's face so white, or his fear.

There were no more thefts from Merhavia.

For the next few months, my grandfather and his friends farmed in peace and tranquillity under German protection. But the Bavarian 304 Squadron was very busy. With the war in its final stages, the Germans were watching anxiously for signs of enemy troop movements. They knew the British were coming, but they didn't know when, or how.

They were very soon to find out.

At first light on 19 September 1918, a strange-looking biplane droned into view. It made a couple of slow passes over the German aircraft lined up neatly on the runway. The lone German airman standing sentry stared skywards. He was still trying to decide what to do when an older pilot, who had seen action on the Western front, peered blearily round his tent-flap. What he saw shocked him to instant wakefulness. Snatching up his helmet and goggles, he began racing for his Albatros fighter shouting, '*Raus! Raus! Englander!*' at the top of his voice.

It was too late.

The strange aircraft, an SE5a of the Royal Flying Corps, was already turning into its attack run. The young British pilot at the controls could hardly believe his luck. He had taken off on a scouting mission, and here were all these pointy-nosed German aircraft lined up for him like tasty plump peapods. This was going to be fun!

Kicking his rudder a couple of times, he pushed his machine into a shallow dive. As the first of the Rumplers swam up into his gunsight, he squeezed his trigger. Bright little orange flashes flickered from the Vickers machine-gun. Firing in short, pithy little bursts, he shot his way carefully along the line of parked aircraft.

Bullets plucked holes in the tightly-stretched fabric of the planes. One Albatros fighter collapsed as its wheel-struts splintered under the impact of the shells, its wings folding lazily skywards. Two of the Rumplers caught fire. Pinned down next to his machine, the pilot who had tried to raise the alarm took a bullet through the back of his thigh.

The war really had arrived in Merhavia.

Next day, the British Empire followed up its airborne calling-card. A squadron of slouch-hatted Australian mounted infantry wheeled into view at the end of the airstrip. Men of the famous Anzac Light Horse, the Aussies rode at a walk through the camp, looking curiously about them. There was very little left to see. The Germans had received an intelligence warning that not just one squadron, but an entire wing of British aircraft – three squadrons, including some of the new Handley-Page bombers – was headed their way. Taking discretion as the better part of valour, they packed up and departed in the night. Before they left, the Germans set fire to everything they were unable to take with them. The remnants of their abandoned equipment and damaged aircraft were still smoking when the Light Horse arrived.

For my grandfather and the others, the arrival of the British was an unqualified disaster. Their new masters simply assumed the colony was German. After all, hardly anyone spoke English. The British troops rounded up my grandfather and the other men at gunpoint, and marched them over to the deserted Turkish army compound in Solem.

Here, amid all the muddy shambles of the hasty Turkish retreat, Shalom and his comrades were imprisoned under close guard. Seeing that their long-time foes were now unable to defend their belongings, the Arab villagers swept into Merhavia in the night. They stripped the place virtually bare.

After a few days the British realised their mistake, and released all their prisoners. But for my grandfather and his comrades, surveying the wrecked and looted shells of their homes, the defeat and departure of their German allies was the end of the road. Everything they had worked for was destroyed, shattered, gone. Packing up what few possessions remained to them, they quit Merhavia for good. They moved just a few miles north, to join a much better defended Zionist community.

Ironically, given what had just happened, the new place was named after the British Foreign Secretary who had so recently made a declaration favouring the Jews. It was called Balfouria.

CHAPTER
THREE

Bassam Abu-Sharif

W hen he was eight years old my father, Towfik Abu-
Sharif, was taken by his parents for the first time to the
madafeh in his home village, just north of Jerusalem. His father
was the largest landowner in the surrounding district, and the
head man of the village. My grandmother was the village wise
woman, who used plant-remedies to treat the community's sick
and injured.

The *madafeh* was the meeting-place where the villagers
discussed the problems of the day in council. In that year,
1922, the council's talk was all of Jewish immigration. It had
been worrying the villagers for years. It was worrying them now
more than ever.

'When the Jews first came here, we felt sorry for them,'
my grandfather began. 'They were sad people, they were
oppressed. We opened our schools to them, so they could
find shelter there. But now we see their aims: they want
our lands, they want to rule us – perhaps they even want
us out altogether.' There was a murmur of agreement from

17

the assembly. 'The British are helping the Jews to take our country from us,' said another man. 'They give the Jews arms and ammunition; they train the Jews; they help them to settle. What can we do? We must do something.'

My grandfather led a delegation to Jerusalem to petition the British authorities. 'Under British rule,' they said, 'it is illegal for an Arab to carry arms. It is not illegal for a Jew to carry arms. You give Arabs caught with weapons long terms in prison. Why do you not do the same to Jews?'

This injustice, and many others like it, heated the blood of my grandfather and his peers. The British made soothing noises. They promised that something would be done soon about Jewish encroachment into Arab lands, they said they would limit the ever-increasing number of Jews coming into Palestine. They did nothing.

Every year, violence between Arab and Jew escalated. By 1929, the whole of Arab Palestine was in full-blooded revolt – against the British Mandate *and* the Jews. And it was not only the Arabs who were up in arms: in the cities, especially Hebron, Jaffa and Jerusalem, the Jews were attacking Arabs in their homes. The war for Palestine was beginning in earnest.

My father Towfik by then was a fifteen-year-old boarder at Rouda College in Jerusalem. He was not allowed out of school without permission. Everywhere there was violence and blood. The new Jewish settlements in the city abutted the old Arab quarters, so that there was no escaping the circle of terror. The only answer the British could come up with to the bloodshed was more bloodshed. Their only remedy to the unrest was to shoot Arab demonstrators. On one of his rare trips outside the school, Towfik saw two British soldiers shoot an unarmed Arab in a disturbance near the Damascus gate. They threw the badly injured man onto a horse-drawn cart. By the time he arrived at the hospital, he was dead.

When he was nineteen, my father went on to study at the American University of Beirut (AUB). In 1936, in his third year at the AUB, there was a general strike in Palestine and a second nationwide Arab revolt. If anything, the violence was even worse than it had been in 1929.

Like many of his fellow-students, my father felt he must return home to defend his country. Many of his classmates did go. But a tutor persuaded Towfik to finish his final year. He was not, when it came right down to it, a man of war. His chubby face concealed a piercing intellect, but it also spoke the truth about his nature. He was a jolly man, and a gentle man. He was a man of peace. I hope I am like him.

Uzi Mahnaimi

Nine years after he arrived in Balfouria, Shalom Mahnaimi met the woman who would become my grandmother. Like him, Hannah Ilgovsky was from Lithuania, but she came from a much wealthier background. Her brother David was a millionaire property developer. David doted on his clever sister, and could not reconcile himself to her departure from the family home. He arrived in Balfouria in 1928, when he heard that Hannah had given birth to her first child – my father, Gideon.

David took one look at the dirt-poor conditions Shalom and his sister were living in, and threw up his hands in horror. His cherished baby sister – how could she possibly be languishing with a new-born baby in this muddy hole, 'Balfouria', married to a big-eared socialist with nothing in his pocket and a head full of dreams?

David began plotting to subvert Shalom's dogged idealism. He proposed planting a citrus farm, with my grandfather as its general manager. Shalom would oversee and manage the plantation; and Hannah would live in a nice new home, built by David, in the style and comfort she was accustomed to.

Shalom resisted. He was a poor Zionist and a socialist. But, above all, he was a man of spirit, a man who kept watch on his own special dream. If he accepted, he would be secure for life. But what would he lose? David tried to put pressure on him: 'Look how badly Hannah's health has suffered in this damp,' he said. 'And she's just had a baby. She would be so much better off in a new home. Come, surely you can't refuse to do what is best for her? You love her, don't you?'

Shalom, although moved by this moral blackmail, would not give in. He resisted for four long years. But at last he agreed. David built Hannah a huge villa in Rehovot, then a very small town south-east of Tel Aviv. No more discomfort, no more danger: Rehovot was a world away from the hard-core Zionist communities of the *Izrael* valley. The new house had every modern convenience. The citrus groves flourished and made money; my grandmother's health improved.

But what of Shalom Mahnaimi? Fired with the unquenchable spirit of the very first pioneers, a fighter for the new land of Israel – what had he become? A farm manager, a man at arm's length from the land he loved so much. He realised too late how right he had been to resist the money.

At the age of thirty-seven and for twenty years a Zionist pioneer, my grandfather was still in his prime.

But his life was over.

Bassam Abu-Sharif

My father came back home to Jerusalem in 1937 with a first-class degree in Economics in his pocket. He was plunged straight back into the whirlpool of Jewish–Arab violence. He joined the Palestine Arab Party, signed petitions, wrote to the Mandate, raised nationalist consciousness in his home village. But the lure of a job, at a time of vicious unemployment, was overwhelming. He had passable English. He was widely-read in classical Arabic literature, and an expert on Arab customs and folklore. Offered an announcer's job with the Arab section of the Palestine Broadcasting Service, he took it. The radio station was run by the very people he mistrusted most – the British.

The three sections of the service – Jewish, British and Arab – shared the same handsome Jerusalem building. But while Towfik broadcast his talks on Arab lore and traditions, his country burned.

The British cracked down hard on the 1936 Arab rebellion. By 1939, their search and destroy operations had just about put paid to any organised Arab activity. But they did not quell Jewish acts of terror. Jewish terrorists who objected to 'British propaganda' on the radio planted a bomb in the studio next to my father's. The Englishwoman who made the children's programmes was killed outright. The explosion also blew both legs off an Arab engineer, Najib Mansour, who had been a friend of my father's. Mansour died from loss of blood.

As the British prepared to pull out of Palestine, the bitterness simmering between Arab and Jew came to the boil. By the beginning of 1948, war was inevitable.

Uzi Mahnaimi

A small piece of roughly-printed cardboard, about two inches by one, was all that saved my grandmother and Gideon from the ovens of Auschwitz.

Every summer, Hannah took her son off for a long holiday in Lithuania, to escape the murderous heat of Palestine. A child of the wind and the sun, of the Middle East, my father was utterly different from his cousins in the Baltic. He lived like a little Arab boy: he ran about barefoot, he was always climbing trees, he was mischievous. He was not interested in being indoors, in playing parlour games, in music or in reading books. He was a little pagan. He was part of a new breed, the breed of my grandfather, a completely new phenomenon in Jewish history.

Shalom's dream of the strong Hebrew had come to vibrant life in the form of his own son.

Gideon's cousins despised him thoroughly for his weather-beaten urchin manners; they thought him a little Middle Eastern monkey. They couldn't understand how this tyke could possibly look so like themselves, yet be so strangely different. '*Asiat!*' they shouted after him, '*Asiat!*' ['Asian!'] But Gideon was unmoved by their taunts. He thought his cousins hot-house flowers: pasty-faced, bookish, boring. He returned their contempt with interest.

My grandmother and Gideon stayed for three months, until early September. It was almost too long. There was the smell of war in the air, rank and pestilent. Rumours had reached Hannah that a new wave of anti-Semitic persecution was brewing in Germany, not just the usual, routine harassment Jews suffered everywhere, but a kind of vast, systematic pogrom organised by a man called Adolf Hitler.

On 1 September 1939, as Hannah and Gideon were nearing the end of their holiday, fifty-three German divisions blitz-krieged their way into Poland. In Lithuania, there was chaos, and panic.

When she heard the news, my grandmother ran straight to the railway station with her little boy. She found an insane scrum of people scrabbling and even fighting to get out of the country. With the most amazing luck, and a great deal of money, she managed to buy the last two first-class tickets on a train heading south out of Kovno. It was only when she was standing crammed up with Gideon in a corridor solid with terrified people that she discovered where the train was going: to Turkey. But as long as she got herself and her child out of northern Europe, Hannah didn't care where they were going. The fear was around her heart, as dry as ice. There was that smell in the air again, the smell of war. Hannah knew.

*   *   *

My father was born to be a warrior. The violence between Arab and Jew was inescapable in his childhood, his own part in it inevitable.

But it was something infinitely worse than the outrages in Palestine that overshadowed his consciousness as he grew up: the Holocaust. All his cousins, all the little boys and girls who had teased him and called him '*Asiat*', their parents, grandparents, all his other relatives, all their friends, adults or children, it made no difference; they, and millions like them, had been murdered in the Nazi concentration camps.

When he first heard the rumours about the death-camps, Gideon found them hard to believe, as so many did. It was particularly hard to believe the numbers involved. 'Six million,' people whispered. 'Seven million Jews they killed . . . *seven million!*' How could it possibly be true? Then came the proof: the concentration camp survivors, wave after wave of them staggering dazedly into Palestine, with the hideous blue Nazi tattoos branded into the flesh of their forearms; the newsreel footage shot by British and American military cameramen, of their soldiers liberating camp after camp, Treblinka, Theresienstadt, Dachau, Belsen, Auschwitz and all the rest. It defied belief, it was impossible, but the genocide had happened.

The systematic slaughter of the Holocaust branded its horror into the minds of all those who learned about it then. It has left its indelible stain on the souls of all who are human and have learned about it since. It marked my father's mind, as it marks the mind of all Jews. To this day, I cannot bring myself to visit Germany.

Gideon reached manhood with one very strong conviction: that to survive as a Jew meant learning how to defend yourself – to the death. He trained his body hard, he ran, he lifted weights, he became as strong and as fit as he could. He knew that for him, in his turn, the test was coming.

★   ★   ★

My father's first real contact with Arabs was when he stared at them over the sights of his rifle. He didn't hate them, but he knew they wanted to throw him out. So in 1946, Gideon joined the Haganah. He was eighteen.

The Haganah was the covert Jewish defence force – covert because the British had outlawed all armed militias, Jewish or Arab. Haganah members bought, stole, smuggled, manufactured and stockpiled weapons. For long months Gideon and his colleagues trained secretly, hardening themselves physically, learning to shoot, to maintain their weapons, acquiring some basic military fieldcraft, a working knowledge of tactics. For a young man like my father, who was naturally athletic, naturally adventurous, it was all very exciting. Like his father before him, he would defend the land.

The word 'Haganah' means 'defence' in Hebrew. Its members were trained, in principle, to defend the Yishuv [the Jewish community in Palestine]; they were not trained for offensive action. Gideon accepted proudly an invitation to join the Palmah or 'shock companies', the élite unit of the Haganah. His Operational Commander was a man called Yitzhak Rabin.

As the British Mandate threw off the reins of government, the fighting intensified. At the beginning of April, with widespread Arab attacks on Jewish settlements, with Jordanian, Iraqi and Egyptian forces infiltrating Palestine, the Zionist leader David Ben-Gurion decided on a pre-emptive strike. The Haganah, some 42,000 strong, was sent into action. The cruel 'war of independence', in which one in every hundred Yishuv Jews would die, had begun.

My father was sent north into Galilee, to the ancient town of Sephat. About 1,500 Jewish people were living in the Jewish quarter under Arab siege. Gideon's job was to rescue them. Even at this stage, the Haganah troops knew they were in a war to the death. The Arabs could lose as many wars as they liked, but the first one my father lost would be his last. So the Palmah men never had the option of quitting.

My father's unit mounted a head-on frontal assault on Sephat on 6 May. The Arabs repulsed them, inflicting heavy casualties. So the Palmah resorted to guerrilla tactics. They hit hard, then melted into the thickly-wooded countryside around the town, where the steep hills, interlaced by narrow ravines, gave them plenty of cover. They placed mines to disrupt Arab troop movements, they sniped, they lobbed mortar shells, badgering the occupying Arab Salvation Army troops, whittling away at their morale.

The Palmah, though, was chronically short of weapons and ammunition. One clear starry night, Gideon was sent out on a reconnaissance mission. His patrol climbed stealthily up through the densely forested slopes to the north-west of Sephat, until they could peer down into its narrow streets. Having noted the disposition and activities of the occupying soldiers, they stole back down and across the valley below to report. The Arab positions they had carefully noted would be mortared during the course of the day. Gideon got back into the Palmah camp, worn out by his night's activities. To his utter horror, he found that the magazine of his Sten gun was missing, lost somewhere during the patrol. None of the others said anything, but he felt a hot wash of embarrassment and shame. How could he have been so stupid? The Sten was useless without its magazine. And it had been fully charged. When every bullet counted, it was a catastrophe.

Gideon began to run back through the trees towards the town. By now it was broad daylight. Approaching the Arab outposts was extremely risky, especially alone, but he felt he had to redeem himself. As he came back to the hide-out where he had been laid up with the others, he cast frantically about him, right and left. The bright morning sunlight filtering through the trees dappled the ground. In his panic, he could see nothing but the play and counter-play of light. Then, with a rush of wild relief, he saw the edge of the missing Sten magazine gleaming dull black among the litter of the undergrowth. He did not see the Iraqi sniper taking a bead on him. As Gideon bent to pick up the magazine, the Iraqi squeezed off a single shot. The bullet went in through Gideon's left forearm, and came clean out the other side. He stared for a split second at the blood spurting out of his wound, then adrenaline took over. In a flash he snatched up the magazine, turned, and ran full-tilt back down the hill, clutching the oblong piece of metal to his chest as though his life depended on it. Two hours later he stumbled back into the Palmah camp, ashen-faced, exhausted, but triumphant. His comrades caught him as his body crumpled to the ground. He might have been slightly damaged, but his honour was intact. For my father, this was the only thing that mattered.

A few days later the Palmah launched a further all-out attack on Sephat, following a short barrage. After twenty-four hours of the bloodiest house-to-house combat, they took the town.

When he was searching the offices of the departed Arab garrison, my father found a revolver, a Webley .38, in the desk of the Arab commander, Fawzi Kaoukji. I still have it.

Though they had triumphed in the north, still more work lay ahead for Gideon and his men. They were sent into battle against the Jordanians for the much larger Arab towns of Lydda and Ramle, down south near Tel Aviv. This time, although it was very fierce, the battle did not last so long: both towns fell quite soon to the Haganah forces.

The Palmah operations officer Yitzhak Rabin asked Ben–Gurion what should be done about the Arabs who were left behind in the conquered towns. They were not, after all, even on the Israeli side of the proposed UN partition line. Thinking that it would be critical for the survival of the Jewish state to enact the 'transfer policy' he had long considered, Ben–Gurion gave the nod to expel the Arabs.

The Palmah was chosen to carry out the mass expulsions. My father, by now an officer, had to lead his men into the individual Arab houses, and throw the Palestinian families out of them at gunpoint. Many of the householders refused point-blank to budge. The Palmah men systematically set about instilling panic among the Arabs. They shot into the air, kicked down barricaded doors, broke in windows with

26

their rifle-butts, exploded grenades near the homes. The people became terrified. Gideon and his squads chivvied them out, the women and children crying piteously, clutching whatever they could carry. Once evicted, they were herded into groups and told to walk east, towards the river Jordan. The summer of 1948 was a very hot one. Some of the refugees ran out of water on the way to the West Bank. Nobody cared for them. A few of them died of thirst by the roadside. In one mad scrabble for water, a small child fell down a well and perished.

Once the Arabs were out of their homes, Palmah engineers razed the buildings with bulldozers and explosives so that the refugees could never come back.

The 1948 invasion of Israel by the Arab armies was a tragedy for the 6,000 Israelis who died. It was also a tragedy, and not the first, for the Arab population of Palestine. The first big mistake of the Palestinian Arabs was their refusal to accept either the British partition plan of 1937 or the similar UN plan put forward in 1947. Either would have given them control over most of modern Israel. They rejected both plans out of hand.

CHAPTER FOUR

Bassam Abu-Sharif

In 1947, when the UN proposed the partition of Palestine, we were living in Irbid, in northern Jordan. My father had become a banker. We were out of the fighting over Palestine, and we stayed out of it.

In 1948 the victorious Israelis confiscated everything the Totahs (my maternal family) owned: all the shops, all the houses, all the land, and a small hotel, The Regent, which belonged to my uncle Youssef. My mother's family home, the home of the Totahs for generations, is still there in the Old City of Jerusalem.

An Israeli family we shall never meet now lives in it.

In 1950 we moved from Irbid, in the north of Jordan, to the capital, Amman. It was there in 1956, when I was ten, that my own political consciousness began to stir. I found the Suez war, between the British, French and Israelis on one side and the Egyptians on the other, fascinating. Up to then I had been leading a very easy and pleasant life, attending a good school and spending my time with the children of the rich. Gamal

Abd-El Nasser, the Egyptian leader, who stood up for Arab interests against the international bully-boys, was my hero. As a ten-year-old, the Palestinian question had been far from my thoughts. But, with the Suez crisis, I began to read and to interrogate my parents about our history.

It seemed to me, in my naive way, that a very serious injustice had been done to the Palestinian Arabs. Didn't they have the right to live as other people lived – at peace in their own country? It was one thing that a new state, Israel, should have been born in what I grew up calling Palestine; it was quite another that Palestine's original inhabitants should be dispossessed and forced into exile. When I asked my mother about it, I discovered that our own family was very much part of the complicated jigsaw puzzle I was trying to piece together. Some of her family's own properties, she explained, had been taken from us by the Israelis in the 1948 war. My grandfather's beautiful house, in Mea'Sharim, which happened to be in the most Orthodox Jewish sector of Jerusalem, had been stolen. The Israelis had come with guns in the night, she said. They had evicted the Arab families by terror. Israelis now farmed profitably on the Palestinian acres they had taken, used our glasses and the very dishes we had eaten from, sunned themselves in our gardens.

I thought about all this, long and hard. Our family had been driven from their lands, their homes, by force. Injustice had been piled upon violent theft. How could we Palestinians have allowed it to happen? There was now a Palestinian Diaspora, just like the Jewish one before it. Our people were scattered to the four winds.

The older I grew, the more I talked with members of my family, the more I read, the more I understood the word injustice. We must have justice, I thought; only justice. But how were we going to get this justice? That was a question to vex the thoughts of a sixteen-year-old boy. To my mind, at the time, there was only one answer. His name was Gamal Abd-El Nasser.

To most Arab youths growing up in the 1950s, Nasser represented a dream and a symbol: a symbol of Arab nationalism, a dream of Arab unity, of Arab liberation, and of Arab progress. Arabs everywhere watched the battles Nasser waged with the Western colonialist states, and fought them as their own individual battles. I imagined myself there at Nasser's side, as he did battle with the enemy for control of the Suez Canal. For me, he was the only hope we had of getting back our lands and homes. When Nasser spoke about the wrong that had been done to the Palestinians, in 1948 and since, I felt pride, and anger, and the will to act.

Abd-El Nasser was my mentor, my hero and my guiding light. By the time I went up to the American University of Beirut in 1963, I had fallen completely under his spell. I was seventeen, and spoiling for a fight. I had no need to rebel – I had a cause. Nasser-led Arab nationalism was going to save my people: and I was going to be in there at the kill. On day one on campus, I signed up with a new organisation, the Movement of Arab Nationalists (MAN). Its slogan, the recruiting officer told me, was 'Fire, Iron and Revenge'.

MAN was a very strict organisation, aspiring to a degree of physical as well as political purity. Discipline was the key-word: group members were expected to behave almost like monks. We weren't supposed to smoke or drink alcohol; we were supposed to help others, whatever that meant; we had to take and carry out orders without question; above all we should stand ready to sacrifice ourselves for our nation, for the good of the people of Palestine.

As a member of this élite order, you were banned even from drinking Coke. One day, I was strolling along with a friend when a huge arm suddenly snaked round my neck from behind. Before I knew it, I was in a stranglehold, while the man who had hold of me stamped my can of Coca-Cola flat into the ground.

'That is a product of the imperialist USA – it is filth!' snarled the huge MAN member who had me in a headlock. 'And that's the rubbish that supports the bastard Israelis. Use your head, fool!' He let me go.

In my first year with the movement, I was full of sound and fury. I did everything I could to advance the cause – distributing pamphlets, organising seminars, whipping up demonstrations. But I felt a lack of direction. Bassam Abu-Sharif wasn't exactly changing the course of history by handing out political tracts to his fellow students.

Then something happened that brought my life into much sharper focus. One morning, early, I was sitting up in bed reading when there was a knock at the door. A man stood on the threshold. I recognised him vaguely as an older student I had seen around campus. 'Come on,' he said, 'El-Hakim wants to see you.'

'Me?' I replied incredulously. 'El-Hakim wants to see me?'

'Yes,' he replied impatiently. 'Come with me now. I will wait.'

I jumped out of bed, my thoughts whirling. 'El-Hakim' was the codename used by George Habash, the secretary-general of MAN for the AUB – and Lebanon. It means 'doctor' in Arabic – Habash was a qualified doctor of medicine. Why would the leader want to see me, a tiny little cog in his machine, a babyfaced little freshman? I threw on my clothes, ran a comb through my hair and flew down the stairs after the messenger.

Following in his hurrying footsteps, I reflected on what I knew about George Habash. The intellectual circle Habash had joined in Beirut included thinkers from throughout the Arab world: Dr Ahmed al-Khatib from Kuwait, Hani al-Hindi of Syria, and a man whose brilliance gleamed among even this high-powered intellectual company, Dr Wadi Haddad. It was Haddad who had founded the political party of which I was now an eager member – MAN.

These men thought as Nasser did, as I did: that the Arabs, while they remained fragmented, would remain weak. The proof of this lay in the 1948 war. Yes, the armies of the so-called

31

Arab League had 'invaded' Israel, but it had been a half-hearted effort. There had been almost no co-operation between the various forces. Why? Because the leaders competed with one another for a hollow pre-eminence. Their narrowness and lack of vision had cost the Palestinians their country. The old guard, we reasoned, had to go. Nasser, with his dream of pan-Arab unity, would sweep them aside. The Arabs would no longer be weak. We would become strong, we would get justice for Palestine.

Habash lived in a small apartment in West Beirut, near Corniche Mazraa. Like all MAN members, he was considered an outlaw by the Lebanese government, which looked on the movement, typically, as an internal political threat. My guide and I trotted along the echoing, dawn-lit streets without a word. We halted before an unassuming apartment door, up three flights of stairs.

'Knock twice,' he said – and was gone.

Nervously I raised my hand to the door. Habash's wife, Hilda, opened it. 'Please come in,' she said warmly. 'You are welcome. Sit down. George will be out in a minute.'

When he appeared, Habash was still in his pyjamas and robe. But somehow, he had the aura of a statesman. He was calm, slow-speaking, fatherly. He radiated charisma. There was something priestly about him standing there, his robe fanned out around him. Like a priest, he believed in absolute justice; like a priest, he wanted to lead, but to keep his white robe pristine; and, like a priest, he would have to cross the swamp of ordinary human affairs, sullying the hem of his garment. He began to speak, his words measured and stately. As he wove his spell of words, he carried me with him. I thought him a romantic, but he had a will of iron.

He began quizzing me about my background and family, my hopes and aspirations: general questions meant to put me at my ease. I relaxed a bit. Then he asked me what I was intending to study. 'I have a scholarship to study medicine,' I replied.

He smiled. 'Look,' he told me, 'if you want to continue with your political life, I have to advise you that studying medicine is not the way. Anyone with an eye to the future should start studying economics.'

I thought about it. I could change disciplines after my first year, because we operated under the American system of high-school education. Hilda brought in coffee, and we began talking about current affairs. He talked, for the most part, and I listened. 'What is the really big question for the Arab mind?' he asked.

'It must always be the liberation of Palestine,' I answered.

'Yes,' replied Habash. 'We all know: only resolve this, and the other pieces of the Middle Eastern puzzle will fall into place.' I was overwhelmed; here I was discussing the future of my homeland with a man who was in direct contact with Nasser. 'What, in the end, is the best way of liberating Palestine?' continued Habash. 'Is armed struggle the best way? Is it the only way? If so, how – and when – should we go about it?' I had no answer to this one. 'Nasser's line is that starting the armed struggle now will drag Egypt into a war for which it is not ready. We should prepare for war, he says, but begin it only when the Arab armies are as one. Can he achieve Arab unity? We must wait and see. But we cannot wait for ever, do you think?'

'There is Fatah . . .' I began. 'Fatah,' said Habash, 'takes the opposite view. Yasser Arafat stands up and pokes fun at Nasser's caution. "Armed struggle now!" is his cry. But who is listening? Perhaps not even the Israelis.' He stopped.

'What do you think?' I asked him.

'I think Arafat may be right. I don't see Arab unity gleaming on the horizon, do you?'

The idea that Habash thought Nasser's agenda might be only a pipe-dream was profoundly shocking to me. It was true that the Arab world was in turmoil. That year, there had been coups d'état in both Syria and Iraq. A proposed alliance between Syria, Iraq and Egypt was causing massive political unrest in Jordan, and on the Jordanian-controlled West Bank. The demonstrators wanted Jordan and Palestine to become the fourth corner of this pan-Arab axis. But Jordan's King Hussein was absolutely opposed to this. Hundreds of people on the West Bank had been imprisoned, some even shot in the rioting.

At length, Habash came to the point. 'My son, many of our colleagues in the movement are in prison now, and their families have no money. What I would like you to do, if you will agree, is to go into Jordan and pass money to these families.'

I was very taken aback. George Habash, the leader of the Movement of Arab Nationalists, asking me, a seventeen-year-old student, to do something like this? 'Why did you choose me?' I asked him finally, to play for time.

'I asked for reports on potential candidates from people I trust in the movement. You were recommended to me as someone who's serious, as someone who's a doer. Here is a job that needs doing. You are also someone who is not known to the intelligence services in Jordan, and on top of all that,' he grinned at me, 'you look unbelievably young and innocent. You see why you are ideal for our purposes?'

I smiled rather weakly. I did indeed see. 'OK,' I told him, with my heart pounding, 'I'll do it. When do you want me to go?'

'Tomorrow.'

I went back to my room, packed my bag, and waited nervously. I lit one cigarette, then another while the first one was still burning. It was all very cloak and dagger. I would have to skip classes. How would I explain to my Mum and Dad that I was back in Jordan, when I should be at college? What would happen if I failed in my mission? Would I be drummed out of MAN? Would I be arrested, imprisoned, even tortured? After tossing and turning for a long time, I finally fell asleep. In the small hours of the night, someone knocked at my door. The stranger on the threshold passed me a small piece of paper; it had a name and a telephone number written on it. 'Go to Amman,' he told me in a low voice. 'When you get there, take a taxi to Nablus, and ring this number. Ask the name on the

paper to meet you somewhere, but not at his place. Got it?'
'Yes,' I said, I've got it.' He handed me a large brown bulging
envelope. 'There are 3,000 Jordanian dinars here,' he said,
counting the banknotes out in front of me. 'Please sign this
receipt.' I signed. In 1963, 3,000 dinars was a lot of money.
Then this man did something strange. Once the money was
safely stowed back in the envelope, he taped a small object
very carefully to the inside of the package with Scotch tape,
then sealed down the flap. 'Don't try to open it, or you will
regret it.' He smiled. He'd set a small explosive charge in with
the money. The envelope was now booby-trapped.

I'd asked my father to meet me at Amman airport, which is
about twenty miles outside the capital. When I arrived later that
morning, he was waiting for me with a big smile of welcome.
The terminal was crawling with Jordanian soldiers. 'What's
happened?' he asked me, as I came up to embrace him, his
grey eyes boring into mine. 'Why are you here?'

'Oh, it's nothing,' I replied as nonchalantly as I could. 'I
didn't have any classes for the rest of the week, so I thought I'd
go and see some friends in Nablus.' In short, I lied to him.

My father said nothing, but I knew he didn't believe me; not
for a second. 'Let's go home, then, shall we?' he said gently.

'No,' I said hastily. 'No. I have to . . . that is, could you drop
me at the taxi-station in town? I need to get down to Nablus
straight away.' We drove in silence, broken only by the need
to show our documents at the numerous army road-blocks on
the way to Amman.

When we reached the Abdali taxi-station, my father turned
to me and took me firmly by the arms. 'Take care, my son,'
he said gravely. 'These are dangerous times in Jordan. Don't
play with fire.'

I rented an ancient Chrysler taxi for the trip to Nablus. The
Jordanian army was stopping everyone on the road. They
demanded my papers, but I felt no fear. Why should they be
suspicious of me? Everything was straightforward, everything
was going like clockwork. The package felt warm in my pocket,

bomb and all. There was a small café at the taxi-station in Nablus with a black pay-phone in a booth at the back. I stuck in a *jeton*, and dialled the number on the scrap of paper.

A man's voice answered immediately. 'Mohammed Yasser?' I asked. 'I am at the taxi-station. Can you come?'

'What are you wearing?' demanded the voice on the other end of the line.

'A blazer,' I told him. 'Colour: black.'

'I'll be there in five minutes,' he said, and there was a click.

A few minutes later, a short fat man wearing a suit and tie waddled up to me. He was visibly uneasy, glancing about him all the time to see if anyone was watching us. I felt sure that anyone who *was* watching must certainly notice him. But with the nervelessness of the totally inexperienced, the serendipity of the ingénue, I felt completely relaxed. 'Hello,' he said, squeezing my hand briefly. 'Would you like some juice?' We went inside. As soon as we sat down, I reached into my pocket to give him the envelope. With an urgent flap of his hand he signed me to keep it hidden. 'Not here!' he hissed. I really was a total amateur.

We went outside after the drink. 'That is my car over there,' he said, pointing to a dusty brown Mercedes. 'Let's go for a drive.' We began a tour of Nablus, with my driver acting out a little charade, playing tourist-guide, pointing out the sites of interest. All the time, he was looking in the rear-view mirror, to see if we were being followed. When he was sure we were not, he pulled over to the side of the road, switched off the engine and turned to me. 'What?' he asked me.

'Here is the money,' I blurted, handing him the envelope. He grabbed it and dismantled the booby-trap, squirrelling the cash away into his inside jacket pocket. 'I need a receipt, please,' I told him. He wrote me the receipt. 'Would you like to stay with us one night?' he asked, to my surprise. 'No, I will go back at once,' I replied.

'OK, good,' he said. 'It is better.'

When I got back to Amman, my father was astonished to see me again. 'You said you were going to stay with friends; now

you turn up unannounced a second time on the same day!'
'Well, yes,' I mumbled, 'Umm, we spent the day together, but
I didn't much like the atmosphere. So I came back.'

'All right,' said my father. 'You are welcome. Stay. Spend a
few days with us.'

'No,' I said hurriedly, 'I'd better go back tomorrow morning,
to prepare for next week's classes . . .' I stopped, aware of
his intent gaze. On my father's face was written a very clear
statement: 'I don't believe you.' I had never before lied to him.
Now I had lied to him twice in the space of a single day. But
what I was doing for the Palestinian cause made it worth it.
Didn't it?

I arrived back in Beirut very early the next morning. Habash
had instructed me that if all went well, I was to come straight
round to his apartment from the airport. Hilda answered the
door again.

'Did it go well?' asked Habash, when we had shaken hands.

'Very well,' I replied, and told him what had happened.

He laughed when I'd related my story. 'That easy?' He
smiled.

'Yes, that easy.'

'Bravo, my son, bravo. You have done very well for us. Come
and visit me very soon. We must keep in touch.'

When I got back to my room, the realisation of what I had
just done hit me squarely in the chest. I sat down on the
bed with a thump. Most of the leading members of MAN in
Jordan were in prison. The whole organisation in Jordan was
effectively crippled. Supplying money for the cause, as I had
just done, was extremely dangerous. I got up and walked over
to the wash-basin, where there was a mirror. I looked just the
same, but I felt different. I had just completed my first mission
for George Habash. I felt I had grown up.

That was my first expedition on behalf of MAN – but it
was not my last. I spent a very politically active three years at
AUB, calling strikes, organising demonstrations, carrying out
further missions for Habash and the cause. But in 1966 my

activities caught up with me. One morning, very early, there was a knock at the door. Three gentlemen from the Lebanese Interior Ministry were standing there. They were not the kind of gentlemen you argue with. 'You will pack,' they ordered me. 'You have five minutes.'

'Why?' I asked them.

'Don't ask questions!' one of them shouted. 'We are going to the airport. We have orders to deport you. You are a political undesirable.'

I spent a miserable few months kicking my heels at home, reading constantly, trying to keep in touch with my studies and with the MAN leadership. Then a minor miracle occurred: Khalil Jumblatt was made Lebanese Interior Minister. One of his first actions was to rescind all political deportation notices in force. I could go back and finish my studies. On 5 June 1967 I graduated from the AUB with a master's degree in Economic Administration.

That same day, Israel launched the air-strikes that began the Six-Day War.

CHAPTER
FIVE

Uzi Mahnaimi

By 1967, my father was head of the IDF's combat intelligence branch. He worked at military intelligence headquarters in Tel Aviv. One day at the beginning of May he came home looking very grim. 'The Egyptians have blockaded the Tiran Strait,' he told us. 'This means that the Gulf of Eilat is closed to Israeli shipping. It is an act of war.' He said seven divisions of the Egyptian army, complete with Soviet-supplied armour, had been moved up into the Sinai peninsula. Nasser had ordered all UN observers in the region to leave. 'The Egyptians are sitting here,' he said, 'right on our doorstep. I don't think they will knock before they come in.' Syria, Iraq and Jordan were also getting ready to attack. But the Israeli government was unsure what to do, so for thirty days it did nothing, except call up the reserve forces. And for thirty days the whole of Israel waited, terrified, for the Arab onslaught, like rabbits caught in headlights.

Like my father and just about everyone else in the country, I was filled with foreboding, sure we would be taking very heavy casualties. Every day that went by we expected the Egyptian Air Force to begin bombing us. Yet again, it seemed, the Jews were facing mass slaughter. Parks in towns throughout Israel were excavated as temporary graves for the avalanche of expected dead. I dug a fox-hole in our back garden. But amid all this alarm and trepidation, one group of people stood out for their complete insouciance: that super-confident brotherhood, the pilots of the Israeli Air Force. These gentlemen insisted that there would be few, if any, Israeli casualties; such was their own superiority, they assured us, that the Arabs would be destroyed before they could fire back. Hardly anybody believed them.

We listened to Egyptian radio sometimes, broadcasting in Hebrew, just to laugh at the Arab announcer's excruciating accent. At the beginning of June I tuned in to hear President Nasser boasting to his forces in Sinai that Egypt was ready for war, let it come, they would win it. Yitzhak Rabin was the Israeli Chief of Staff, Aba Eban was the Foreign Minister and Moshe Dayan had just been appointed Defence Minister. At the end of those thirty nail-biting days of inaction, they took the fateful decision: the Israelis would wait no longer for the hammer-blow to fall. The IDF would strike Egypt first.

Bassam Abu-Sharif

When I heard the news that the war had started, a thousand birds started singing in my heart. Nasser had acted! At last the Israelis would learn about Arab strength. We would avenge the humiliations of 1948; we would regain the lands, property and freedom that were rightfully ours. We would have justice.

I wanted to go home at once. I had to find out what was happening. Had the Arab armies crushed the Israelis? Had they accepted peace conditions? I had to know, to be there. This was the moment all Arabs had been waiting for. I wanted to breathe deep the liberated air of Jerusalem, and of my tortured country, Palestine. I wanted to savour the moment of triumph.

Other Palestinians at the AUB felt the same way. Hundreds of us clambered into specially chartered buses. We were travelling with light in our eyes and joy in our hearts. We were singing on the bus.

But when we reached the border, we found a platoon of Syrian soldiers in the way. 'You must go back!' they shouted. 'Go back! No Palestinians are allowed into Israel.' I got off the bus to find out what the hell was going on. Of course it couldn't be true. Why should we go back, when our country was being liberated? Did Israel matter any more? It must just be the Syrians being awkward, I thought. I asked the officer in charge if the war was over. Had the Israelis accepted terms? He looked away, shuffled his feet, said he didn't know. All he did know was that Israeli forces had taken and were occupying the Golan Heights. He spat when he said this. This news was extremely worrying. Taken the Golan? This must mean either that the Israelis had the Syrians right back on the defensive – or had defeated them. Surely the Israelis could not have defeated four Arab armies, including the mighty Egyptian army, in a matter of a few days?

We waited for hours in the shimmering heat. There was no more singing. The Syrian captain finally came back. 'Syria is negotiating a ceasefire with Israel,' he told us truculently. 'In the meantime, no Palestinians are being allowed into the West Bank.'

I reasoned with him. Why should he help the Israelis? How could we harm any ceasefire negotiations? Finally, after a lot of discussion and persuasion, he ordered his men to open the barriers. But though they let us cross into Syria, the soldiers still wouldn't let us travel on. Instead they herded us up into a makeshift camp on a mountainside near Damascus. They kept us there overnight, under armed guard.

At daybreak, I demanded our release. 'What the hell are you doing, keeping us here on this bloody mountain? We have a right to freedom of movement. You have no right to arrest us. Let us go to our homes.' At length, they agreed to let us pass. Pressing our luck, we asked for small arms – there might be pockets of Israeli resistance we could mop up. To our surprise, they handed out Russian-made bolt-action Seminov sniping rifles.

'Here,' they said, 'Greet the Israelis with a bullet.' Then they waved us off on our way south to Jordan.

We saw the smoke first, tall black columns of it snaking skywards, before we saw the carnage. Part of me knew at once what had happened, but my mind refused to acknowledge it. We were approaching the Suweileh junction south-west of Amman, Jordan's capital. Here the road forks, one way leading to the Jordan valley and the West Bank, the other heading south towards Aqaba. Before us was a scene of utter devastation. Jordanian army tanks, armoured cars, trucks and jeeps were sprawled across the road, burning after the last Israeli air-raid. Many of them held charred bodies, still smouldering. After seeing the first one, I tried very hard not to look at them. There were more Arab corpses, soldiers and civilians, littering the roadside.

Long lines of dejected Jordanian infantry, their shoulders hunched in defeat, trudged towards us through the wreckage of their armoured vehicles.

Among all this shambles struggled an unending stream of new Palestinian refugees. There were thousands and thousands of them. Most were on foot, carrying their small children and belongings. Those who had transport were trying to weave their overladen vehicles in and out of the shattered army and the teeming civilian column. Everything was happening at a snail's pace, a tragedy in very slow motion.

I stood among the great press of people, letting them flow around me. The sense of their misery was overwhelming. I could almost feel it physically. I groaned aloud. I wanted to stretch out my arms and stop them all, make them face the other way, force them to go back. I wanted to shout at them, to scream at the top of my voice: 'Go back to Palestine! Stay in your homeland and fight!' But the exodus continued, unceasingly, relentlessly, sweeping by.

I stopped a Jordanian sergeant, his face a mask of sweat, fatigue and filth. 'What's going on?' I asked. 'What has happened?' 'It is over,' he replied dully. 'We are occupied.'

I fought my way down through my fleeing people to the Allenby Bridge. The words of the Jordanian sergeant resounded in my head: 'We are occupied.' I was filled with a kind of sick dread. Dread for my people, dread for my family, dread for my home. In a moment my dreams had been shattered, the whole focus of my life had gone. I could have sat down on the spot and wept until death.

In a while I tried to collect myself, to do something, anything, to relieve the blackness all around and inside me. I wanted to go home, to make sure my relatives were unhurt. I could still go. As I drew near the bridge, I concealed the Seminov. 'It'll be useless anyway,' I thought.

I arrived at the narrow green-painted crossing-point. Instead of the usual friendly Jordanians, dozens of Israeli soldiers confronted me. I couldn't take it in. This was Jordanian territory, the whole of the West Bank was Jordanian territory. What was going on? What were all these Israelis doing here? They had tanks and heavy weapons, they were placing sandbags around freshly-dug machine-gun posts. I approached the heavily-armed picket at the eastern end of the bridge. The Israelis stared at me over their weapons in contempt. 'You!' barked the sergeant in command. 'Turn round and get back!'

'I want to go home,' I shouted back. 'I live in Jerusalem!'

'Not any longer you don't!' sneered the sergeant. 'Now fuck off.'

I stared at him. This Israeli with his gun, this petty tyrant, was going to stop me returning to my own home? To the house where I was born? I couldn't get it clear in my mind. 'We are occupied . . .'

Did this mean I would never see our ancestral home in

43

Jerusalem again? The last time I had been there – that was the last time I would ever walk through its door? It was impossible. This simply could not be. The Arab armies could not all have been defeated. I stood there for an hour or more, unaware of time or place. Tens of thousands of Palestinian refugees had fled the Israeli army in 1948. I was watching a new generation being forced from their homes. I turned away, in the end, utterly sick at heart. 'Darkness has fallen over the Arabs,' I thought. 'Everywhere there is darkness.'

It could not be so.

Uzi Mahnaimi

That night, the first night of the war, and every night for a week, my mother and I took cover in the fox-hole I had dug in the back garden. Sleep was out of the question. We could see and hear the Jordanian army shelling Lydda airport, a few miles away. Jordanian forces had also attacked across the West Bank, and in Jerusalem. We were just praying that neither the shelling, nor the soldiers that would follow in its wake, would find us.

I took a call from my father. He was speaking from one of the main Israeli command bunkers under Tel Aviv. 'Hundreds of Egyptian and Iraqi aircraft have been destroyed on the ground,' he told me jubilantly. 'The pilots were right! Our own losses are slight.' I had never heard so much joy in his voice. When he had rung off, I kept the receiver to my ear for a second or two, wondering if I had heard him right. It was stunning news. Could it really be true?

I had been listening to Egyptian radio again that day. My mother had tried to stop me tuning in, because there were endless reports saying that the Egyptian forces had pushed forward on all fronts, that their victorious brigades were mowing down all Israeli opposition in their path. When I heard him saying that, the announcer's accent didn't sound nearly so funny. The broadcast instructed all Israelis living in Beersheba, in the south, to place white flags on their rooftops as a sign of surrender; otherwise their houses would be destroyed by Egyptian tanks. Fearing the worst, many of the people there actually complied.

Even though we'd thought Egyptian radio was exaggerating, what my father had said didn't seem possible. Had the whole Egyptian Air Force, and much of its army, really been destroyed with almost no loss to ourselves? Had the IDF taken the whole of the West Bank and East Jerusalem? And seized the Golan Heights from Syria? Instead of the expected nightmare, the piles of Israeli dead, it was like a dream. In the space of six days, our forces had won a crushing and breathtaking victory.

At the end of that incredible week, my father came home. 'Let us go,' he said. 'Let's take a little trip down to Jericho, to see what it is we have won.'

The next morning we piled into the car in a state of high excitement. We drove down to Jerusalem, and on through into the eastern part of the city. Its ancient streets looked beautiful, the stones glowing warmly yellow in the morning light. Sunlight flashed off the magnificent golden cupola of the Dome of the Rock. Our soldiers and police were everywhere, establishing control. But it was strange that there were no civilians in sight. Where were the Arabs who lived in these houses? We got out at the Wailing Wall, a place forbidden to Jews under Arab rule. None of us had ever approached it before, but had seen it only in photographs. I wasn't in the least bit religious, but I touched it with my hands, savouring the texture of its worn surface. It was the strangest experience. I felt light-headed with victory. I could almost feel the history of the moment, the centuries all spinning down on to this spot, this time. The Jews had come home. We had conquered! I looked up at my father in his military uniform. He looked invincible. We were Israelis; and we were strong.

'Let's go on,' said my father. 'Let's go all the way down to the Allenby Bridge.'

45

At once, on turning a corner in the road, the reality of war came crashing home. Dead Jordanian soldiers lay on the pavements. Their corpses, already beginning to putrefy in the summer sun, gave off a sweet-sick smell I can never forget. Israeli paratroopers had engaged a Jordanian position in that sector of the city, and this was the result. Small working-parties of men were busy piling the bodies into trucks.

As we came out onto the main highway from Jerusalem to Jericho, we drove straight into a wide river of people, all on foot. They were walking away from the city, a broad unbroken flood-tide, flowing silently and changing shape all the time. They were like a river, a river of Palestinians, whole families, young and old, babies and grandmothers, all walking, walking, walking towards Jordan.

Victory, in the Middle East, is traditionally followed by massacre. It has been the way from time immemorial. When you win, you take revenge: you plunder, rape, and kill. The whole of Arab East Jerusalem seemed to be fleeing the expected massacre. We had to pick our way through these refugees every mile of the long road down to Jericho.

'There must be hundreds of thousands of them,' said my father. 'Hundreds of thousands. Why are they all running away?'

Brand-new Jordanian armoured personnel-carriers were strewn all along the route, the very latest US-made M-113s, a type I'd never seen before. Some had been blasted apart, caught by rockets and cannon fire. But some of the APCs were untouched, simply abandoned by their Jordanian crews. Our own army didn't have the M-113, so we got out and had a good look at one.

When we reached Jericho there was more chaos: refugees milling about in every direction, Israeli policemen and soldiers shouting orders, children lost and crying for their parents, nobody knowing what to do or where to go. The Allenby Bridge, just beyond the ancient town, was the scene of greatest confusion. The bridge itself had taken some sort of hit from a shell or a bomb, and was partly destroyed. Bits of twisted metal were sticking up from it here and there. Still, refugees were streaming across it, waved on by the IDF troops, all flooding into the safety of Jordan. Watching them go, I realised that hundreds of other Palestinians were trying to cross back in from Jordan.

My father got out and spoke to an Israeli lieutenant nearby. 'Some of them ran away a few days ago,' the officer said. 'Now they've realised we're not going to massacre them, they want to come back in. But we're under orders not to let them.' Sure enough, his troops were stopping anyone trying to come back across the bridge at gunpoint.

So many refugees, defeated and dejected. They were pitiable, these people; but I could not stop the exultation welling up in me. My father and his friends had beaten the Arabs, they had made them run away. Our soldiers were heroes. Israel was a superpower. The Arab armies were nothing, and less than nothing – paper tigers. I gazed across the bridge, beyond the backs of the victorious Israeli troops, at the furious Arabs behind the barriers. No, we would not allow them in. This land was ours now.

Among the people staring back at me, although I could not know it then, was Bassam Abu-Sharif.

CHAPTER
SIX

Bassam Abu-Sharif

It was a year before I smiled again. I turned back to Amman, mingling with the sorry stream of refugees. Desolate, just as they were, I was still in shock. What should I do? Where could I go? The phrase 'We are occupied . . .' re-echoed in my head, refusing to go away. Looking around me, at all these wretched people, I thought at last that I could at least try to help them. Most of them had only what they stood up in. They had nothing, literally, not even food. I turned my face to the east and began trudging.

When I got back to Amman, I reported to the Ministry of Information. A huge throng of displaced people circulated aimlessly outside the building, weeping, lost, and looking for loved ones. Jordanian radio was broadcasting continuous calls over the loudspeakers for all soldiers to return to their units. I pushed my way gradually inside. 'Look,' I said to a harassed official, 'I am an AUB graduate. I am able-bodied. Can I help in any way?'

'Yes, you can help in the camp. There are plenty who need

help there,' he replied. He meant the Suweileh refugee camp, which the Jordanians, with the help of the UN and other aid agencies, were enlarging as fast as they could to cope with the Palestinian tidal-wave. It was sited right there by the roadside, at the junction where I had seen the catastrophic aftermath of Arab defeat the day before. All the refugees had to do was stumble off the highway into it.

Somewhere among the flood, I later learned, were sixteen of my own family: my uncle Youssef Totah, my aunt Badrieh, Youssef's seven children, his brother and sister-in-law, their four children, and Youssef's fragile and ancient mother. The Israelis had come like a heart-attack in the night. The family had fled in their night-clothes, all somehow cramming into Youssef's open-topped red Opel saloon. They had been attacked by the Israeli army in the small hours of the night. It was the night Badrieh went into labour. She gave birth, in terror and pain, to the sound of windows smashing as the rioting came up the street. It took fifty hours to drive the twenty miles or so from Jerusalem to the Allenby Bridge, the baby screaming, Badrieh bleeding heavily. By the morning of the second day, they had run out of water, and the baby was sick. By the time they reached the Kuwaiti border two days later, they thought the new-born child was dying, dehydrated. But the Kuwaitis would not let the baby across the border, even though she was very sick – the infant had no papers. They all had to sit in the desert, constantly rejoining the queue of cars shuffling its way towards the crossing-point, watching the infant slowly fade. It was only the eventual kindness of a Kuwaiti border guard, who closed his eyes to the tiny wailing scrap and waved her through, that saved her life.

Had I known these members of my family were there, at the time, I might have been able to do something to help. But in that horrible chaos, nobody knew anything.

Suweileh camp was misery piled on catastrophe: a few tents pitched crazily in the desert, abandoned possessions scattered across the sand, thousands and thousands of people, no food, very little water, no facilities, nothing. To see so many hungry children around, crying, the wounded lying untreated, groaning in the heat, the old and the sick lying dazed and listless in the heat, like cattle – this was the nation of Palestine.

A young girl came up to me with a tiny infant on her hip. About seventeen years old, she was very pretty, but sweat and dirt streaked her face, and her clothing was ragged. There was a grim desperation in her eyes.

'Do you want to sleep with me?' she asked. 'Give me five dinars.'

At first I could hardly believe I'd heard the words. I recoiled as if bitten, and staggered away. I sat down heavily on the hot sand. So Palestinian girls had to prostitute themselves now, did they? It had come to that. They had to sell themselves, dishonour themselves just to survive? Anger took hold of me as I stared out across the desert. A blurred image danced in front of me: the girl, with her hand out, offering herself up for money.

I understood now what I had to do. There was no going back. My own fight began here, now. I would not stop until that girl, and the thousands like her, were back in their rightful homes. I would regain our country, or die for it. I could not live a normal life. I could not return to the AUB or become an employee, a salaried exile in one of the Gulf States. Could I just walk away from these people around me in the desert? Turn my back, and try to forget what I'd seen? I could never forget. We must have justice.

I had reached my own personal crossroads. Only one road led to justice.

I did what little I could in Suweileh for a few days, helping to get the camp set up, pitching tents, carrying endless plastic containers of water, shifting the ration-boxes that eventually began arriving, even dressing wounds. Then, one morning, I awoke with the certain knowledge that I must go straight back to Beirut. I had to see George Habash.

I had never seen him looking so drawn and grim. He was

furious, with the same quiet fury I myself felt about what had happened. 'That's it,' he began. 'From this time forward there is armed struggle. There is no other way.' At length he took me by the arm. 'From now on, we work for victory. We will use all necessary means. We're starting talks with other Palestinian groups about how to unite in armed struggle. The useless Arab regimes will not liberate Palestine. We, the people of Palestine, will liberate Palestine. Tell me, Bassam: are you with us?'

I reached for his hand, which he grasped and shook very firmly. 'Yes,' I told him. 'I am with you.'

On 11 December 1967, we formed the Popular Front for the Liberation of Palestine (PFLP). Its manifesto had only one item: the liberation of Palestine from Israeli occupation by means of armed struggle.

Uzi Mahnaimi

For a boy of fifteen, the Israeli victory in the Six-Day War was thrilling. My father had picked up an AK-47 assault rifle on his travels, abandoned in the Sinai by the Egyptians. Sitting up in bed at night, I taught myself how to strip the weapon down to its component parts, then reassemble it, in the dark. I was fantastically proud of this achievement. Soon I would be joining the invincible IDF. I was looking forward to military service, serving my homeland. I felt I had it all to live up to. My grandfather had been one of the few, one of that select band of heroes who had refused to give up, who had founded the state of Israel; my father was a hero of the 1948 War of Independence; now he had helped Israel triumph a second time – and what a triumph!

With this kind of pedigree, there were very few real choices open to me. Like my school-mates, I was from a very special family: one of the founding élite. If you were from the civilian élite, you joined the military élite, which meant one of three

51

things: fighter pilot, Fleet 13 frogman [Fleet 13 is the IDF's special underwater weapons unit] or Sayeret Matkal (General Headquarters Reconnaissance Unit).

Sayeret Matkal is the Israeli equivalent of Britain's Special Air Service or the American Green Berets. This secret force carries out intelligence and combat missions in the Arab countries and abroad. To join it, you had to be the best. Like my peers, I wanted to be the best. My heart was set on it. Anything less would be a personal humiliation. I began running ten kilometres a day; I worked out regularly with weights. But to serve with an élite unit takes more than physical or mental fitness: you need that sense of family tradition. When I ran, I felt this Zionist heritage. I felt the blood of my pioneering grandfather coursing through my veins. I felt the power of the strong Hebrew.

Bassam Abu-Sharif

M y father lost his temper when I told him I was joining the Popular Front for the Liberation of Palestine. He refused to accept it. He tried everything to make me change my mind, he did everything in his power to stop me. He even offered me a blank cheque: 'Here,' he said, 'take this. Go, finish your Ph.D., get qualified. You have been accepted by British, American, Canadian universities. Go! Take up your place. Finish your studies. Then, when you come back, you can do whatever you want. You can serve your country better with a doctorate than by becoming a guerrilla fighter. Go!'

'You say I can serve Palestine when I get back,' I replied, 'but what would I be coming back to? I cannot go back to our home in Jerusalem. I cannot go back to my own country. You want me to work for some Palestinian businessman in Jordan? Where is the honour in this?'

'Ach,' he spat in disgust, and turned away, as if disowning me.

But he had not given up. He mobilised all his friends, lecturers at the AUB I respected, almost everyone he thought might have a ghost of a chance of influencing me – they all came round and tried to put me off. In the end, he even begged me not to go. It meant that much to him. He feared for me.

Though I could see his point of view, deep down inside I knew: a human being whose people have no future is himself without value unless he fights for what is right. I did not want to be part of a people with no future. I did not want to be an eternal foreigner, a displaced person, a landless, homeless, stateless, shamed, despised Palestinian refugee. A Ph.D. What is that, I asked my father, when we have no country? When our homes and ancient rights have been taken from us? My father didn't only want me to be better educated, he wanted his son to be far away from what was coming. Because what was coming, in the struggle against Israel, was destruction, and war, and death. 'You will go to prison,' he told me, 'if they don't kill you first.'

'In the end,' I insisted, 'I would rather be in prison in my own country than be a free man in exile. I would rather be dead.'

'So be it,' he said.

While these arguments were going on, my mother had kept silent. This was very unusual. Finally, I came to her. 'My son,' she said, 'you are right. We have no country. We have no justice. But what can you do? Abd–El Nasser could do nothing. All these Arab armies could do nothing. You are a few young men. What can you do?'

I was astonished. It was such a pragmatic question. This wasn't like her. She just wasn't that type, she was, by nature, more emotional. But now she was cool, and her cool, practical questioning got through to me where my father hadn't. I couldn't answer her. It stung me, this question. What, in fact, could I do? She gazed at me, waiting for a reply. 'Well,' I said, 'it is true that we can do nothing at present. But the important thing is to show everybody that the defeat of the

Arab armies doesn't mean we Palestinians have been defeated. And that's it.'

Once they had seen how determined I was, my parents tried to respect my decision, although they would never be happy with it. It was hell to resist my mother. I was carving out a very lonely path for myself. My mother knew, as I did, that once I joined the armed resistance I'd be cut off from the family – perhaps for good. She put her arms round me, something she hadn't done in a long while, and hugged me. 'Take care, my son,' was all she said. 'Take care.'

Uzi Mahnaimi

My first real contact with an Arab was exactly like my father's before me: looking at him over the sights of a gun. One afternoon shortly after the Six-Day War had ended, I came home as usual from school. It was very hot. Dumping my books in the bedroom, I wandered out into the garden. The young Arab gardener my mother had taken on was watering the flowers. We began quarrelling. It was a squabble so trivial I can hardly remember today what it was really about. I think he must have splashed me with the hose, by accident. Naturally I was convinced he'd done it on purpose. In seconds, we were shouting; in a minute we were both furious beyond reason. All my childish fear and hatred of the Arabs suddenly overtook me. I rushed into the house, ran up to my father's study and snatched his ancient Russian hunting gun from the wall. It was a shotgun, with long gleaming blue-black barrels. I rushed back out into the sunlight and brandished the weapon at the Arab boy's stomach. I had no thought for whether it was loaded, neither did I really know what I was going to do. The red mist had come down. For a moment, the gardener stared at the gun pointing at his midriff. I think, in that instant, that if he'd said another word I would have killed him, but he turned on his heel and ran out through the gate.

My mother came out and gave me hell for threatening to kill the boy 'over your silly childish nonsense', as she put it. Looking back now, my behaviour was ridiculous. But that attitude, the instant resort to the gun, was the result of my upbringing.

As for the Arab, he never came back. We lost a very good gardener.

CHAPTER
SEVEN

Bassam Abu-Sharif

F rom the bitter ashes of Arab defeat Yasser Arafat, George
Habash, Naif Hawatmeh and many others took wing.
These men, and all of us who rallied to them, represented a
spirit. We were all that was left in the Arab world to defy the
Israelis.

In Arabic, the humiliation of 1967 is called *al-Nakbah*: 'the
catastrophe'. It was like a tocsin ringing a single chime: the
call to arms. To say that Arabs were stunned by the defeat
would be an understatement. In less than a week, Israel had
taken territory four times its original size, including the Golan
Heights, the West Bank of the Jordan, the Gaza Strip, the Sinai
Peninsula and East Jerusalem.

However small they were to begin with, groups like the PFLP
found in this catastrophe an opportunity. They rushed headlong
into the vacuum. The people, who had lost faith completely in
Arab nationalism, turned to these groups in huge numbers.
Volunteers queued up to join, to become *fedayin*, 'those who
sacrifice themselves': Palestinian freedom fighters. All wanted

the chance to strike back at Israel. Arafat's Fatah, which he had founded back in 1959 with Abu Jihad, Farouk Qaddumi, Abu Iyad and the al-Hasan brothers, grew to twenty times its original size, then a hundred times greater. In the 1967 talks it was agreed that the Palestine Liberation Organisation (PLO), which Arafat was soon to take over, would be the umbrella organisation for all Palestinian freedom fighters. The group I had now joined, the PFLP, would be a part of the PLO, but also free to carry out its own agenda. Arafat and his comrades had been right all along: Pan-Arab Nasserism had been so much windy rhetoric; all talk and no action. It was time for action.

For the first time since 1948 the Palestinians took control of their own fate. We did not know where the road would lead us; we had no idea if justice lay at the end of it, but it was a road we were determined to travel. The Arab nations that had meddled with our struggle had all failed the people of Palestine. The Palestinians were free, after the Six-Day War, as they had never been before, to think and act as they saw fit. It was a heady drug. In 1968 a Palestinian *fedayi* could travel right across the Arab world with nothing more than his organisation card, and be welcome everywhere. No passport – just the card. Nobody, nobody, in the Arab world then, dared raise a voice against a *fedayi*. If the Egyptian army had tried to stop a group of Palestinian commandos attacking Israel from its territory, there would have been a revolution in Egypt. The same was true of Syria, or any other Arab state. In the aftermath of *al-Nakbah*, the *fedayi* was god. This was the measure of our freedom then.

Fatah had been launching sporadic raids into Israel since its foundation. But they had been small in scale, and largely unsuccessful. Now the PFLP and all the other newly-motivated Palestinian groups joined the attack, playing cat-and-mouse with the IDF patrols. But brave as the guerrillas were, they were attempting the impossible. Every night, they tried to infiltrate through the labyrinth of tiny interconnecting ravines that lies between Jordan and the West Bank; almost every night, the

Israelis detected them. The *fedayin* were captured or killed before they even got near an Israeli target. Deadly as these missions proved to be, there were always plenty of willing volunteers.

While he had destroyed the original Nasserite Arab nationalist version of the PLO by laying bare its essentially romantic ideology, Yasser Arafat, in launching these attacks on Israeli-occupied territory, knew he was himself acting romantically. Habash, too, understood this. There was no way a relative handful of young men, armed for the most part with antiquated hunting rifles, could take on the Israeli tanks, minefields and machine-guns, the well-armed and vigilant army patrols. But these raids were a necessary step. They showed the world that the Palestinian spirit was not crushed. They showed the Israelis that the Palestinian people would never give up, that they would fight with whatever came to hand, by whatever means they could, to recover their dignity and their lost lands, to get justice. But the cross-border raids were never practical. Looking back now, they were a joke. Most of the 'guerrillas' were ex-students like myself, who had undergone 'training' in Egyptian army camps. This training in no way fitted them for the real task in hand. The *fedayin* were undertaking a covert war of infiltration, of sabotage and surprise attack. They needed the skills that can come only from intensive and highly-specialised training: the clandestine movement of arms and men, the making of a secure operational base by means of a cell-structure, a commando's skill in striking a target . . . What they did know was just enough to make them dangerous – to themselves: desert survival courses, strength, stamina and fitness work, a small amount of weapons and explosives training. As a part of an invading regular army, the *fedayin* might have had a role. Otherwise, they were nigh on useless.

Realising that something had to be done about this, Arafat himself went under cover into the West Bank in 1967. He knew that the cross-border raids would never do more than annoy the

Israelis. His aim was to set up his own revolutionary network, inciting a mass popular revolution from within. Only this, he felt, would get the Israelis out. But he found it impossible. Already Israeli internal security, Shin-Bet, had too many spies and informers working among the Palestinian community. The whole time he was in the West Bank, Arafat was constantly aware of being no more than a whisker away from the clutches of the Israelis. For weeks on end he hid out in the cave systems around the West Bank town of Nablus, a sort of nocturnal revolutionary troglodyte. Once an Israeli patrol reached a cave to find Arafat's coffee still steaming over the fire.

After that trip, Arafat knew there would have to be a change in tactics. If Fatah and its satellite groups like the PFLP could not fight on the inside or successfully penetrate the Israeli security shell from the outside, some other means of carrying the attack against Israel would have to be found.

Habash and Arafat, Hawatmeh and other Palestinian leaders had the same ideas, more or less, when it came to formulating strategy and tactics in these experimental days. None of them could come up with an alternative to what was already being tried. Then, at a special PFLP meeting called late in 1967 to discuss forward strategy, the whole picture changed in a flash. The man who changed it was called Dr Wadia Haddad.

In a few short, punchy phrases, Haddad set the meeting on fire. 'Trying to get men and weapons across the Jordan is a waste of time and effort,' he began. 'Armed struggle of that type will never achieve the liberation of Palestine.' There was complete silence in the room. He was only saying out loud what we all knew, but he had actually dared to come out and say it. He had our full attention now. 'We have to hit the Israeli army in a qualitative way, not a quantitative way,' he went on, speaking calmly and clinically. 'This is a particular animal, the IDF; we cannot fight it plane for plane, tank for tank, soldier for soldier. We have to hit the Israelis at the weak joints.' He paused to let his words sink in. 'What do I mean by the weak joints? I mean spectacular, one-off operations. These spectacular operations will focus the world's attention on the problem of Palestine. The world will ask, "What the hell is the problem in Palestine? Who are these Palestinians? Why are they doing these things?" At the same time, such operations will be highly painful to the Israelis. High-profile, sensational operations, carried out by thoroughly trained people in secure underground structures – this is how we shall hit at the painful joints. In the end, the world will get fed up with its problem; it will decide it has to do something about Palestine. It will have to give us justice.'

Haddad's vision was electrifying. He was proposing a form of strategic guerrilla action, a way in which the few could take power against the many. The strategy, if it worked, would put an end to the years of failure and humiliation. He had found a way for the weak to become strong.

Haddad had thought out the tactics we should use, in detail. His first idea was to hijack an El Al airliner, while it was airborne, and hold the passengers to ransom. If that didn't bring the world's media running, nothing would. 'The way I see it,' he said, 'it shouldn't be necessary to use actual violence. We don't even have to hit Israeli targets all the time. But we must be a constant irritation, a bug under the skin of the developed world. We must make them lose patience with Israel and Palestine the hard way.'

This was breathtaking stuff. When he had finished speaking, I felt like standing up and applauding, and I could tell the others round the table felt the same way. The world had tilted slightly on its axis, and it had tilted in our direction. Here, at last, was a new way forward – a chance to get the Israeli boot off the back of the Arab neck. From now on, we would carry the attack to Israel. We would take – and keep – the initiative. I felt exhilarated. It was from this moment that Haddad became known as 'the Master'.

I saw my own role in this new plan of action very clearly. On joining the PFLP I had been made a member of its Central Committee. I'd also become deputy editor of the Front's magazine, *Al-Hadaf* (*The Target*). But here was a chance to play a key role in the new strategy. The outside world, the news companies, would want a spokesman who could put forward the Front's aims and objectives in straightforward language, using the soundbites they so much loved. I was just the man to do it. I had the languages: English, French, Arabic; I had the education; I even had a little press experience from working with the UN in the aftermath of the Six-Day War, enough to know I could get our position across effectively. I thought about it a bit more. It wasn't merely a matter of presenting the PFLP to the press and TV news. What about our operational teams, the people who carried out the hijackings? They would need training in how to communicate. They would have to be capable of controlling a plane-load of terrified passengers; they would have to know what to say at news conferences. The job could be very important in the hard years to come. It might even be indispensable.

It was not so plain to see what George Habash, the actual leader of the PFLP, would do. He had to accept this clever cuckoo Haddad who was threatening to take over his carefully constructed nest. Habash insisted on keeping the PFLP thoroughly tinged with red, to maintain his left-wing credentials against any potential threat from within. In fact the membership of the PFLP was radical, but it was not Marxist. The person who best personified this attitude was Wadi Haddad. If you were to ask any outside observer, Western, Arab or even Palestinian, what came to mind when they thought about the PFLP, they would say, 'Spectacular operations, terrorism, hijackings, kidnaps and so on.' They would not say, 'A Marxist-Leninist organisation.' So the PFLP had an internal conflict, which turned into a bitter personal rivalry between Habash and Wadi Haddad.

Haddad was a free and original thinker. He wanted a free hand planning and conducting his special operations. Our leader was going to have to take a bit of a back seat, on the operational side at least. But then, Habash owed Haddad his freedom. When he first formed the PFLP, Habash had been imprisoned by the Syrians, who saw the new organisation as a threat to their own ambitions in the region. It was Haddad who got him out. Haddad organised a brilliant ambush of the Syrian jeeps taking Habash to gaol. So Habash would let the Master have his head.

And the world would be changed.

I can remember feeling that we were about to make history. Because of my new role, I needed to know about all PFLP operations, in advance, in detail. Haddad was explaining how the special commando he had trained was going to effect the first PFLP mid-air hijack. Once they had seized the plane, the team would divert it to a friendly Arab country; then we would hold its passengers to ransom. Simple, outrageous and, if it worked, deadly effective.

It worked. In July 1968, Haddad's team hijacked a Rome–Tel Aviv flight of Israel's national airline, El Al, forcing the plane down at Algiers. As he had predicted, the world's media crews came down on us like wasps onto jam. The hijack caught the Israelis completely by surprise. They were left powerless and floundering. We had hit back. Israel tried to play for time, to spin out the negotiations. None of it was any use. Haddad had predicted this reaction. He simply kept the passengers bottled up in Algiers until the Israeli government agreed to his terms. After two months it capitulated, freeing a large number of Palestinian prisoners from Israeli gaols in exchange for the aircraft's passengers. We had won our first victory.

It was the first of many. Haddad's strategy delivered every-thing he had claimed for it, and more. The issue of Palestine became the number one item on global news broadcasts; it has stayed there, more often than not, ever since. Israel was knocked back firmly on the defensive, and there was one unforeseen bonus: Western governments had absolutely no answer to the hijacks. They could not risk the lives of innocent passengers, so they gave in to our demands. Thus, even when they were caught and imprisoned, our people were frequently released. The involvement of Western governments at the highest level in our struggle, and their spectacular failure to deal effectively with the hijackings, gave it a true international dimension. It also gave us power. In a matter of months the Palestinian Arabs had sprung up from the gutters of defeat to snap their fingers in the face of Israel and its Western supporters.

The years of hijack had begun.

CHAPTER
EIGHT

Bassam Abu-Sharif

M ost of the people Haddad trained to carry out his attacks were Palestinians who came from within the ranks of the PFLP. All volunteers went through a standard initial military training. Talent-spotters in the training camps then referred the best recruits on for further, more intensive training and from this second, much smaller pool Haddad would select the best again, looking for intelligence, persistence, strength of character, resourcefulness and physical toughness. He then put the hand-picked survivors through his very own special training programme. The few who made it through that went on the missions list.

Haddad's final training was quite exceptional. It went far beyond such things as proficiency with weapons and explosives. Since they would be undertaking operations against airline security guards and staff, the hijackers were trained to fly even the biggest and most modern airliners. They had to know exactly what a pilot was doing at any given moment, so that they couldn't be bluffed. In the event that the aircrew were killed, a hijacker had to be able to take the controls and land the plane.

The trainees practised exchanging gunfire in the confined spaces of an aircraft's cabin and cockpit, just as the El Al guards they would confront did. They were trained how to defeat airport security checks. They studied the laws that would be applied to them in various countries if they were captured; they even drove around the various European capitals, becoming familiar with the roads and traffic systems. In a chase, this knowledge could make all the difference.

In the West, this was the age of revolution. Young people everywhere in the developed world were in revolt – against government, the received social order, the war in Vietnam, the capitalist system. You name it, they wanted rid of it. Many of these dissatisfied youths were active, as students, in their university unions. Thousands were members of anti-capitalist parties; many wanted to do something more concrete than just 'show solidarity' with a given cause. And students could be very dangerous. In May 1968 French students, in alliance with a well-mobilised working class, came close to bringing down their own government. German students, too, were on the boil.

Whatever their shade of opinion, virtually all these revolutionaries saw the Palestinian liberation movement as the number one revolutionary cause in the world at the time. They saw it as a cause to which they should give help, and from which they could also receive help. Haddad's spectaculars proved that a relatively small number of committed and well-organised people could kick the West up the backside, and get away with it. This was like a magnet to these fledgling Che Guevaras. Many of them really hated the machinery of capitalism: the power of big business and big government, which crushed the spirit of the individual. They wanted freedom and power. And they hung their revolutionary aspirations on the peg of Palestine.

The fact that we had independent training camps, and that we could admit chosen people into them, was what really attracted these international radicals. They were looking for guidance, and they sought an outlet: often they wanted a chance to express their frustrated dissent in action. We gave them that chance.

By this time we had training camps throughout the Middle East: Iraq, Jordan, Egypt, Yemen, Lebanon, and also in Algeria. We offered people like this a practical training and a worthwhile cause. So our revolution, the Palestinian revolution, came as a godsend to these disaffected people. 'Committees of solidarity' with our cause soon mushroomed across Europe.

These solidarity committees started to form a network with Palestinian offices around the world. They despatched medical and financial aid, and sent volunteers to work in the refugee camps. Dozens of Scandinavian doctors and nurses turned up to run clinics. Revolutionary student leaders came to our operational bases, believing that the best way they could help us was to take direct action: against Zionism, imperialism, and reactionary forces everywhere.

As the public face of the PFLP, I was the first stop for those who wanted to join the struggle for Palestine. In fact I was just about the only port of call. Though it was never an official role, I was in effect the PFLP's chief recruiting officer. In the late 1960s, in the age of revolution, there were plenty of volunteers.

One day in 1969 two young Germans turned up in my office in Amman. It was their first visit to the Middle East. They impressed me a great deal: very intelligent, highly educated, and sincere about what they believed. The most important thing as far as I was concerned, though, was that they truly wished to help our cause. Their names were Andreas Baader and Ulrike Meinhof.

We wanted to use these foreign volunteers, if they were made of the right stuff. Haddad thought foreigners should even be used operationally, because their presence confirmed the international dimension of the Palestine people's struggle. They showed we had allies inside Western society. Baader

66

and Meinhof were our first visitors from Germany. They stayed in Amman for about a fortnight, holding discussions with all the Palestinian groups, not only the PFLP. They talked to Fatah, they talked to the Democratic Front for the Liberation of Palestine (DFLP). They were carrying out a reconnaissance trip, deciding exactly whom they wanted to work with, and how.

As things turned out, the Baader–Meinhof group, as it quickly became known, was not of much help to the PFLP, although a few of its members did join in the odd PFLP operation. Another organisation was of very great help to us, though: the Red Brigade. The Brigada Rossa in Italy, the Japanese Red Army, ETA in Spain, Action Directe in France, all these Red Brigade units were affiliated, with one another and with the PFLP. Haddad, the Master, carefully nurtured these interconnections, gradually building a network that stretched across the whole of Europe and the Middle East.

Haddad's strategy for these groups was the same, exactly, as he had elaborated it to us in December 1967. They were to hit at the painful joints, by means of direct action. The more spectacular the direct action, the better. But the enemy was enlarged, for these foreign groups, to include, besides Israel, 'imperialism and the forces of reaction'.

Haddad acted as a kind of conductor: when he was planning one of his spectaculars, he orchestrated groups from various countries. He called this 'pooling'. So in one operation you might find activists from Latin America, Germany, Palestine and Spain all operating as a team, all trained by him, all working to the Haddad master-plan.

Uzi Mahnaimi

When I was growing up, I thought all Arabs were demons. Every Israeli child believed this. Many still do. It was the way we were brought up, the way we were taught but, most of all, it was the result of our having absolutely no direct contact with Arab people. What we did not know, we feared. What we feared, we demonised. The spectacle of these Arab terrorists hijacking innocent civilians, threatening and killing them, only increased my own fear and loathing of the race. We had to smite the demons, to drive them out. My own time to do so was at hand.

As soon as I finished high school at the age of eighteen, I began the entrance tests to join Sayeret Matkal, my own personal Holy Grail, the Israeli Defence Force's super-élite. The man who interviewed me was its deputy commander, Yoni Nethanyahu, who later headed the raid on Entebbe. He asked me what I knew about the secret force. 'Not very much,' I replied. 'I know its job is to strike targets deep inside Arab countries.' He told me a little more about what sort of thing his commandos got up to – enough to make me even more desperate to get in. He asked me what sporting activities I took part in, what sort of distance did I run every day? He was pleased with my answers. I left his office on a cloud of euphoria. I was sure now that they would accept me for training. Once in, the rest was up to me. I still had a preliminary field test to get through, but, fit as I was, I couldn't see that being a problem.

It was on this test that the roof fell in on me. I'd had some niggling problems with my back, but I never took the pain very seriously. But this field test pushed candidates for selection to the extreme edges of their fitness, and beyond. It proved too much for me. Right in the middle of it, my back gave out completely. Not only could I not finish the test, they had to call a doctor in. He examined me, shook his head, and that was the end of it. It was a crushing disappointment: all my dreams of glory dashed in the dust. Far from being allowed to pass through the heroic portals of Sayeret Matkal, even my standard military service was postponed while I received treatment.

My world had just caved in, but I still wanted to join the army.

The only thing was that I didn't like the idea of becoming an officer. The peer-group pressure on me to take a commission was intense. All my father's friends were high-ranking military officers; all my friends were the sons of these men. My school-mates were all queuing up for commissions. It just wasn't possible for me to resist. I had to join the army, and I had to become an officer. It was a conveyor-belt.

One day I was in the car with my father and one of his high-ranking intelligence colleagues. They asked me what I was going to do, finally, when I was called up for military service. 'Well,' I began, 'I don't really think I want to be an officer . . .' The sudden drop in temperature stopped me. There was a long silence in the car. Then my father's friend said, 'Come on, Uzi, what do you mean, you don't want to be an officer? You want to be a corporal or something? Of course you will become an officer.' He glanced at my father, and smiled. 'It's in the blood,' he said.

I got in nine months later, when my back problems had cleared up.

Bassam Abu-Sharif

One morning in the autumn of 1969 my secretary knocked on the door. 'There is a young man waiting to see you,' she announced. 'Another recruit. I told him you were very busy, and probably wouldn't be able to see him today. But he won't take "No" for an answer.' It was true I had a lot of work to get through that day, and this stranger had no appointment. Still, I didn't like to turn people away. 'Who is he?' I asked. 'I have no idea,' she replied disparagingly. 'But he is not an Arab. He says his name is Sanchez. He has just come out of the blue.' I kept the unwanted visitor waiting for more than an hour while I got through the most urgent tasks. After about ten minutes, though, I stuck my head round the door to take a quick look at him, for safety's sake. On first sight, he did not particularly impress me. He was obviously tired: slumped back on the reception couch, surrounded by his luggage – three large bags and a black box. He clearly intended staying in Beirut some time. I wondered at once what was in the box. When I had finished what I was doing, I went through to him.

He had a very calm, quiet face. It wasn't only that he was young, he had what you would call a baby face. Yet there was an air of seriousness about him that was quite at odds with his looks. I guessed he must be about nineteen. 'Welcome,' I said in English. 'How can I help you?'

The stranger jumped to his feet. 'Thank you,' he began. 'Are you Mr Bassam?'

'Yes,' I replied, and we shook hands. It struck me that he did not yet even have a beard.

He launched into what must have been a prepared speech. 'I am a student,' he told me. 'I come from Venezuela. I have been studying in Moscow at Patrice Lumumba University. I've been following your struggle. I want to join the PFLP because I'm an internationalist and a revolutionary.' He stopped, gazing at me with his big round eyes. I studied him. He explained eagerly that he had met Palestinian students in Moscow, who had told him about the PFLP's ideology and its struggle against Israel and the West. This rang true: the PFLP had a very strong student organisation in Moscow. He had come from Moscow to Beirut airport overnight and then direct from the airport to my office.

As he was speaking, I studied his soft round face, assessing him, wondering what to do with him. I was used to making judgements about people within the first ten minutes of meeting them, but I could not quite make up my mind about this one. Despite his youth, he was a very cool customer. An angel face, but deadly serious. And he was so elegant: beautifully turned out, in a well-tailored suit and silk tie of the very best quality, with fine hand-stitched leather shoes on his feet. Not the kind of revolutionary student I was used to meeting.

'You want to join the PFLP?' I asked. 'To do what?'

'To be a fighter,' he told me earnestly, as if this were the most natural thing in the world.

I smiled. 'It is a tough thing to be a fighter.'

'I can take it,' he said, bristling visibly at my smile. He could see I found it hard to believe someone so innocent-looking, so elegant, could be of much use as a revolutionary terrorist.

I did find it hard. Which just goes to show how wrong you can be about appearances.

'Tell me about yourself,' I went on. 'How did you come to be a student in Moscow?'

'My father is a leading communist politician in Venezuela,' he stated. 'In Caracas. That's how I won a scholarship to Moscow – they reserve places for Communist Party members. But I don't wish to be a student any longer. I wish to fight for the cause.' As he spoke these words, he stiffened suddenly to attention, inclining his head in a sharp nod.

I was startled. For a moment this boy had become a military officer – a cavalry officer of the old school. The more I questioned him, the more he intrigued me. He was very polite, very well educated – and explosively intelligent. He spoke English, Spanish and French with equal ease. He was extremely well read. He had delved deep into the rich and exotic mines of South American literature, but he was also on good terms with the major works of North America and Europe. We chatted a bit about the books we both liked. There was something underneath the babyish charm, I thought: some steel that we might be able to use.

My secretary came back to see how we were getting along. I made up my mind: Mr Sanchez was worth going further with. I asked her to fix him somewhere to stay for the night. The standard PFLP basic training course in the searing heat of Jordan's deserts weeded out the time-wasters pretty quickly. We would see . . .

As he stood up to leave, the young man took my secretary's hand. With an elegant flourish, he stooped gracefully over it, brushing her fingers lightly with his lips. She was only slightly more amazed than I: here was the true Latin American gentleman. The man was a chameleon.

'By the way,' he said on his way out, 'I have a present for you from Moscow.' He walked through into the outer office and returned carrying the big black box. Inside the box was something that looked very like a complicated gun but, to my surprise, it was a camera, of the very best Russian manufacture, complete with an assortment of long lenses.

The next day, over coffee, I told him that I would put him in touch with some people who would begin his training. He accepted the news coolly: it was just as he had expected. I asked my driver to take him to Shatila refugee camp outside the city. From there he would be taken to Amman, in Jordan, to the initial training camp. 'There's just one thing,' I said as he rose to leave again. 'I can't remember if you told me your full name?'

'Ilich Ramirez Sanchez,' he replied. 'My father named me after Lenin.'

'OK,' I said. 'From now on, don't tell anyone else your true identity. Round here, we all use a *nom de guerre*.' I thought for a moment. He was a Venezuelan. 'What about the name "Carlos?"' I asked.

He flashed his even teeth at me. 'Carlos will do just fine,' he said, and strode out.

Why 'Carlos'? The name Carlos derives from the Arabic name Khalil, 'Al-Khalil Ar-Rhaman', or 'The Beloved of [God] the Merciful' and refers to Abraham, who is important to both Jews and Muslims. 'Khalil', when the Moors took it to Spain, eventually became 'Carlos'. I thought it might suit a South American who wanted passionately to fight for an Arab cause.

It was just my own little joke.

*   *   *

A very special war broke out between Wadi Haddad and the Israelis once the hijacks started. To Israeli intelligence, Haddad was public enemy number one, and they learned very quickly from his own tactics. Right from the start, the Israelis were seeking to kill him, and anyone connected to him, in any way they could. Mossad began killing PFLP members, or even people who backed the group financially, in places like Paris or London, wherever it could spot them. Haddad joined battle with Mossad on the streets of foreign capitals – as Zadok Ofir, a Mossad station officer in Brussels, found out to his cost. Ofir had been trying to recruit Arab double agents among the Arab community in the city, and his efforts had been reported back to Haddad. Haddad aimed one of his own operatives, 'Sami', at Ofir. Ofir fell straight into the trap – and recruited Sami.

One day Ofir asked Sami to meet him in a Brussels restaurant. Sami agreed, but he had other things on his mind than what he would be having for lunch. When they had been talking for a short while, Sami excused himself and went to the toilet. Behind the cistern, he found a pistol that had been taped there for him beforehand. He quickly stripped off the tape, cocked the weapon, and walked back into the dining-room holding it casually down by his side. He strode up to Ofir, shot him several times in the chest, and walked out. Amazingly, although seriously wounded, Ofir survived the attack. Sami did not. It took Mossad two years to track him down, but in the end they found him and killed him.

Zadok Ofir, I discovered much later, was the man who had trained Uzi Mahnaimi in espionage and counter-terrorism.

At the same time as trying to kill PFLP members all over the world, the Israelis were also attempting to close down all our special operations cells. But Haddad somehow always managed to keep one jump ahead: ahead in ideas, ahead in techniques, he kept on surprising them. By changing his operational shape all the time, he held on to the initiative.

One of the ways he stayed ahead of Israeli security was by making brilliant use of technology. A steady flow of first-class chemistry and engineering graduates came to the PFLP from the Arab universities. Haddad put them to good use. He set up scientific laboratories; his research teams came up with new metal alloys that were, under certain circumstances, undetectable by airport X-ray machines. They kept up a steady flow of technological discovery, including things that were so weird and idiosyncratic that they were bound to defeat detection. Some of it was real James Bond stuff, like the strange fact that lobster shells can't be penetrated by X-rays.

One lab developed a suitcase that looked and felt exactly like a normal Samsonite case, except for one small difference: it was made of a fibrous material that had explosives woven right through it. This mixture, moulded into the appropriate shape, was then baked. Result: a functioning, normal suitcase that was also a bomb.

Haddad's happy band of strange scientists also dreamt up a form of liquid explosive that looked exactly like red wine. It was about this time that a South American volunteer of Arab origin came to us. He looked Spanish, sounded Spanish and had a South American passport. His cover was perfect for us. On top of this, he was very enthusiastic. So enthusiastic, in fact, that he asked to be sent on a suicide mission. There's not much even the best security can do about suicide bombers, so Haddad took him on gladly.

The 'red wine' explosive mixture was put into a standard Chianti flagon, which was sealed with an authentic-looking red wax seal and pasted up with real Chianti labels. Haddad sent the would-be suicide bomber to Tel Aviv airport with this exciting little present for the Israelis. But the man found out it is not all that easy to kill yourself. All he had to do was pull the seal clear of the jar; the explosives would take care of the rest. At the last second, his nerve failed him. With his forefinger hooked through the detonating wire, he hesitated. He looked around wildly. Panicking now, he half-dropped, half-placed the wine-flask on the floor by the check-in desk. He turned and walked quickly away. But as he was scurrying off, an alert El Al security man noticed the abandoned jar and came running after him. 'The wine, sir, is it yours?' he called. It was enough. At this polite challenge, the volunteer collapsed. He was arrested and taken to prison. Once in custody, he confessed everything.

About six weeks later he got back in touch with the PFLP. It was true, he said, that he was a coward; it was true that he had failed. But he was sorry, really sorry. He wanted the Master to forgive him, could he please be given a second chance? Where could he meet the Master again? Of course this was a pretty crude and feeble attempt by Mossad to plant a spy in our nest. And, of course, we saw through it at once. 'Don't worry, I will pardon you,' responded Haddad. 'Come. We will have a little talk, you and I . . .' Strangely, the volunteer never showed up.

This was the first in a new phase of activity Haddad planned: the suicide bombings. It was one of the hardest to carry through with success. One of the Palestinians groomed for this very special form of operations was an intelligent young man who used the name Abu Harb. During his flying training, he proved to be an excellent pilot. Wadi Haddad got hold of a twin-engined light plane, and made Abu Harb practise landing it very early in the morning in the mountains of Lebanon around Baalbek. The road between Shatora and Baalbek was closed especially for this training.

The Master had worked out a detailed air route for Abu Harb from the Bekaa Valley to Tel Aviv. Studying each hill, each valley, each fold of land along the route, Haddad had seen that a plane could fly along the valley bottoms from the Bekaa and come out virtually on top of Tel Aviv. Israeli radars would have the plane on their screens only for a couple of minutes, by which time it would be too late for them to intercept the flying-bomb and shoot it down before it crashed on the city.

Haddad's plan had been simple: stuff the light plane to the gills with high explosives, then get Abu Harb to fly the pre-planned route and crash it right into the middle of Tel Aviv's tallest building, Shalom Tower. He expected the tower to fall on other nearby buildings, compounding the damage caused by the crash debris and the initial explosion. The Master attended the final practice sessions. Luckily for the Israelis but unfortunately for Abu Harb, he crashed on his very last practice landing, and was severely injured. This put an end to the entire operation. It had taken two and a half years to set up, and came to nothing in a moment. But Haddad never worried for a second about failed operations. He just walked away and moved on to the next idea.

These are examples of operations that went wrong. But even if one of his inventions or schemes failed to pay off, Haddad was always coming up with something new. It was impossible to predict where, how and when he would strike next.

When the PFLP hit a financial crisis in 1972, Haddad set up a special operation to raise funds. He experimented with the German postal system, finding out exactly how long it took a letter posted in a certain mail box in a certain Frankfurt street to reach the desk of the General Manager of Lufthansa. Once he had established this, he got his men to hijack a Lufthansa airliner to Aden. As they were taking control of the jet, a letter from Haddad hit the General Manager's desk. Inside was a key, a demand for five million dollars in mixed used notes and a set of instructions. The key opened a car left in the car-park of Beirut's international airport. The instructions said that the person carrying the ransom money should go to the car, open it and look in its glove-box; there he would find further instructions. If these instructions were not followed, the letter said that the airliner would be blown up at a given time.

One hour before the deadline, a small private jet landed at Beirut. A lone German man clutching a heavy bag got out, looked around nervously, then made his way to the car-park. Immediately one of our fighters recognised the man as someone who had served previously as a member of the German embassy 'diplomatic' staff in Beirut. The German was a spy. He got in the car, opened the glove-box, read what he was supposed to do and set off. A team of twenty different PFLP vehicles followed him at various stages of the appointed route, to make sure he really was alone. The German parked at the appointed spot. As he pulled up, a dozen cars surrounded him. 'Please don't kill me,' was the first thing he said, 'I have the money – don't kill me!' You could understand his nerves.

He was taken to a café, where German-speaking guerrillas chatted with him about the films he had seen recently. Meanwhile, other guerrillas were counting the money. It was fifty Deutschmarks short of the five million. At the bottom of the money-bag was a note, signed by the General Manager of Lufthansa: 'We apologise for the missing fifty marks – it was impossible to get the full amount on a Sunday.'

The German was taken back to Beirut airport. 'The deadline has almost expired,' he said, looking at his watch. 'In fifteen minutes they will blow up the plane. How can we get it back now?' 'Easily,' said the local PFLP commander. 'Get on to the control-tower radio here and send the following three words to the tower at Aden airport: 'Martyr Abu Taláat'. He did so: it was the code for the aircraft's release. Lufthansa got its airliner back.

And the PFLP no longer had a financial crisis.

CHAPTER
NINE

Bassam Abu-Sharif

The next time I saw 'Carlos' was in July 1970, in the PFLP-run 'foreigners' training camp outside Amman. He was one of about ninety foreign recruits undergoing advanced instruction there, near the ancient ruined city of Jarash. Carlos joined in the general weapons courses, gaining greater proficiency with light arms and explosives. He attended the numerous political lectures and seminars. The officer in charge of this camp was an Iraqi major called 'Qadir', who had deserted from the Iraqi army and come over to us. Major Qadir told me that this student, Carlos, was not run-of-the-mill. He learned extremely quickly, he led and dominated discussions, he had great courage.

At the very end of their course, the foreign trainees got a little surprise. They were attacked without warning, in the night, by seasoned PFLP fighters using live ammunition. The idea was to see how they stood up under fire. There were always a few who panicked at this final test of their mettle. It was the nearest thing the PFLP had to a passing-out parade.

Live mortar rounds started exploding near the training camp at about four in the morning. It was still pitch black. Machine-gun fire ripped overhead. The trainees had been told that if the camp ever came under attack, they were to withdraw across the nearby river, re-group on the slopes above, and await orders. When the tracer eventually stopped flying, I walked down into the abandoned camp with the major. Everyone seemed to have carried out orders, but the camp was not entirely empty: there was one student left in it. It was Carlos.

He was lying back on his kit, perfectly at ease, smoking a cigarette. 'What the hell are you doing here?' I demanded. 'You're supposed to be under attack. Jump to it!'

He looked me straight in the eye, and replied evenly, 'That's rubbish.'

'How would you know?' I asked, flabbergasted by his cheek.

'Because if it was real, I'd be dead by now,' he drawled.

I couldn't help laughing at this. 'Your place is not here,' I told him. I turned to the major. 'Take him to the professional camp tomorrow,' I said. This Carlos was a man who clearly stood out from the crowd.

Very few foreigners made it through to the PFLP's professional camp. The next day the instructors there interviewed Carlos, put him through a number of tests, and accepted him. This camp was a completely different proposition. The training was very heavy indeed, both physically and mentally, but once again Carlos sailed through it all. If they made it past this stage, trainees were sent either on to the People's Republic of China or to the alternative finishing school, codenamed 'H4', run near the border with Iraq by that country's army. Carlos was sent there.

Uzi Mahnaimi

On the very first day of my basic infantry training, three members of the Japanese Red Army Faction terror gang threw hand-grenades across the passenger concourse of Lydda (now Ben-Gurion) airport. They opened up on the survivors with sub-machine guns. Twenty-seven people were killed in the carnage, dozens more injured. Their leader, Okomoto, was working for Wadi Haddad and the PFLP.

The airport was just outside Tel Aviv, so close to my family home that I felt the attack almost as something personal. But no sooner had the shock-waves from the airport massacre begun dying away than there was yet another terrorist slaughter. Eight members of a shadowy new Palestinian group calling itself 'Black September' grabbed eleven Israeli athletes and officials at the Munich Olympics. Golda Meir's government refused their demand to release 200 Palestinian prisoners from Israeli gaols. With Israeli co-operation, five German police snipers ambushed the terrorists at Fürstenfeldbruck air force base outside Munich, as the gang was trying to fly out. All eleven athletes were killed in the ensuing firefight.

These attacks were devastating to the people of Israel; the whole country reeled under them. I realised how naive my euphoria as a fifteen-year-old had been, how utterly misplaced those feelings of triumph at the Allenby Bridge. We had not won a final victory in the Six-Day War. The Palestinians were not going to give up. The real war was only just beginning, and in joining up for my three years' compulsory military service I was certain to become part of it. It was not a war that would figure in the official military histories. It was a war of terror and counter-terror, a conflict that might last ten, twenty or a hundred years. And it was a war in which Israelis were being hit. We were not, after all, invincible. We were very, very vulnerable.

Bassam Abu-Sharif

In September 1970 Haddad went for the big one: a multiple hijack. By now, we had the world by the throat. Our operations had transformed the situation in the Middle East: we felt invincible, unstoppable; we could do just about anything we liked. The mighty Israelis had been obliged to back down and meet our demands, they'd had to release our prisoners, broadcast our statements. We had taken power. If we could seize one airliner successfully, why not seize four? Haddad's plan was to hijack three New York-bound flights: El Al flight 219 from Amsterdam, a Swissair DC-8 out of Zurich and a TWA Boeing 707, flight 741 from Frankfurt. We knew that American hostages had the highest news value. Once in control of the planes, our commandos would land them all at a disused British military airfield in Jordan: Dawson's Field. We would then play the respective governments off against another, to force the release of Palestinian political prisoners held in Europe. Leila Khaled, who had already proved her courage and nerve in a previous hijack, took on the toughest assignment – the El Al hijack. Also in her team was a Nicaraguan volunteer, Patrick Arguello, and two Palestinian men.

Above all things, Haddad loved a challenge. Leila was wanted by police forces everywhere and especially, of course, in Israel. Her photograph had been shown on news-stands all over the world. It was impossible, therefore, to get her past Israeli security and on to another El Al flight. But for Haddad, the more impossible a job looked at the outset, the better he liked it. He wouldn't rest until he had thought of a way round the obstacles.

At the time, a top-class German plastic surgeon was operating on wounded PFLP fighters in one of our camps. Haddad asked him to carry out extensive surgery on Leila, in fact to remodel her face completely, so that she would still be beautiful but, to the police, unrecognisable. She then joined an El Al flight posing as the newly-married Mexican wife of her Nicaraguan 'husband', Arguello. She was wearing a sombrero and a neat little bolero waistcoat. She looked very demure, and very pretty. The deception worked like a charm. She passed even the intensive scrutiny of the Israeli security men at the El Al desk in Amsterdam.

The hijack itself, though, went horribly wrong. Although they let her and Arguello through, El Al security spotted the other two members of Khaled's team while the aircraft was still on the ground, and immediately took them off the flight. Undeterred, Leila and Patrick decided to go it alone. Once the aircraft had levelled off, they leapt from their seats. But the Israeli pilot, trained in counter-measures, banked sharply and put the aircraft into a steep dive. The hijackers were thrown off balance. In the confusion, the Israeli security chief on board shot Patrick Arguello dead. Six or seven passengers jumped on top of Khaled, biting, kicking and scratching her. She pulled the pin from a hand-grenade and dropped it, but the device failed to detonate. After a mighty struggle, she was bound tightly with neckties and taken to prison in London.

Meanwhile, Leila's comrades, who had been thrown off the El Al flight, decided to do a little hijacking on their own initiative. This was strictly against orders, but they pulled it off. They simply bought new first-class tickets at Schipol airport for cash and hijacked a PanAm Boeing 747. Taking this huge aircraft was definitely not part of our original plan. It was so heavy that we were unsure whether the packed sand strip at Dawson's Field would bear its weight. We decided the two men should take the plane to Beirut, wire it up with explosives, then explode it on the ground at Cairo airport. It would tell Nasser what we thought about his decision to start negotiating with the Israelis.

The Swissair DC8 and the TWA Boeing 707 landed as arranged at Dawson's Field. I was on the ground there, waiting. When I got to them, the passengers were terrified. Since we had no steps for the aircraft, they had to come down the escape chutes. When they got to the bottom of the chutes, many passengers set off running wildly into the desert. They had no idea where they were going, or how they would survive if they ever got there. Quite soon after they had begun running, the heat would hit them, they would realise they were at greater risk wandering around without food, water or shelter in the middle of a vast stretch of sand than they were with us, and they would come back, looking sweaty and sheepish.

I asked one American who had done this where he thought he was. 'Somewhere in Africa?' he asked dazedly. 'No,' I told him 'You are in Jordan, and we are Palestinian guerrillas.' 'In Pakistan?' he asked, completely bewildered. 'No,' I said patiently. 'We are Palestinian. From Palestine. You know, the country that is now occupied by Israel.' But he didn't know. He had obviously never heard of Palestine. We will just have to go on hijacking until every American in the world has heard of it, I thought.

Instead of setting off at top speed into the desert, some hijacked passengers tried bribery. One woman, also American, emerged from the aircraft clutching her handbag fiercely to her chest. As soon as she reached the bottom of the chute, she rushed up to the nearest PFLP guerrilla, opened her bag, took out a big roll of dollar bills and shoved them into the surprised man's hands. I strolled over to her. 'Lady,' I asked, 'what the hell do you think you're doing?' She looked at me, uncertain what I meant. Then she understood my question for what it was: extreme disapproval. 'Oh, nothing, nothing,' she said. 'I was just giving him a tip.' 'A tip! A tip for what?' I asked her incredulously. 'For hijacking you here? Put it back in your purse, lady. We are not thieves. This is not a robbery.' Crestfallen, she tucked the dollars back into her purse.

I called all the passengers into a group. There were more than three hundred of them, so many that I had to use a megaphone. 'Look,' I began, 'I'm sorry, we have just hijacked you to the desert in Jordan. This is a country in the Middle East, next to Israel and Syria. We are fighting a just war, a war for the liberation of our country from Israeli occupation. The reason you're in the middle of it is that we want to exchange you for prisoners who were taken in Israel and other countries. By "we", I mean the Popular Front for the Liberation of Palestine.

There's not much else I can tell you. You relax tonight; there is food and drink here for you. We'll talk again tomorrow.' Some of the passengers burst out laughing at the idea of being able to relax, having just been hijacked to a desert airfield seething with heavily-armed PFLP guerrillas, and encircled by Jordanian tanks and infantry. I could see the incongruous side of it myself.

Just then, news came that our commandos had blown the PanAm jumbo jet to pieces on the ground in Cairo. The TWA aircraft captain was inspecting his own 707 at the time with the rest of his crew. 'Do you know what has happened?' I asked him. 'No, what?' he replied. 'Our guys have just blown up a PanAm 747 at Cairo airport.' He let out a long whoop of delight. 'Yahoooo . . .! PanAm! Scratch one for the opposition!' This was a new perspective for me on our little venture. 'Well, it's not good news for us,' I told him. 'We wanted that PanAm to land here.' 'No way,' said the captain. 'You've got a TWA plane – that's good enough!'

Three days later, quite unexpectedly, yet another airliner arrived at Dawson's Field. It was a British Overseas Airways Corporation VC-10. It had been hijacked from Bahrain. Haddad was very surprised: this, too, was a completely unexpected development. He had not ordered the hijack. Who had done it?

The control towers at Beirut and Amman airports were in constant touch with us at Dawson's Field. All sorts of officials and ministers were attempting to negotiate on behalf of the passengers. The Beirut controller radioed to Amman that there was a hijacked BOAC flight on its way, and could it have permission to join the merry throng at Dawson's Field? I was with Haddad when the news came in.

'But this was not planned,' he exclaimed, suddenly alarmed. 'We must get ready. This plane might well have a very special passenger-list – like Israeli commandos, for instance.'

Beirut tower told us the hijacker was alone, and insisted he was a *bona fide* Palestinian who wanted to help our cause.

UZI'S PHOTOS

Pilots from German Squadron 304 dancing in Merhavia, Christmas 1917.

German pilots in Merhavia with pioneers, Christmas Eve 1917.

Turk soldiers searching for weapons at a pioneer's house in Merhavia. Our German friends (*right*) are on guard.

Merhavia and Squadron 304, a short time before the British army arrived.

Merhavia pioneers gathering for a photo opportunity.
Shalom Mahnaimi is in the second row from the top, on the right.

Shalom Kreiner's
passport in 1912, with
his mother's handwritten
confirmation.
His father, Haim-bear,
refused to let him go
to Palestine.

Shalom, after work, in his best clothes,
with friends in Merhavia before Friday
dinner.

Shalom, first on the left, during the wheat harvest in Merhavia, 1916 - the first Zionist
settlement in Emek Izrael, near Nazareth, and the hard core of Zionism.

Shalom Mahnaimi (*far left*) and his balalaika, with pioneer friends in Merhavia.

Rabbi Haim-bear Kreiner and his wife Fani: my grandfather's parents. They emigrated from Lithuania after the First World War to join their Zionist children, a decision that saved them from the concentration camps twenty years later.

Shalom Mahnaimi and his wife Hannah Ilgovsky - my grandfather and grandmother - at their wedding in the early 1920s.

Top left: Uzi's parents, Gideon Mahnaimi and Ra'aya Schneider at their wedding in 1951.

Top right: Ilana Mahnaimi, in army uniform, in the Sinai desert a couple of days before the beginning of the Yom Kippur war.

Left: Uzi and Ilana Mahnaimi, relaxing in the spring of 1991 at a Tel Aviv cocktail party to celebrate the end of 45 days' threat of Iraqi missiles during the Gulf War.

Uzi on the summit of Mount Hermon after the Yom Kippur war.

Below: Uzi and father Gideon on the banks of the Suez Canal after the Yom Kippur war.

Maya Mahnaimi,
London 1994.

Below: Tamar Mahnaimi,
Folkestone 1994.

Bassam and Uzi: the first meeting in Amman, January 1995.

23 October 1991. A couple of days before the Madrid peace conference: the first meeting of an Israeli journalist with Arafat at the PLO Headquarters in Tunis.

'OK,' replied Haddad. 'Let him give me a sign.' The hijacker's voice crackled faintly over the airwaves: '*Wara kusa*'. I started laughing. *Wara kusa* is a traditional Arab dish of vine-leaves stuffed with courgettes in a special sauce; it happened to be one of Haddad's favourites. 'Yes,' said Haddad, a broad grin splitting his features. 'This man is definitely one of us. Let him come.'

It turned out that a Palestinian worker in Bahrain heard on the news that Leila Khaled had been imprisoned in London. Leila was a heroine to this man, as she was to all Palestinians, so he decided to do a bit of freelance hijacking to show support. Single-handedly, he would force the British to release the queen of freedom-fighters. The Palestinian worked in a metal-working shop. In his spare time he fashioned an imitation pistol, took it to the airport, and calmly hijacked the first British airliner he laid eyes on.

As the desert grew very cold at night, we put the passengers back on the planes to sleep. They were already beginning to adapt to their situation. A strange sort of community spirit was springing up. They were forming friendships, talking animatedly in little groups, sometimes singing quietly together. I went on board to tuck them in and help keep them calm. 'Don't worry, it's only a hijack. Nobody will be hurt,' I said in my best bedside manner, while my PFLP colleagues went around wiring detonators to large lumps of plastic explosive placed under their seats. One man lost his cool: 'You expect us to be relaxed?' he shouted. 'Relaxed? Look at that guy! What the hell is he doing?' 'He's just laying a few explosive charges,' I said. 'Not for you, though. Don't worry. It's just to blow up the plane in case anybody tries anything.' The poor man subsided back into his seat, muttering wildly to himself.

Just then I saw one of the Canadian stewardesses lobbing a carton of 200 cigarettes to one of our fighters. The man caught it, drew back his arm, and threw it straight back up at her as hard as he could. The carton spun up into the doorway, hitting the stewardess squarely in the chest. 'Who do you think we are?' shouted the man, outraged. 'We are freedom-fighters . . . We are not a gang! You think we want your lousy imperialist cigarettes?' He scrabbled in his pocket, pulled out a packet of twenty cigarettes and waved it furiously in the air. 'We have our own cigarettes; we don't need yours.' He launched into a lengthy diatribe about the political basis of the hijackings. I went along to console the poor woman, who had burst into tears, terrified.

No one was allowed to touch anything without first asking permission from us. One of the TWA security men came up to me. 'I need to check the bathroom at the rear,' he said. 'There's some kind of blockage. It's beginning to stink.' 'OK,' I told him, 'go ahead.' The man came back clutching seven sodden passports. They smelled terrible. I inspected them gingerly from a safe distance. They were clearly all Israeli. So, all the passengers with Israeli nationality had stuffed their passports down the pan, had they? Well, well. 'It might be an idea to wash them,' I said. When the steward came back, I took them. Enormous tension spread through the plane. I could sense everybody watching me. I said nothing, and left.

Examining the passports, I found that three of the Israeli citizens were cabin staff, two were rabbis and two were passengers with dual US-Israeli nationality. Next day we released all the women, children and old people; but we kept a small group of passengers with high political value: all the diplomats – and all the Israelis who'd ditched their passports.

One of the rabbis who had tried to flush away his passport signalled that he wanted to talk to me. He was actually from New York. He was certainly scared, as anyone would be, but he asked me to give him some books to pass the time. I sat down next to him, and we began a discussion. Naturally, he was very much against the idea of taking innocent third parties to advance our cause. We ended our talk without reaching any common ground. The next day we picked up the discussion where we had left off. I enjoyed matching wits with him, and found myself looking forward to our daily exchange of views.

In the end, having listened to the case I put for the people of Palestine, the rabbi said that, in my place, he would do the same. Whether he said that under the strain of the position he was in I cannot tell, but he did say it. Later, when he was released, he was interviewed on television. All he would say to the assembled press was, 'These people deserve to live, and they have a just cause.' He refused to say anything further.

Talking to the people we held hostage, sometimes *tête-à-tête*, sometimes in a group, made me realise how few, still, knew anything at all about the plight of the Palestinians, despite widespread media coverage of our previous hijackings. The image the Israelis projected – of poor little Israel surrounded by murderous Arabs trying all the time to gobble it up – was widely accepted. The Israelis were still way ahead in the propaganda war, but we were catching up fast.

Wanting to hit back at us in kind, Israeli police seized 450 Arabs living in the occupied territories. Some of the detainees were members of our own families; most of George Habash's relatives were rounded up. We were sent a message to say that if we harmed any of our hostages, the Israelis would do the same to the people they were holding. It was exactly the kind of reaction we expected from them, and we ignored it.

Next came rumours of a joint US–Israeli plan to attack us at Dawson's Field. The Pentagon had ordered twenty-five Phantom fighter-bombers over to Incirlik airbase in Turkey. These threats meant we would have to raise the stakes even higher. Wadia Haddad told me to bring two journalists down to the airfield at four the next morning. I picked a Visnews (now Reuters Television) cameraman, and a photographer from an Arab newspaper. 'Film the planes blowing up,' I told the newsmen. The three aircraft exploded in spectacular fireballs as we fired the charges. Then we paraded the hostages: each man was held tightly from behind by a PFLP guerrilla; each had a gun at his head. 'You can kill one or two of us,' Haddad told the Jordanians, 'but we will kill the rest of them.' The Jordanian army withdrew. We then split the hostages into small groups, dispersing them around the whole of Jordan to make it impossible for any would-be rescue missions.

Dawson's Field finally put the PFLP and, far more importantly, the issue of Palestine, on the map. All our demands were met, all our imprisoned fighters were released. The British even allowed Leila Khaled to go free. As for me, I had become notorious. I had given half a dozen lectures to the passengers during the hijack, as well as press and TV interviews. Mistakenly, some journalists saw me as the mastermind behind the whole show. I even finished up on the cover of *Time* magazine, under the headline, 'Pirates of the Air', shouting at the passengers through my trusty megaphone. I had become 'The face of terrorism'.

The hijack at Dawson's Field was a very big success for the PFLP; it attracted unprecedented world-wide media coverage but it had its black side: Dawson's Field triggered another disaster for the Palestinian people.

By 1970, King Hussein of Jordan had hundreds of thousands of Palestinian refugees living inside his borders, even outnumbering Jordan's original population. Heavily armed PLO fighters were using the country as a base for guerrilla operations on a massive international scale. The *fedayin* operated outside Jordanian control. By now, though, Hussein was extremely worried about the numbers and the power of the PLO guerrillas in his land: not least that they might end up overthrowing him. It had happened in Aden. Hussein's determined fight to regain control gave rise to daily gun-battles between his security forces and our fighters.

The Dawson's Field operation was the straw that broke the back of the camel. Though he had originally come out strongly in favour of the Palestinian cause, now Hussein felt he stood to lose everything, including his country. The United States and Israel made it very clear to him that unless he got rid of the Palestinian 'terrorists' operating from his territory, they would come in and do it themselves. Faced with this ultimatum, Hussein ordered his tanks and loyal Bedu infantry into all our camps and training bases. In the ensuing fighting, hundreds of PLO and Jordanian troops were killed and wounded. Exactly how many died is impossible to say, but one thing is for certain: the dead were all Arabs. Our own Arab brothers had taken up arms against us: a catastrophe for the Palestinian cause. We called it 'Black September'.

Under the Jordanian army onslaught large numbers of Palestinian *fedayin*, including myself, fell back to the Ajlun mountains near Jarash, in the north. Here we regrouped. In the summer of 1971 the Jordanian army came after us again. This time, they were determined to drive us out once and for all.

While these battles were raging across the beautiful Jarash hills, Carlos arrived back on the scene. He had completed his training with the Iraqis. Now, like the rest of us, he found himself pitched headlong into the middle of a war zone. He proved to be a real fighter, brave in the face of Jordanian armour and artillery, an excellent soldier. He also showed the quality that Major Qadir had glimpsed in him: ruthlessness. Not only was he nerveless under fire, but he could take life without blinking. The Jordanians shelled and mortared us daily; under this intense fire, Carlos stood out again and again for his sheer *sang-froid*, joining in several successful counter-attacks on Jordanian army positions. He was blooded. But not even a thousand Carloses could postpone the inevitable. By the end of the year, all PLO groups had been kicked out of Jordan.

Although most PLO fighters went to Lebanon or Syria after Black September, Haddad himself had to keep on the move: Syria, Iraq, Yemen, Lebanon, he was everywhere and nowhere at the same time. I went to Beirut. Carlos came with me. After his performance in Jarash, I recommended him for operational work. He went to learn the black arts of terrorism at the feet of 'the Master'.

Over the following weeks and months Haddad put Carlos

through his own special training programme. Once again, the student studied hard and learned well. The Master was pleased with him. He was now ready.

Carlos went on the missions list.

CHAPTER
TEN

Bassam Abu-Sharif

I fell in love with the woman least suitable for me in the whole world.

I met her first in Beirut, immediately after the battles of Black September. I'd been back in the city a few days, when a group of student friends from the American University came round to celebrate the fact that I'd escaped from Jordan in one piece. So many of my friends hadn't.

With them, the happy throng brought a young woman, a third-year mathematics student. Her name was Amal Khoury. She was ardent, intelligent and beautiful. I knew nothing about her, I had no idea what sort of family she was from, but she was striking. As the evening wore on, I noticed that her eyes were changing colour gradually, from green to brown. It was amazing. When she first came through the door, I was beginning to cook supper. By the time I'd finished making the meal, I was entranced by her.

There was something in the air between us, some rapport, that lovely inexpressible tension you feel when you're really drawn to somebody. I didn't quite know why I felt what I did, or what to do about it, and I had absolutely no idea what she thought of me – I wasn't what you might call a good catch. We started talking about the political situation in Jordan. She burned with the will to get justice for the people of Palestine. I loved this bright fire inside her. I wanted to warm my hands by it.

I asked her why she supported our cause so strongly, because she obviously wasn't a Palestinian. To judge by her accent, she was Lebanese. She said she was a member of the Syrian Socialist Party (PPS). The PPS believed the whole region, Iraq, Syria, Palestine, Jordan and Lebanon, should be united: this was what they meant by 'Syrian'. It was a sweet dream, the old dream of a united Fertile Crescent, much like Nasser's classic piece of Pan-Arab self-delusion, with about as much chance of becoming hard reality. But the PPS also supported the liberation of Palestine by armed struggle, which was something we certainly did agree about. We talked on as the sun went down. Most people went home, but Amal and her best friend stayed. I suggested we go to the Commodore Hotel, for a drink by the pool. We stayed there talking until three o'clock in the morning.

Every two or three days our group of friends would meet, which meant Amal and I would meet. We went on circling one another gently in this way for a few months. One Sunday there was a move to drive up for lunch in Ehden, which is a very beautiful village in the north, on the slopes of Mount Lebanon. The water is clear there, tumbling down from the heights, the food is good, the fruit is very sweet.

On the way back to Beirut, Amal suggested we call in at her home village, Diq al-Mahdi. This name, Aramaic in origin, means 'the beautiful view'. I was expecting – what? A small village house? Instead, we pulled up outside a palace. A gleaming white villa spread its handsome wings against the hillside. Bright sprays of bougainvillea splashed their brilliant contrast against the dark shrubbery of its gardens. Behind all this again, the tall cedars of Lebanon stood in magnificent sentry. Amal smiled impishly at me. 'This is my home,' she said. 'Would you like to come in for coffee?'

We went in, the whole group of us, to be greeted by her mother, who rang rather majestically for refreshments. Signs of enormous wealth were everywhere, from the superb paintings on the walls to the antique Sèvres porcelain the coffee arrived in.

I discovered a great many things about Amal that afternoon. She was from one of Lebanon's oldest and most important Maronite families. They were extremely wealthy, with extensive business interests in Africa – factories, all kinds of things. To me, the most extraordinary thing was not the money, but the fact that Amal was a Christian. I was a Muslim. This meant trouble, so I avoided the issue. I didn't tell her mother the truth: that I was a Palestinian Muslim and a member of the PFLP; I mumbled something to the effect that I was a Jordanian student. Mrs Khoury and I got along very well. 'You must be sure to come back and see us,' she said as I was leaving. I smiled and nodded my agreement. I intended to.

As we were driving back down to Beirut, Amal dropped her grenade. 'I must tell you something,' she began, looking straight ahead through the windscreen. I knew at once from her tone and her stare that this was going to be bad. I braced myself, waiting for the axe to fall. 'I am engaged to be married,' she went on, 'to a Christian man. My cousin.' She held up her left hand. One of the world's largest solitaire diamonds was glittering on her ring finger. Strangely enough, I had never really noticed it before. At that second, as I stared at the ring, and the impact of what she'd just said came home to me, I realised how much I was in love with Amal. I felt the world slow down. The next few seconds of my life were going to be crucial. 'Why didn't you tell me this before?' I asked finally.

Amal brought the car to a halt by the side of the road. 'I suppose I didn't want to put you off,' she replied, smiling gently. I looked back into her eyes. 'Amal,' I said, reaching for her hand, 'there is something I ought to tell you, too.' She watched me intently. 'I, too, am engaged to be married. To a Muslim girl – in Amman!' We both burst out laughing. Somehow we'd forgotten to mention these awkward little details until then.

A few weeks later Amal handed me a piece of stiff white card. It was an invitation to her wedding. Not surprisingly, my name wasn't on it, but her cousin's was. She meant to show me that her own 'awkward little detail' was turning into a very big problem, for both of us: the wedding day was approaching fast. She had even been having fittings for her wedding-dress.

In April 1972 I travelled to Denmark, to speak at a mass political rally. There was going to be a huge march through Copenhagen, a very big show: I was sharing a platform with a top Vietnamese freedom fighter. Just before I left for the airport, Amal came to see me. Still nothing was really resolved between us. She said quietly, 'I wanted to tell you something before you go.' She stopped. The fear of all lovers, the fear of loss, came at once into my heart. 'What is it?' I asked nervously. 'I've just broken off my engagement.' She held up her hand again. The glittering diamond had disappeared. 'Really?' I stuttered, pulling myself together. 'Well, I split up with my fiancée weeks ago!' I brandished the piece of paper that released me from my wedding contract in front of her twinkling eyes. 'We were both going to be married, and we've both broken it off,' she laughed, slipping her arms round my neck. 'What does this mean?'

'It means,' I replied happily, 'that we shall have to marry each other!' There was silence between us as we thought about the implications. 'Look,' I said finally. 'I love you. I want to marry you. But now I know who you are, the sort of family you are from, I think it's my duty to tell you that life with me would be very tough.'

'I don't care,' she replied. 'We can build our own life together. Isn't that the point?'

It was the point, but what were we to do? She was a high-born Maronite heiress, I was a penniless Palestinian guerrilla. We knew, if they found out about it, that both our families would stamp on the relationship. It was against every tradition, on both sides. The Maronite Christians of Lebanon are deeply conservative, in general, and politically right-wing. They regard themselves as in every way superior to Muslims, never mind Palestinians. Maronites like to call Palestinians 'refugees'; to them the word is a term of abuse. A favourite Maronite saying is, 'One Palestinian in the sea – pollution; all Palestinians in the sea – solution.' Great joke.

Amal's family did not subscribe to this type of narrow racism. But would they let their darling daughter marry a Palestinian? We both knew the answer to that one.

So we didn't tell them. Sameeh, though, Amal's brother, had cast himself in the role of jealous guardian. Sameeh was extremely suspicious of me, and extremely possessive where his sister was concerned. He obviously didn't believe I was a respectable Jordanian. He took to following Amal in his car whenever she tried to visit me. She had to sneak out of the house when she knew he wasn't about.

Despite this little piece of nonsense, we carried on seeing one another as often as we could, almost every day. Like the youth of Sparta, we kept our love secret, which made it even more intense. It became so intense that we knew we had to get married.

But how on earth could we?

CHAPTER
ELEVEN

Bassam Abu-Sharif

B y 1972, the Middle East was approaching melt-down
point. The massacres at Lydda and Munich gave rise
to a new Israeli policy with one very simple objective: to
eliminate the leadership of the PLO. The idea was that by
cutting off the head of the monster, the body would naturally
wither away. The Israelis set about their self-imposed task of
killing all the PLO's men of calibre using the methods of the
terrorist assassin: the parcel-bomb and the car-bomb. Their
professed targets were the PLO's operational commanders. In
practice, they killed whomever they could get.

I was still officially a deputy to Ghassan Kanafani, the editor
of *Al-Hadaf* (*The Target*), the PFLP magazine. In fact, we did
just a little bit more than putting out a periodical. Both of
us travelled the globe more or less continually, giving public
lectures, holding seminars, putting the case for the Palestinian
Arabs – and damning the Israelis. In 1969 I gave twenty-three
lectures in twenty-three American universities. In 1971, I went
round fourteen different universities in the United Kingdom

doing my stuff. In 1972 it was the Scandinavian countries: Sweden, Norway, Denmark. Despite the label 'terrorist' that many tried to hang round our necks, everywhere we found young people who were sympathetic, and eager to learn more about our cause.

The Israeli government feared this concerted PFLP programme, hated us opening the world's eyes to the truth about Palestine. Often enough, I would find myself speaking on the same platform as a Vietnamese liberation leader. Naturally I'd always take the opportunity to draw a parallel between the US role in Vietnam and the Israeli occupation of Palestine. This kind of thing did Israel great damage. We were winning hearts and minds, we were gradually counteracting the one-eyed Israeli version of what was happening in the Middle East. Bit by bit, Ghassan and I were turning opinion around in countries that had previously been friendly towards the Jewish state.

The Israelis didn't want to lose the propaganda war, so they decided to shoot the messengers: in this case, Ghassan Kanafani and me.

On 8 July 1972 at ten in the morning, Ghassan was taking his pretty twenty-one-year-old niece to enrol at the American University of Beirut. They got into his car in the garage underneath his house, and Ghassan turned the key in the ignition. The ignition circuit had been wired up to a large block of plastic explosive taped under the driver's seat.

The huge explosion blew Ghassan, the girl and the car to pieces. I rushed down from the office to find those pieces scattered all over the garage. The bomb was obviously the work of Mossad. I felt intense hatred. How could they have killed my friend and colleague in this cowardly, cold-blooded way? And that innocent, lovely girl! Ghassan's murder re-motivated me, re-kindled my determination to fight all the harder.

Seventeen days later, on 25 July, it was my turn.

The book had been hollowed out. Nestling in the excavated space were two explosive charges wired to go off when the uncut section of the book was lifted. For a microsecond I saw the blocks of plastic explosive, the black wires and the tiny bright red detonators. Instinctively I swayed back. That movement probably saved my life.

They had meant to blow me into three separate pieces. One of the charges had been tamped to direct its blast upwards, blowing my head off at the throat; the other was designed to explode downwards, cutting off my legs at the trunk. Somebody had wanted to make sure.

The table the booby-trap was resting on happened to be made of iron. The massive force of the downward blast blew a hole straight through its thick surface, ripping open part of my stomach wall and my right upper thigh, and peppering me with shrapnel fragments.

The other half-kilogram of explosive blew off the first and second fingers and the thumb on my right hand, as well as two fingers on my left hand. It also blinded me in the right eye, opened a gaping wound across my throat, and blew my right eardrum in. It broke my jaw apart, on both sides, smashed my lips and teeth to pieces, and sliced open large wounds in my chest and trunk. Those were the main injuries. The tiny reflex sway I made backward, in the split second after glimpsing the bomb, was what saved me from outright decapitation. If that table had been made of wood, my legs would certainly have been severed at the thigh. I'd been lucky, really.

I did not lose consciousness at once. I felt no pain. All was black. Everything was spinning. Although I did not realise it, I was completely deaf. I remember telling myself, 'OK, that's the end. Maybe I'll see Ghassan now.' I thought I was dead. Then, suddenly, I felt the floor crashing up hard into me. 'I'm still alive,' I thought. 'If I'm not dead, they didn't want to kill me. They wanted to kidnap me! I must move, quickly.'

Even blind, I knew the layout of the room. I got up, staggered forward until I bumped into a wall, and began feeling my way out of the office. When I reached the door, a current of air brushed my face. I felt pain for the first time, a massive pain that gripped me like a huge pair of pliers that seemed to have taken hold of my whole body. I also felt that I was very wet; something was drenching my chest and legs. What was that?

I had just shuffled through into the corridor outside when I felt two strong hands seize my upper arms. 'Who are you?' I asked. There was no response. I still hadn't realised I was deaf and blind. 'It's them,' I thought. 'They're kidnapping me!' I began to struggle. I could feel that they were taking me downstairs, putting me in a car. 'Who are you?' I kept asking. 'Who are you?' But my kidnappers made no answer. Suddenly a great wave of tiredness swept through me. Very well then, I thought, I can do no more. If they were taking me, so be it. 'OK,' I mumbled, 'take me to the AUH' [American University Hospital]. 'Please just take me to the AUH.'

It was then that I began suffocating on my own blood. I was choking, unable either to spit out or swallow the blood that was filling my throat. I spiralled down into unconsciousness, choking.

Uzi Mahnaimi

Intelligence agencies have their own internal dynamic. Once an agency exists, it has to do something. There is an operational momentum which means that if the preferred target cannot be hit, you move on to the next person down the list, or the one after that, until you do find someone who can be hit.

In 1972 it was impossible for someone working in the Mossad office with particular responsibility for executions not to have noticed Bassam Abu-Sharif. He was a constant thorn in the flesh of Israel, not as a terrorist but as a very successful propagandist for Palestine. Someone did notice. 'He is not – perhaps – one of the hijackers himself,' they reasoned, 'but he is the apologist for hijackers; he works with Wadia Haddad. We know where he is – in the PFLP information office in Beirut.

He is easy to reach there. We almost got Haddad in Beirut, but he was lucky. Why don't we hit Abu-Sharif instead?'

So the Mossad man wrote a memo to his boss suggesting Bassam Abu-Sharif as a target for assassination by parcel-bomb. 'Why not?' came back the response. 'We can't get all the bastards, but we can get this one. He's an easy target, we'd be better off without him. Go ahead, why don't you. Send him a present.'

Bassam Abu-Sharif

It was eight days before I heard my first noise. The sound was coming from a place that was very far away, a distant echo of a life I'd once had, the sound of someone shouting my name: 'Bass-aa-am . . .'

'Yes,' I croaked, then winced in agony. I hadn't realised that my jaws were wired tight shut.

'Do you recognise me? Do you know who I am?' asked the voice.

'Yes,' I mumbled. 'Your name is Khaled Abd-El Rahman.' It was my bodyguard. 'Amal?' I mumbled sleepily, 'Where is Amal?' Then I drifted back into the blackness. For the doctors, this was the first proof that I could hear anything at all. Wrapped up as I had been like a mummy, they had formed no real idea of whether I would see, or hear again – or even live.

Next day I awoke feeling slightly more alive, and signalled for Khaled. I said to him, 'You know me very well. I can't see anything. There is only pain. Tell me exactly what happened to me. Exactly.'

'It was a parcel-bomb,' he began, hesitatingly. 'You have lost all your hearing in one ear, but you can still hear a little with the other one. Your jaw is broken, top and bottom; you will need plastic surgery to replace the missing gum at the front, and new teeth all round.' He paused.

This was as difficult for him as it was for me; maybe more so.

'You have a 15-centimetre by 3-centimetre gash in your throat,' he continued. 'Large lumps of both your thighs and your stomach are missing; two fingers and the thumb on your right hand are missing or badly mutilated, as are two fingers on your left hand. Oh, and you have shrapnel all over your face and body, many small pieces. But you will live. Whether you will see again, we do not know.'

That gave me something to think about.

As I lay there in the hospital, with a tube down my throat and my jaws wired together, there was nothing to do but think. The only bit of me still working properly was my mind. I thought very deeply about life – and death. Sometimes it felt as though my head would split under the pressure of the myriad thoughts seething about inside. I thought in detail of what I would like to do to the Mossad men who had sent me this bomb, to the ones who had killed Ghassan. I devised exquisite tortures for them, repeated endlessly. Nothing was too bad for them. But, as the days passed and my anger cooled a little, I began to have a different thought.

I thought that violence was not the way. This did not mean the Israelis had frightened me into giving up the struggle. I would still fight, with all I had, for a Palestinian state. But now, having suffered it at first hand, I knew violence would never work. My feelings about peace, about negotiated settlement, the unfocused feelings I had experienced as a student, when I'd read a document about peace in the Middle East written by a Quaker man called Fisher, these feelings all became much sharper, much more profound. Almost everyone I knew expected me to want revenge: 'an eye for an eye' and all that: exactly appropriate in my case. What I actually felt, what I had at first tried to deny to myself but now could not, was, 'Why war?' By the end of my stay in hospital I did not feel the desire for revenge on my attackers. I felt something strangely like pity for them.

101

At some point the killing had to stop. Having suffered it at first hand, I knew: violence was not the way. Peace was the way.

On the morning Mossad blew me up, Amal was supposed to be coming in to see me. For some reason, she couldn't make it. When she phoned the office, they wouldn't tell her where I was. The more my colleagues tried not to tell her anything, the more anxious she became. 'Where is Bassam?' she insisted. 'You must tell me where he is.' Finally someone told her I was in the operating theatre, in hospital. 'What?' she demanded. 'What has happened to him?'

'Oh,' replied one of my colleagues, unable to tell her the truth, 'he has had a small accident – an injury to his finger. He has just gone in to have it looked at.'

Amal jumped into her car. Her brother, as ever, followed. She hurried into the hospital thinking I had had nothing more than a minor accident. But, in the elevator on the way up, she met a friend of ours. He was crying. Amal felt a rush of fear. 'What's wrong?' she asked urgently. 'He's hurt more than his finger, hasn't he?' The man made no answer, but dropped his head, staring at the floor. 'I only hope Bassam will live,' he mumbled at last. Amal ran out into the ward where they'd taken me, his words echoing in her head. She found dozens of people milling about, but no one with the time to answer her questions. Then she caught sight of Khaled, who had brought me to the hospital. He was kind enough to tell her what had really happened.

No one was allowed to see me; I was in any case unconscious. But Amal stayed as close as she could all day, to hear the results of the surgical investigations. She went back home late, her eyes red from weeping. She explained to her family where she had been, whom she'd been seeing in Beirut. In fact they already knew, because of Sameeh the shadow. Far from showing any sympathy, they gave her seven kinds of hell for seeing me. So this was why she had broken off her wedding to a suitable Christian boy? For some Palestinian terrorist?

From that day on, Amal was locked into the house. And just in case she ever did escape, her maniac brother confiscated her car-keys. She languished at home, consumed by anxiety, fear and frustration. No knight-errant came to her rescue. After a few days, though, she did manage to escape. She hurried down to Beirut and sat for about fifteen minutes by my bedside before the Khoury clan caught up with her.

Her family went on doing everything they could to stop Amal seeing me again. Not only was I a bloody Palestinian, but I was a terrorist Palestinian. What could she be thinking of? How could she possibly know such a man, let alone be involved with him? There wasn't even much of him left now, was there? Amal was undeterred. On odd afternoons, while I lay swathed like a mummy in my bandages, she would steal a few precious minutes at my bedside on some pretext or other. Lying broken and unconscious, I never knew she was there.

Three weeks later, the medics decided to remove the bandages from my eyes. There were no fewer than ten doctors in attendance, including several consultants. But where was Amal? Khaled told me, 'Bassam, outside there are many beautiful girls; each one is asking to come in and see you. But the doctor says you have to choose one, and one only.'

'Who is there?' I asked. So and so, he replied – they were names I did not know, Palestinian women who supported the cause, who cared. 'And there is one outside I do not know,' he went on. 'She is very persistent. Her name is Amal.'

A huge wave of love and happiness rushed through me. 'OK,' I said. My heart was beating faster. 'Let this Amal in.' It was her. She came to me. I could not see her, but I could hear her and smell her wonderful scent. We could not embrace, because of my injuries, but the touch of her hand on my face was enough. It was my beloved. I could hear her sobbing, with anguish, happiness and relief. I found that one of my own tear-ducts, too, was still working.

Dr Lowin was the consultant who had carried out the remedial surgery on my eyes, so to him fell the task of unwrapping them. The room fell very quiet now. 'Bassam,' he said gently, 'you remember I told you about the risks before I operated . . .?'

'Yes,' I replied. 'Go ahead.' The last bit of bandage came away. There was absolute silence. I could hear the stillness of an extreme tension in the room.

'What do you see?' he asked me finally.

'Nothing,' I replied. 'I see nothing. Only blackness.'

'Pass me a torch,' he cried. 'A torch, quickly!' I could hear the other doctors scrabbling in their pockets for their little eye torches. I sensed the instrument as he placed it up to the iris of my left eye. 'What do you see?' he asked.

'I see nothing,' I replied. 'But I can feel the heat of the torch.'

'That's good,' he breathed softly. 'Now I'm going to draw back my arm. Let me know if you see anything.'

'Wait,' I said. 'Wait . . .! I see light. I see light!' Gradually a patch of greyness formed across my vision, then I could make out light and dark patches, indistinct shapes; in a little while, I could see. The consultant stood at the bottom of the bed, beaming at me. 'How many?' he asked, holding up five fingers.

'Five,' I said. I tried hard to smile back, but it still hurt too much.

'And now?'

'Three.'

'My dear friend,' he said, 'you are going to see.'

At this, a huge shout went up outside. There was a long rip of automatic rifle-fire. One of my friends, Sharif, had gone to the steps of the hospital and announced that I would see. Though I had not known it until then, there was a crowd of people outside, waiting on the news. I was truly amazed at the noise. How could there be such a crowd?

I could see Amal's face for the first time in weeks. I could see that her cheeks were shiny with tears, and that she was trying bravely to smile and laugh through them all at the same time. It was the best thing I'd ever seen in my life.

In a little while, after we'd said our hellos, she told me what she'd been going through. Her parents and her brother never let up for a moment, but she would not give in. It was a constant battle for her at home. The Lebanese are known in the Middle East for their strength of will. I discovered then that Amal had a will stronger than steel, a will as strong as faith itself. 'It isn't a question of being determined,' she told me. 'It's just the way it is. And this doesn't matter, either,' she said, pointing at my bandages. 'We are in love. We must be together. Nothing's going to change that.'

'Well,' continued the doctor, when the cheering had died down a little, 'you will be able to see, but you will not be able to read. The yellow spot in your retina is destroyed.' This was not good news. I had to be able to read. Information was my business. 'Is a strong will of any use?' I asked him. 'Yes,' he laughed, 'you can try. You can try to train your eye. Who knows? Perhaps I'm wrong. Relax for one month, then I shall come back and give you instructions how to train it to read again.' He came, I trained it for some days – and I could read.

This was just as well, because my jaws stayed clamped together with silver wire for the next ten weeks. Unable to talk, I was fed by means of a plastic straw. One of the worst things was being unable to yawn. I finally left hospital two months after first catching sight of Amal again. My normal weight is about 80 kilos. On leaving my bed, I weighed 36 kilos: I was a skeleton.

But with Amal by my side, I was a very happy one.

CHAPTER
TWELVE

Uzi Mahnaimi

After basic infantry training, I applied to join military intelligence. This was not because I wanted to follow in the footsteps of my father, but because I still had back problems. Army intelligence struck me as being one of the better options. I began by doing a course in combat air reconnaissance, including air navigation, aerial photographic interpretation and various other skills. This was followed by a further three months on a basic intelligence course. Then I applied for officer training. I was in the middle of the Negev desert, half-way through this, when the massed armoured divisions of the Egyptian and Syrian forces attacked Israel. It was October 1973. The Yom Kippur war had started.

To say the Arabs had caught us with our pants down would be understating the truth. It was headless chicken time. Yom Kippur is the main religious festival of the Jewish calendar. No work is permitted, everything is closed right down. I was playing tennis on base with another officer cadet when a sergeant came running. He was shouting something about an Arab attack, his words whirling away on the desert wind. We dropped our racquets, ran inside and turned on the radio. At Yom Kippur, even broadcasting is outlawed, but we heard an announcement: 'This is an emergency broadcast. An hour ago, forces of the Egyptian and Syrian armies attacked Israel . . . All IDF units report back to base immediately . . .' I stood there for a minute or two trying to take this in, while the radio went on repeating its message. It was quite unbelievable. The Arab armies had rolled into Israel at the height of the most important festival of the Hebrew year, and the entire IDF, its men and women, its commanders, had all been caught napping – in many cases, quite literally. What a monumental cock-up!

A Syrian tank division had almost reached the shores of the Sea of Galilee before the IDF had even begun organising basic resistance. The Arabs had disguised their preparations for war brilliantly. There had been advance Israeli intelligence of the attack, but nobody had drawn the right conclusions from it. Israel was lucky not to go under in the Yom Kippur war. For the first week or so, our forces took a pasting. Several factors helped to save us. About one week into the war, the US government finally responded to our frantic pleas for help and established an air bridge to Israel, shipping over massive amounts of war *matériel*, including some much-needed modern weaponry such as Sidewinder missiles for our air force. Then, the Arab invaders were tactically stupid. The Egyptian tank brigades had been trained to cross the canal – but that was all. They crossed the canal, and rolled to a halt. Their commanders were not trained to take the initiative. Once they'd stopped, we had time to re-group and counter-attack. If the tanks had kept going, consolidating en route, who knows? It might have been a different story.

Once the country woke up to what was happening, everyone was mobilised for action at panic speed. They plucked everyone out of my own course, although none of us had quite completed our officer training, and sent us straight off to fight at the front. Most members of that particular course

107

never did finish their training. In fact, their families never saw them again.

Because I'd completed an air reconnaissance course, I was teamed up with a pilot, and sent to war in a single-engined Dornier aircraft, armed with nothing more lethal than a Hasselblad camera. Our mission was to watch along the Jordanian border for signs of aggression and the slightest sign of military activity. The high command was extremely nervous about the Jordanians joining in with the Syrians. On past form, it was only too likely that they would. We flew for nine hours at a stretch, in numbing discomfort, with our parachutes strapped on tightly the whole time. One lucky shot was all it would take to bring down our minuscule plane.

It was all the most fantastic adventure. I had no thought of personal safety. I was enjoying myself. Looking down onto the 'enemy' lines gave me an incredible charge. I couldn't wait to get into action – real action, that is, not this aerial swanning about. My gung-ho attitude wasn't a sign of courage, but simply foolhardy enthusiasm. Extreme youth often likes extreme conflict. What I failed to realise was that we were lucky – we had the quiet sector. This time round, the Jordanian army had decided to stay at home. At the time I thought we were pretty unlucky. Then something happened that made me think again.

One of the other airborne reconnaissance crews, a pilot/observer team in a Dornier just like our own, was in the hottest battle zone, spotting over the Golan Heights. On the third day of the war, they took off on their second mission. As they were approaching the Syrian lines, they decided they would make a name for themselves by being very daring and getting down for some close-up photographs of the Syrian armour. They got a bit too close. Three Syrian SAM-6 missiles hit their little plane in rapid succession, blowing it into very small pieces.

A few days later another spotter crew was shot down, this time over the Egyptian border. Once again, both crew members were killed outright. Suddenly I didn't feel quite so rash. I knew there'd been a shortage of trained crews even before the war broke out. It was obvious we must be next in line to take on the Golan sector. Sure enough, the order I'd been dreading came through. It meant almost certain death or capture – difficult to say which was worse. Then, right at the last second, our first trip up to Syria was cancelled: the Yom Kippur war proper had ended in a ceasefire. I was heaving a great sigh of relief at this reprieve when I got a new set of orders: I was to join a front line armoured brigade, as deputy field intelligence officer, in the Golan Heights.

Up here, on the spectacular high grassy plains, amidst the broad rolling plateaux and the sporadic mountains of the Golan Heights, a completely different war was going on. The USA might have negotiated a high-profile peace settlement, but the uncomfortable truth was that we were still fighting with Syria. Never say die . . . It was a scrappy, low-key, unofficial war, but it was none the less deadly. We called it the 'war of attrition'.

Instead of my bird's-eye view of the fighting, now I was right down in the thick of it. I arrived at the front to find the bodies of Syrian troops killed in the first attacks still lying all around our positions, still stinking. I had a jeep, a radio and a Kalashnikov. My job was to become expert on the ten-mile deep strip inside Syria: the bit where the battles took place. If anything moved in that area, it was my job to spot it and decide whether to call down fire on it. I got to know every Syrian position, intimately. Every day, besides making my own solo spotting trips, I would join the regimental commander and his radio man on an overview recce. We drove slowly along the border, inviting gunfire, staring through our field-glasses at the Syrian lines. Having chosen the main artillery targets, we would call up a few salvos, then watch the fall of shot for its effect. The Syrians, meanwhile, were doing the same thing back to us, their shells whizzing over our heads as we watched ours whistling over to them. It was absurd, like being caught up in a movie about the Wild West, only with much bigger guns. It was a shoot-out at a gigantic 'OK Corral' – and we had our very own Boot Hill cemeteries. The Golan Heights are a huge graveyard for both armies.

The Syrians were good at getting their special forces reconnaissance units deep in behind our lines to direct their artillery. Their use of camouflage was outstanding. If we ever captured one of these forward observers, which was an extremely rare event, he looked like a large walking piece of the Golan turf, covered from head to foot in the long yellowy grass peculiar to the region. These spotters were the biggest threat to my personal safety as I jinked manically along the front in my little jeep. I could feel the thinness of my skin, the ease with which it could be punctured by a piece of hot shrapnel – or a sniper's bullet. When I was alone, I drove very, very fast.

And the Syrians were implacable. When they weren't shelling us, they were firing batteries of high-explosive Katyusha rockets at us; when it wasn't that, it was a mortar barrage. Then there were the air-strikes. Worst of all, though, were the periodic tank battles. These were vicious, fought at very close quarters, and cost both sides more lives than all the other forms of warfare put together. So we fought our daily duels. One of the strangest things was trying to kill people in some of the world's most inspirationally beautiful scenery.

I got used to the distinctive flat drone of the Syrian 'Sagger' anti-armour missile's rocket motor, as the fat black weapon whizzed past a few feet above my head. What I didn't get used to was the skill with which one of the Syrians used it. This man could make the missile do horrible tricks. He could make it weave and undulate low over the ground, steer it high into the air, then whack it down vertically with devastating accuracy into the middle of one of our positions. This was definitely not in the manufacturer's handbook. The closest call I had in the Golan Heights was when a Sagger controlled by this magician landed a few yards away from me. I still don't know why it didn't kill me. I remained stuck in the middle of this vicious combat for another nine months.

Israeli units, particularly our tank brigades, outfought both the Syrians in the Golan and the Egyptians in Sinai. One single Israeli tank commander knocked out thirty-five Syrian tanks in the course of the war, but we didn't always have it our own way. We lost a lot of men and a lot of tanks; sometimes, to tell the truth, we ran away. In the end we won because of two things: we out-thought them, and we out-fought them. But then, we had a lot to lose.

Bassam Abu-Sharif

I had been down into the abyss; now I had to climb back. Not only my body had to be rebuilt. I faced a challenge on both the personal and the political planes. On the personal front, the challenge was to get back to normal as quickly as possible, which meant working eighteen hours a day. This was partly to say to the enemy, 'You may have done this to me, you may have thought I was finished – but look, here I am, back again.' I also wanted to rebuild my social contacts. I was worried that people might avoid me because of my disfigurement.

But the first thing I wanted to do, above all else and at once, was to marry Amal. I knew I would never persuade her parents that I was a suitable husband; what I didn't know was that it would take me two more years to convince them that I was even a possible one.

The plastic surgeons struggled slowly to rebuild my face. For months I was in and out of hospital. One evening in April 1973, just as I was getting back on my feet and learning painfully how to walk again, there was a telephone call. It was Arafat's personal bodyguard. 'Get out of your apartment at once,' he yelled. 'You are in great danger.' Shuffling slowly outside on my sticks, I found that four other PLO leaders who shared the apartment block with me had also been warned to leave. We were just wondering what to do when we heard gunfire. It was right on top of us – no more than a hundred metres away.

111

Our bodyguards came running, cocking their weapons as they spilled out into the street. The shooting was rolling closer; there seemed to be a full-scale war going on just around the corner. There was no possibility of moving to safety – where was safe? But with the bullets flying as they were, we were better off inside. I staggered back into the apartment, then Arafat's bodyguard rang again, to tell me what was happening. The Israelis had sent three commando teams into Beirut on Operation 'Spring of Youth'. One squad had blown up Arafat's office, another blasted the offices of the DFLP and the third went for Verdan, where we lived. The commandos had killed Kamal Adwan, Kamal Nasser and Abu Yussef, three of our best operational leaders. It was a catastrophe.

Arafat had been very lucky to escape. His personal body-guard, who was fluent in Hebrew, was leaning out of the PLO Chairman's office window when the attackers came. Below in the street he heard some men speaking the language very quietly, their voices carrying clearly on the still night air. Hebrew in Beirut meant only one thing. Without a word he turned, grabbed Yasser Arafat, bundled him down the back stairs of the building, thrust him into one of the cars that was constantly on call and drove away with him at top speed. A few seconds later the whole office-block they had just vacated was blown apart.

If Amal and I were going to get married, I thought we had better hurry up and get on with it. The way things were going, I wasn't going to be around much longer to enjoy my nuptial bliss. Although we could snatch only moments together now, we were still as much in love as ever. Her parents were still just as virulently opposed: it was stale-mate.

Then, quite suddenly, about a year after the bombing, while I was still convalescing, Amal's father Elias said he wanted to meet me. This was a great shock. 'Am I going on trial?' I asked her. 'What's in his mind? Does he hope to persuade me to give you up?'

'I have no idea,' she replied serenely. 'He just wants to see you.'

I thought if we were going to meet, I should take her father out to dinner. This was my big chance; probably my only chance. The trouble was that I had no money. I shot round all my friends, vacuuming the pathetic scraps of cash out of their pockets. It was pitiable: they were all as poor as me. At the end of this exercise in scrounging, I'd scraped together just under 120 Lebanese lire, about 40 US dollars. 'What am I going to do with that?' I asked myself. This was going to need some very careful planning.

I picked a place in Hamra Street I'd been to once before. It did good food, but it wasn't over-priced. On purpose, Amal and I got to the restaurant early. I went through the menu like a maniac, calculating the likely cost of the meal down to the last penny. Supposing he wanted steak? Amal had told me he drank Scotch. Nightmare! Scotch cost a fortune in Beirut – how many Scotches would he drink? I worked out that 120 lire would just about cover the bill if he had two Scotches, one steak and a salad, while we had very little. Amal said she'd have a salad, while I would pick at an hors d'oeuvre. We'd just have to hope he didn't notice . . .

The big night came round. Amal's father arrived a bit late. The first thing he did was order a large Scotch. I had to join him in another. That was two, already. Or was it four? I could see him glancing at my damaged face. If he was surprised at all, he concealed it very well. After looking at the menu for a while with an air of profound contempt, he looked up at me. 'What a lousy restaurant,' he said, loudly enough for the hovering head waiter to hear. 'It's a Western place. Let's go to an Arabic restaurant where we can get some decent food.'

'Oh my God,' I thought. 'I'm done for!' A slow worm of panic started turning in my guts. As we stood to leave, I tried to pay for the drinks. 'I'll take care of that,' he said breezily, pulling out an enormously fat wad of notes. 'Well,' I thought, 'it's OK. Don't worry. You still have the

120 lire,' and I clutched the notes in my pocket like a drowning man.

'I know,' said the unstoppable Elias when we were outside on the pavement. 'We'll go to Suqarat.' This was a famous Lebanese place, with famous prices to match. As we were being shown to our table, Amal's father said casually to the waiter, 'Bring us a bottle of Scotch to start with, would you? Black Label.' 'Certainly, sir,' said the man, hurrying off. 'That's it,' I thought. 'The show's over. Bankruptcy. No wedding. We might as well all go home now.'

'Let's order,' said Elias, as soon as we had sat down. 'I'm hungry.' 'Let's,' I muttered, swallowing hard. 'What will you have?' I asked Amal. 'Oh, I'll have the lobster, thank you,' she replied brightly. 'I've heard it's very good here. Mmm, and a green salad. And some vegetable mezze to start with . . . and . . .' Every time she ordered something, I kicked her foot under the table. 'Stop ordering!' I wanted to shout. I couldn't think what had got into her. Soon we had a table covered in the world's most expensive food and drink. 'Well,' I said to myself, eyeing the spread, 'there's no way I can pay that bill! Might as well get drunk; bound to finish up in prison anyway . . .' I reached for the bottle of Black Label and poured myself a very large glass. We had one thing in common, Elias and I: a taste for fine Scotch.

We drank, we chatted, the ice began to break. Having hated Amal's father in the abstract, I rather liked him in the flesh. He didn't really seem to dislike me. Emboldened by this and by many glasses of Scotch, I turned to him. 'Look,' I said, 'Let me be frank about this. I am in love with your daughter. I want to get married to her. But I would never do that without your permission. We shall not elope. We need your blessing. I never want Amal to regret marrying me against the wishes of her family; I never want her to feel guilty. May we have your permission?'

He gazed back at me evenly. 'How are you going to support Amal if I grant it? My daughter lives rather well. Have you any idea how much her monthly budget is?' 'No, I don't,' I replied, crestfallen.

'What sort of income do you get at the moment?' he continued mercilessly.

'Six hundred lire,' I stammered. It was embarrassing. The meal in front of us certainly cost more than twice that.

'I can't simply throw my daughter away, you know,' said Elias. 'Amal spends at least 10,000 lire a month. I ask you again, how are you going to support her?'

I was silent for a moment, then said, 'We will fight together, Amal and I. That is the only answer I can give.'

His face remained expressionless as he studied me. 'I know that Amal wants you,' he said at length. 'She is my daughter. I love her. I want to make sure her future is a happy future. You are lucky: Amal's mother has taken a liking to you. She doesn't like what you are, but she likes you. I will have to talk to the family. Oh, and by the way,' he finished, with a twinkle in his eye, as he picked up the enormous bill, 'I think I'd better take care of this, don't you?'

CHAPTER
THIRTEEN

— ◆ —

Uzi Mahnaimi

In order to win my wife, I had to lose both my best friend and my mother. I met Ilana Kresic just as the Yom Kippur war was coming to an end. Like just about everyone else in Israel at the time, she was in the army. She was based in the Sinai desert, at a training depot, teaching new immigrant recruits who had difficulty with their Hebrew to read and write a bit better. We met at the home of a mutual friend – one of my best friends, as it happened.

Ilana was stunning – really beautiful. She looked incredibly sexy in her extremely non-regulation army mini-skirt. She had masses of long jet-black curls, and a wonderful wide mouth. Her main activities seemed to be laughter and having a good time: not necessarily in that order. As an antidote to months of all-male company in the Golan and the daily fear of violent death, she was perfect. And she was nobody's fool. The sheer fun of being in her company was irresistible. There was only one snag: this heaven-sent woman and my best friend appeared to be going out together, seriously. It was obvious he had long-term plans for her. Within about fifteen seconds of meeting Ilana, I had long-term plans for her, too, but with me instead of him. It ruined a beautiful friendship.

I saw my new girlfriend whenever I could, which is to say, not very often. It was certainly never often enough. Military duties ate my time. I fretted when I couldn't be with her. Then, later on in 1974, we got a big break. I was posted to teach at the military intelligence school in Tel Aviv; Ilana had already been moved to a base near there. It meant we could now meet every day, as all lovers want to.

Ilana's family had immigrated to Israel from Yugoslavia in the early 1950s. Her father was a Croat, her mother was a Serb and, like virtually all Serbs, a nationalist. The family had left Serbia because her father, a committed communist, had run into trouble with the Yugoslav authorities under Tito. Israelis pride themselves on their classless democratic society. In theory, my parents should have been happy to socialise with Ilana and her parents. In practice, they were not happy. It was not so much that they tried to avoid the new immigrants; it was just that, as members of one of Israel's founding families, my parents had their own impenetrable social network. My father was never actively unpleasant to Ilana's people; it just didn't occur to him to pass the time with them. My mother, though, was another story. Forgetting her own rather humble immigrant roots, she contrived to look down on them.

When she understood that my mother was patronising her, Ilana was furious. At first I tried to ignore it, in the hope that it might go away; at last, I had to agree there was no justification for my mother's snobbery. To cap it all, she told Ilana that if grandmother Mahnaimi had been alive, our wedding would never have been allowed to go ahead. Why? Because in Judaism the blood-line passes to the child through the mother's side, not the father's. Ilana's own mother had been a Christian when she arrived in Israel. She and Ilana had converted to the Jewish religion together. But for my mother, this joint conversion was not enough. If Ilana hadn't been born a Jew, she could never actually be a Jew. She was *gioret* – a special category that describes a converted female. My mother told Ilana nastily, 'Your children will never never be Jewish. They will never be true Mahnaimis.' For Ilana, as for me, this comment was enough and more than enough.

My parents came to our wedding, which took place in our back garden in 1975. We stood under the canopy, we put on the rings, there was much laughter and rejoicing. But the damage had been done. I had been forced to make a choice between my wife and my mother. I chose my wife.

Bassam Abu-Sharif

N ow began the marathon. I never knew it was possible for one human being to have so many aunts. There seemed to be dozens of them. We began a round of excruciating pre-wedding visits. Encased in their hard corsets, they were like very large beetles, glowering at us from their dusty shellac carapaces. They disliked my nationality, my background, my occupation, my politics, the damage to my face and my missing fingers. 'Look at him,' they muttered to one another. 'He is all distorted: blind in one eye, half-deaf. No fingers. He probably can't even give her children. And he's as poor as a church mouse; just wants to get his hands on her money.' And they would give a loud communal sniff. By the time we got to the end of these grillings, two of Amal's aunts disliked me so much that they offered me a very large cheque to go away and never come back.

My last interview was with Amal's uncle, Azar. 'Come into my study, my boy,' he said. 'Make yourself at home.' We sat down in a room lined from ceiling to floor with books, smelling wonderfully of leather. Azar was knowledgeable. He enjoyed spreading his learning before me like a peacock's tail. For the next two and a half hours, we talked about every subject under

118

the sun, except the wedding. Finally, when I was just about to give up and go, he said, 'OK, I like you. I am not going to stand in the way of your marriage.'

'Thank you,' I replied solemnly. At least there was one person who wasn't entirely against me.

Still, the ordeal wasn't over. Some of the Khoury clan asked Christian political leaders in the region to intervene. The leading Maronite political family, the Gemayels, got involved. Bashir Gemayel later became President of Lebanon, only to be assassinated within a matter of days and be replaced by his brother Amin. The Gemayels' opposition was very serious for us. In my case, it could easily turn out to be fatal. By 1973, there were at least 250,000 Palestinians in Lebanon, many of them armed resistance fighters. The *fedayin* were operating increasingly as a state within a state, undermining the very peculiar, and very delicate, Christian–Muslim political balance in the country. Palestinian groups were also using Lebanon as a base for attacks into Israel, bringing down the usual indiscriminate Israeli fire not only on their own heads, but on to innocent Lebanese civilians. It was pretty much a re-run of pre-1970 Jordan. Christian feudal lords like the Gemayels most certainly did not approve of Amal, a member of their own clan, getting married to a Palestinian Muslim interloper. It would be much easier to get rid of the interloper.

At this moment, my own family arrived on the scene. I had finally plucked up the courage to tell them I was in love, and, what was more, about to marry a Christian woman. I wanted their blessing for the marriage. But my mother, like most of Amal's relatives, was dead against the match. Her own son, marry a Christian? In a church? Never. Never in a million years! She would die first, she declared, and had a fit of the vapours to prove it. My father, though, was more open-minded. He listened patiently to my tale.

'Look, Dad,' I said, 'I want to marry Amal: the Christian way, the Jewish way, the Muslim way, in a church, in a mosque, in a synagogue, any way at all. I just want to marry her.'

He thought for a little while, then said, 'My son, you must do whatever you want. I will help you if I can.'

So our fathers sat down and talked. The Scotch came out. At first they just talked, then they told jokes. At last they agreed the wedding should go ahead the following spring, the spring of 1974 – if Mr Khoury could square things with the Christian warlords.

To spare my mother's feelings, they reached a face-saving compromise on the venue. Instead of getting married in a church, we would bring the church to Amal's house: the ceremony would take place there. But first, we had to go and see the chief Maronite patriarch in Beirut, Monsignor Farah. He insisted on seeing us separately, which was highly unusual. I feared the worst from this interview, and I was right. First, the Monsignor advised Amal very strongly against marrying me, then he told me that under no circumstances was I to marry Amal. He was very much against the precedent we were setting. In fact, he told us, he would have none of it: he disliked the whole idea so much that he refused point-blank to officiate at the wedding. By this time, though, nothing in the wide world was going to stop us, short of death.

On that April day, after all the fighting and fussing, in the long flower-bedecked hall in the great house, it came down at last to Amal and me. We walked up to the makeshift altar, Amal looking radiantly beautiful in white. I was in my one and only suit, but it was very carefully pressed. We knelt before the Maronite cardinal, a deputy of the Monsignor, who had gone out on a limb with his church in agreeing to marry us. He raised his arms to begin the service. The moment she saw him raise the Christian cross above my head, my mother fainted. Two strong ushers carried her unconscious to the car. Oh well, I thought, at least there she will miss the rest of the ceremony.

I hadn't bought Amal an engagement ring – everybody knew by now I couldn't afford one – and she had enough diamonds to be going on with. But we'd bought her wedding ring together in Beirut. It had cost 80 Lebanese pounds, and Amal had paid for half of it. I slipped it on her finger, and kissed her. I felt slightly light-headed. Were we married now?

I had asked Amal's father for a simple low-key wedding. Several thousand people came to it. Several thousand! There had just been a spate of political assassinations in Beirut. The city was very tense. I'd asked Elias to play it cool with the reception because I thought our wedding might be the cause of yet more trouble. 'Listen,' he told me. 'She is my daughter. I want to celebrate her marriage. You have nothing to do with it. OK?'

'OK,' I said.

It was the social event of that year. Politicians from every side, dozens of diplomats, businessmen, hundreds of relatives from both our families, relatives we never knew we had, journalists from all corners of the Middle East, everybody gathered at the Khoury palace for the big jamboree. Hundreds of armed fighters from every faction in Lebanon came: Shi'ites, Druze, Fatah, PFLP, Maronite, Phalange . . . Sworn and bitter enemies, whose normal mode of exchange was a bullet, shook hands, drank and talked together.

Amin Gemayel came. My own boss, the PFLP leader George Habash, turned up; talk about two extremes of the political spectrum. With them they brought about five hundred armed men – each. These private armies kept careful watch over the proceedings, and one other. Yasser Arafat had agreed to come, but the driver who should have picked him up took his own family out in the car for the day instead. The PFLP and Fatah were engaged in one of their bitter little periodic fights at that time and the driver was a PFLP supporter, so, he amended the guest-list to exclude Yasser Arafat simply by not going to pick him up. Arafat still blames Amal to this day for missing the big bash.

Carried away by the general atmosphere of goodwill, a Lebanese politician stood up and made a speech about the importance of the occasion: about the symbolic significance of a Christian marrying a Palestinian, about how it gave all of

121

us hope for the future. When he sat down, another politician stood up and made pretty much the same speech, but with slight variations. Not to be outdone, a different party leader rose to his feet and gave the theme another working over, just in case there were any finer points that the first two might have missed. Then people began reciting poems. Then there was another speech. Meanwhile the wine flowed, and everyone got very jolly. My mother was revived, put on her best martyred face, cried a bit, then forgot about things and joined in the fun. She even danced with Elias on the long terrace at the back of the house. Finally we cut the cake.

I had asked all the various faction leaders to stop their men firing their guns into the air, the custom at almost any celebration in Lebanon. With the volatile cocktail of groups at our wedding, I thought shooting into the sky could very easily turn into shooting one another. But as Amal and I stepped into the car that would take us down to Beirut, a solitary guerrilla raised his Kalashnikov skyward and fired a long burst.

We were married.

The day after our wedding we were married again, this time, by a Sunni mufti. My mother attended this ceremony very happily. In a Maronite marriage, there is no possibility of divorce for either party. In a Muslim ceremony the man, normally, has the right to divorce his wife. Instead of accepting the standard contract, I asked the mufti to re-write it so that Amal, and Amal only, should have the right of divorce. She was, after all, still a Christian.

CHAPTER
FOURTEEN

Uzi Mahnaimi

P ray to all the gods you know that an intelligence service
never targets you for recruitment. You will be the exception if you manage to resist. Most of the agents I recruited
never knew why they became spies. They became spies because
I knew them better than they did themselves. I saw where they
were weak.

The notion that spies work for money is mistaken; of course
spies do take money as it can help in recruiting them, but money
is rarely the motivating factor. No more is political belief. A spy
is always someone with a personality flaw. The first job of the
spy's eventual master is to spot that flaw, then to work on it,
and finally to exploit it mercilessly.

People agree to spy for all kinds of reasons: some harbour
resentments about the way they have been treated; some like
the idea of adventure; others are small people who want to be
big: they want the feeling of secret power that spying gives them.
This category of recruit is the biggest, by a long chalk, and it
is by far the most useful. The clerk who feels he is screwing

the hierarchy that is crushing him, the private soldier getting his own back on a bullying officer . . . resentment of this type is the most valuable category of weakness. Once you begin exploiting the particular personality flaw which gives your agent the illusion of secret power, you can do just about anything you want with him or her.

After a year or so teaching navigation in the military intelligence school, I opted to work for a very special unit: a counter-intelligence service known as Unit 154. Its job was to recruit Arab agents to spy on the armed forces of hostile Arab countries. First, though, I had to get in.

There was a whole battery of basic intelligence tests to go through, but the worst were the psychological tests. Israel is a country totally governed by psychologists: they infest the place. Even Israeli schoolchildren have to go through psychological testing in order to progress academically. The whole country is psychology mad.

So I went through the psychological mill. Finally, after his teams of head-shrinkers had palpated my brain until it resembled something a bit like candy-floss, the chief psychologist came to a decision: I was not, he pronounced, at all suited for service in Unit 154. At the time this revelation came as a bit of a shock. The shrink said there was no problem with the actual level of my intelligence – well, thanks, Doc – but that my personality wasn't suited to rigid hierarchies and routine discipline. Now, twenty years later, I think he was absolutely right.

But Unit 154's commander at the time had his own ideas. He called me in to see him. 'Uzi, take a seat,' he said breezily when I appeared on his threshold. 'The shrink says you're totally unsuited to army life.' My heart plunged into my army-issue boots. Then he grinned.

'It's all right,' he said, 'I just wanted to congratulate you. *I* am unsuited to army life. Anyone suited to army life is by definition psychologically inadequate, and probably insane. Now, do you still want to be a member of my unit?'

'Yes, I do.'

'Right then,' he said, stretching out his hand across the desk. 'That's settled. You're in.'

At once I was sent to a kind of boarding school and plunged into an eight-month immersion course in Arabic language and culture. It gave me the most profound shock. There I was, twenty-two years old, from a good Zionist family, well educated, but without the slightest knowledge of this amazing culture that had always surrounded me. I knew nothing about the Arabs, except that they were all demons. Now I spent all my waking hours learning classical and colloquial Arabic; I learned to read the language, I learned how to write it. I studied the classic works of Arab literature, listened to Arabic music, ate Arabic food, attended seminars on Arabic customs and art. I went to bed and dreamed in Arabic. We all stayed for some days as guests in the homes of Arab villagers. This experience, above all, gave me the most severe culture shock, but I found it fascinating. All of a sudden a new world had opened up for me, a world whose riches shook all my entrenched preconceptions about the Arabs – and about myself – to the foundations. At the end of the eight months, I could speak Arabic fluently, read an Arabic newspaper, my eyes had been opened to an entirely different system of thought. Though I had not become friendly with any Arabs, I had a whole new perspective on the Arab people.

At the end of this induction period I was posted officially to Unit 154. Now began a whole range of new courses that taught me the craft of spying – its theory and practice, the sophisticated modern technology of espionage, the older methods of transmitting information, 'tradecraft', the works. There was a tremendous amount to absorb. It takes weeks just to learn how to spot for sure when you are being followed. The first time you fail to notice someone following you is usually the last. At the end of the basic training, nobody was more surprised than the chief psychologist to discover that I had come out top of the class.

Then I began training for my specific job with Unit 154. This was to recruit Arab agents from the occupied territories who would themselves then recruit other Arab agents in the target countries. This sounds unwieldy, even improbable, but if you can get it right, it can produce gold.

You can be taught the theory of spying until you are blue in the face, but there is only one way to find out if you will make a good spymaster: by doing the job. There is a great deal you can learn that will help you, but essentially you either have the innate ability to recruit someone or you do not, there is no in-between. The working assumption in Israeli intelligence is that you can recruit anyone, anyone at all. There is an Arab proverb for this, as there is for most things: 'For every closed door there is a key that will open it.' This was the rule we worked to.

I was a typical naive Israeli *sabra*. I had been brought up, like most Israelis, to believe that lying and deceit were wrong. Now I was being taught to lie globally, institutionally, in detail and in depth. The whole point of my new life was to deceive; it was deceit and nothing but deceit. It had never occurred to me to manipulate people, consciously and ruthlessly. Now I had to do it for a living. They were teaching me a philosophy that was exactly the reverse of the way in which I had been raised. It was like being shoved headfirst into a barrel of garbage. When I understood some of the things the instructors were telling me, I felt like a virgin at a Hell's Angels initiation ceremony. I got my second big shock since joining the Unit.

One of the things I found hardest to accept in the beginning was that the agent has no human value. You spend hours with him, days, even; you teach him everything he needs to know, you go through his courses with him, help him, socialise with him, look at his family photographs, you know the names and ages of his children. Then, at the end – wham! – the knuckleduster in the face: you throw him away. 'The agent is not a human being; you must never think of him as one. The agent is just a weapon, a means to an end, like a Kalashnikov – that is all. If you have to send him to the hanging tree, it is normal, don't even think about it. The agent is always a cipher; the agent is never a person.' So endeth the first lesson.

This kind of lesson was the hardest for me to learn. Once you have sent a man you know well to hang, knowing that he will hang, you have lost a certain kind of special naivety about life, a protective innocence you can never recapture. Your moral virginity is gone, and for good.

Much later I was to discover that this dictum of disposability applied almost as well to me. My superiors were out to get what they could out of me, and they'd use any ploy they could to extract it. They manipulated me in exactly the same way I manipulated my agents. They tried to convince me, for example, that the job of spying for Israel was the world's most important job. For a long time, they succeeded with me, as they did with all of us. I really believed that the job I was doing was incomparably meaningful, just and important. Of course, like much of spying anywhere in the world, its value was questionable. At the end of the day there was no big difference between myself and the agents I 'controlled'. Really, I was as much of a stooge, but I had more senior management. When this finally dawned on me one day, I decided to leave.

Nobody tells the truth all the time. Most of us use a little bit of deceit now and again to get what we want. But, as the course went on, I found myself looking at people in a totally different way. I started seeing them as targets of opportunity, to be used and manipulated at will. I started taking this manipulative attitude home with me; it became second nature. When I realised I was doing this to my friends, to my family, I was appalled. I saw how my colleagues, too, were unable to switch off their professional deceit in their private lives. It was not a pretty sight.

There were sides of this work, then, that were very dubious. Much of what we did was grey, routine, even bureaucratic, but the job was also thrilling. It was far more interesting than even the best spy thriller could convey. The intense satisfaction I got from actually recruiting an agent, the excitement of seeing the hard information we needed come on stream – there was nothing to touch that. In Unit 154, we always likened what we did to a successful seduction, except that the thrill of good espionage was greater even than the thrill of good sex.

How does a young Israeli soldier, newly trained in spying, recruit an Arab who doesn't want to work for him? There are many ways. One is to exploit the overwhelming power of the Israeli civil administration in the occupied territories. The Arabs in the West Bank and Gaza were entirely at the mercy of the Israeli state, and we used the state's machinery without mercy. Unit 154 was only part (and not the best one) of a huge interlocking machinery of military intelligence. I got information, masses of it, on likely targets for recruitment.

I was directed by the needs of the military intelligence research department, which has specific priorities at any given time. Every year, it puts out a list of intelligence requirements. It may be they need someone in the Egyptian Air Force, or inside the PFLP.

I would be directed to a starting-point, to make contact with an Arab. This Arab, say, had a relative who worked for the Egyptian Air Force. Now it was up to me to work out an approach strategy. The crudest way was to get the police to pull him in for questioning. I might arrange a little traffic accident, for example. The target Arab would find that he had driven into an Israeli car; actually, the driver would be working for me, and make very sure that he wasn't really hurt. As far as the Arab knew, though, he had injured an Israeli. A policeman who just happened to be on the spot would arrest my target and bring him in. I'd keep the guy locked up for a while, interview him in the role of plain-clothes policeman, get to know him. If I thought he could be recruited, I'd work out the approach best suited to that man's particular character, and ensnare him. Very basic, but sometimes effective.

Another simple ploy was to use the inland revenue. I'd get the income tax inspectors to sink their teeth into an Arab I wanted to work for me. He'd suddenly get a huge and very threatening demand for 'unpaid taxes'. Once the target was good and worried, I would step in, a knight in shining armour, and 'rescue' him. Then he owed me. A crude, but very common, example of how we used to get at people using the bureaucratic machinery of our occupation.

Once I had succeeded in getting an Arab to work for us, the objective was to use him to extract information from a hostile Arab country. About 90 per cent of our effort went into penetrating countries like Syria and Egypt, as opposed to getting people inside the Palestinian terror groups. Why should this be? The head of Israeli military intelligence came round to talk to us one day about the overall intelligence picture. This is what he had to say: 'The focus for Israeli military intelligence is the Arab armies. This has always been true, and it is likely always to remain true. If you can succeed in recruiting just one Syrian officer during your careers, that officer will be worth more than all the agents we can place inside the PLO put together. Why? Because if the terrorists launch a successful attack, two, or ten, or a hundred Israelis can die. This is terrible. But if the Syrian army launches an attack of which we have had no warning, it will be a disaster. Israel itself might die.' Having walked along the knife-edge of the Yom Kippur war, I knew exactly what he meant.

Given this, it was no surprise that my first operational posting with Unit 154 was to Sephat, in northern Israel. Sephat was where my father had fought so determinedly in 1948, and it was very near to Mahnaim, where my grandfather had first turned his hoe.

My target mission was Syria.

In the run-up to the Yom Kippur war, three Israeli Air Force men were shot down and captured by the Syrians. They were held in some hell-hole in Damascus. We asked the Syrians to give them back, but they refused point blank. Israeli policy was then, is now and ever shall be, that prisoners of war must always be rescued – at just about any cost. There is a very good reason for this. One of my own friends, also a pilot, was shot down in his Skyhawk over Syria. The Syrians kept him shackled to his cell wall by the legs and arms for the year or so that they held him. During this entire time he was kept hooded, except for the few occasions when they gave him food or water. More days than not, soldiers came and beat him. But these official beatings weren't enough for them: they encouraged other prisoners in the gaol – Arab felons – to come in and beat him too. The door to his cell was left permanently open. So you made a big effort, if someone was taken. The next time, it might be you.

To get back the men who were captured, the IDF mounted Operation Argaz, or 'Trunk'.

Every now and again, at fairly predictable intervals, half a dozen or so senior Syrian officers made a tour of their positions in southern Lebanon. The aim of Operation Argaz was to kidnap them. Ehud Barak, the IDF's former Chief of Staff, was the leader of this operation, which was carried out by Sayeret Matkal.

Twice the ambush team came within a hair's breadth of snatching its juicy prize. Twice the operation was called off because of a last-second hitch. Then, as the Syrians were passing through a south Lebanese village one day in a seven-car convoy, a small flock of sheep spilled out suddenly on to the road in front of them, blocking their way. The convoy ground to a halt. The drivers of the first two staff cars jumped out of their vehicles and rushed up to the shepherd, shouting and waving at him to get his flock out of the way at once, or else. But the shepherd was a Sayeret Matkal officer with another, and much more deadly, flock under his control. At his signal, ten heavily camouflaged commandos rose from the ground like ghosts from the grave and stuffed the muzzles of their guns up the noses of the startled Syrians.

130

The operation was a triumph. The Sayeret Matkal men captured six officers with the rank of brigadier or above. But one of the Syrians, a colonel called Muftahar A-Shara, who spotted what was happening much more quickly than his colleagues, escaped into the undergrowth on foot. This man was to be a key player in the subsequent story.

The commandos took their captives away to a very comfortable and well-appointed gaol inside Israel, where they were interrogated at length. Meanwhile, negotiations with the Syrians for a prisoner exchange got under way. A couple of weeks later, the Syrians released the Israeli Air Force men and a further IDF prisoner of war in exchange for their captured top brass.

Israeli General Headquarters thought the Syrians would have learned a little lesson from this episode. We confidently expected it to be the end of the story. Instead, it was only the beginning, especially for me.

The Syrians have a vendetta mentality. If you attack them in any way, they must stab you back. This is normal. But, to the Syrians, having the last stab is what counts: it is everything. The colonel who had escaped the ambush could neither forget nor forgive the humiliation he had been part of. He brooded and schemed. At last, he came up with a plan for revenge. He would kidnap an Israeli intelligence officer. Only by achieving this most difficult of things could he pay back the disgrace and humiliation suffered by Syria; only thus could he have the last stab.

The Shin–Bet officer in charge of security in the Golan Heights during and after the Yom Kippur war was a man named Ilan Cohen. Possibly infected by the Wild West atmosphere of the place, he was given to driving about unescorted. This was a very dangerous and very irregular practice for any Israeli so close to the Syrian border. For a high-ranking Shin–Bet officer, it was virtually suicidal.

It didn't go unnoticed. A Syrian intelligence unit spotted Cohen swanning around on his own and recognised him at once. The head of the local Shin–Bet! Here was a perfect target for the colonel, and the stupid Israeli was completely unprotected. It could hardly be better. At once, the Syrians set up an ambush for him near Majdal–Shams, a very pretty little Druze village right in the north of the Golan, nestling among the hills, entirely surrounded by apple orchards.

A few days later, as Cohen was driving out of the village, a pro-Syrian Druze team closed the trap it had set. Whacking his foot down on the accelerator, the Shin–Bet officer escaped the ambush, but only by the most amazing luck. The Syrian colonel was furious that his prey had escaped the net, but the setback did not make him give up. On the contrary, it made him even more determined. His men had very nearly got Cohen: he had seen that it could be done. He was still going to teach these Israeli bastards a lesson, but it would just have to be done in some other way.

Shortly afterwards, I arrived in Sephat to begin work. I had been in the job for a few weeks when I took over responsibility for running two young Syrian agents. Let's call them Ahmed and Selim. They were brothers in their late teens who had been recruited by my colleagues in Unit 154 about a year before I took control. They lived in a Golan village that had been taken by Syria during the 1973 war, then recaptured by Israel, then returned to Syria as part of the 1974 ceasefire agreement. When I met them, both brothers were coming up for service in the Syrian army. One of them clearly had officer potential.

Ahmed and Selim were what we called 'cross-border' agents. At special points in the border our agents could cross safely into Israel from Syria. The brothers were making the crossing together about once every two months, at dead of night. Before agreeing to take them on, I read several times through the files we held on them. I didn't like everything I read. I couldn't put my finger on it, but something in their background made me slightly uneasy.

As their case officer, I would usually be at the border crossing-point to meet them, with my partner, when they came over. The crossing-zone was mined, and, from our side at least, scanned by electronic sound and movement detectors. There was a complicated procedure to go through when agents wanted to come across, but the brothers knew the routine. They had been over several times, they knew when to stop and when to come forward. With them it always went like clockwork.

Over the course of our first few meetings, my new agents gave me quite a bit of general information. We would sit with the maps spread out before us and they would show me what Syrian army movements there had been in their area, the position and type of any new Syrian weaponry, minefields, weak points and so on. They would also bring me up to date about the situation in Damascus, the morale and economic well-being of the Syrian people, that kind of thing.

This was all well and good, but we had much bigger plans for them. The idea was that when the clever brother, Ahmed, completed his officer training, as he undoubtedly would, he would start passing us much higher quality information. As he moved up through the ranks and gained greater responsibility, we expected to receive some really high grade material. The other brother would act as the go-between. It was a simple plan. We were very optimistic about its succeeding.

When you sit with an agent, it isn't all spy, spy, spy. You have a bit of a yarn with them now and again, crack a few jokes. This is good for business. One day, when they had made their latest report, I was sitting with the brothers chatting about this and that. We fell to talking about cars, as they both loved cars, especially big expensive foreign ones. Ahmed told me proudly that a friend of his in Damascus had just bought himself a brand new Range Rover. At the time, I thought nothing of it but, as I was dropping off to sleep that night, an alarm-bell started ringing in my head. I thought about what the boy had said. This was 1975, when Range Rovers were relatively new on the market. They were certainly very rare in the Arab world, and extremely expensive. How come two local yokels from a village in the Golan had a friend who could afford a Range Rover? It was the kind of vehicle senior

Syrian army officers swanked about in. I thought about Ahmed and Selim a bit more. They were very self-confident – almost arrogant. Agents are not usually quite so self-confident. And there were one or two other tiny things that were niggling me. No, I decided, something wasn't quite adding up here. Something was wrong.

The next morning I went to my unit commander. I said to him, 'Listen, I think there's something not quite right about the Syrian farm-boys.'

He looked at me as if I'd just defecated on his office carpet. 'What? What's wrong?'

'I don't know. I can't quite put my finger on it, but something about them is bugging me.'

'Come on, Uzi,' he replied. 'This is our future you're talking about. In a year or so these guys will be giving us the gravy. There's nothing wrong. Don't be so suspicious.'

I was only partly convinced. 'OK,' I said. 'But why don't you organise a few extra checks on them, just to be on the safe side?'

The next time the brothers came across the border we took them down to Tel Aviv for a weekend spree. It is very good policy to reward agents from time to time. We took them to the best restaurants, slipped them some extra spending money, gave them an all-round good time. But my unit commander had decided to act on my suspicions: he had asked Shin-Bet to keep Ahmed and Selim under the tightest surveillance for the whole time they were in Tel Aviv.

They took the job very seriously. They bugged every room in the hotel suite we had booked for the brothers: not only with listening devices, but with concealed cameras and one or two other slightly more startling surveillance gadgets even I didn't know about. On top of that, the Shin-Bet men tailed the Syrians continuously, whether we were with them or not. At the end of the weekend jaunt, after forty-eight hours of continual following and constant monitoring of their bugging devices, Shin-Bet had absolutely nothing to report.

I had been wrong. The brothers, it seemed, were squeaky clean.

Then, just as my partner and I were getting ready to collect them for the return journey, bingo! One of the farm-boys suddenly muttered, 'Shit! We should have killed him.'

We were in the monitoring room with the Shin-Bet duty officer at the time. There was dead silence as we stared at each other. Something was very wrong. 'Shit! We should have killed him' meant there was something very wrong indeed.

I rang my unit commander on the urgent contact number. He was very surprised, but also utterly professional. 'Take them straight down to interrogation,' he said. 'And be careful. Don't stop anywhere.' We went round to the hotel as scheduled to pick the boys up, behaving as if nothing had happened. But instead of taking them on to the main road south out of Tel Aviv, we drove directly over to a secret interrogation location.

The interrogation teams are a breed apart in Israeli intelligence; not a breed you would ever want to meet. I watched them operating on the Syrians through a one-way mirror in the wall of the interrogation room. They did not hit the boys. A very experienced Shin-Bet interrogator was in charge, with a very easy-going, attractive manner. For a long time, though, he didn't get anywhere.

The brothers maintained they were innocent. We had heard wrongly, they said, they were just having fun, it was a remark taken out of context, it meant nothing. The Shin-Bet man was very slow, very patient, very leisurely. Still they admitted nothing. Then, finally, without any great drama, the truth began to come out.

Ahmed and Selim were both Syrian double-agents. All the time we thought they had been working for us, they had been working for the Muhabbarat – Syrian intelligence. They had been double-agents from the very first moment we recruited them.

Syrian intelligence had monitored our Unit 154 guys as they made initial contact with the brothers, watched as we cultivated them, watched as we gradually reeled them in. The Muhabbarat had instructed Ahmed and Selim to co-operate with Israeli intelligence; ordered them, in fact, to offer themselves up for recruitment. 'Get yourselves recruited by the Israelis,' they were told. 'Make sure you get recruited.' Eager as we were to have a mole or two inside the Syrian army, we had fallen for it.

Now that the farm-boys had started talking, I went through and joined in with the interrogation. 'Why did the Muhabbarat do all this,' I asked. 'What was their objective? What was your objective?'

The elder brother – Ahmed – looked at me. 'You were the objective.'

'Come on,' I said. 'That can't be true. I am not so important. What do you mean; I was the objective?'

His reply turned my blood to ice.

'We were told to kill you,' he said steadily, staring me straight in the eye. 'Kill one of the Israeli intelligence officers, cut off his head, and bring it back. Bring the other one over alive, as a hostage. That was our mission.'

The 'Israeli intelligence officers' in question were me and my partner.

The border zone these agents routinely came through to meet us was about 400 metres deep. The brothers said an élite Syrian commando unit had been waiting for them just beyond the 200 metre strip on the Syrian side. Two kilometres behind this, a mobile command post had been set up. The officer in charge of the operation had been waiting to meet them there, with their captive – and the severed head. This was the Syrian colonel, Muftahar A–Shara – the same officer who had come so close to capture himself in Lebanon three years previously. Bizarre as it sounded, gruesome as it sounded, this was their mission. The boys had been told their orders came down from the highest level: from President Assad himself. We were able to confirm from reliable independent sources that the operation had indeed been ordered by Assad.

'Whose head were you going to cut off?' I asked.

'We hadn't decided,' replied Selim. 'It just had to be one of you.'

'What was the point of that? Was it meant to be a trophy?'

'No, it was not as a trophy,' said Selim. 'It was to prove that we'd really done the killing.'

I looked the brothers over with a fresh eye. I had never given much thought to their physique. It was what they'd had to say that we'd always been interested in, not how much they could lift. Now I realised that they were both very big, very brawny, typical well-fed country boys. They had great hambone fists, broad shoulders, barrel chests. They were much stronger, physically, than I was – or my partner, for that matter. I wondered what would have happened if they had started smashing at our faces with those fists. I thought about the consequences if they had succeeded in overpowering us. It was a very uncomfortable thought.

This had been a very sophisticated and well-planned revenge mission. We were lucky the brothers had failed. Right at the end of the session, the Shin–Bet interrogator asked why they had not gone ahead and killed us. They said my colleague and I had behaved in a different way that night: super-alert, with the adrenaline pumping, they thought they'd noticed a change in the normal pattern of our behaviour. This had made them hesitate. That was all that had saved us.

Still the story wasn't quite finished. A couple of days later, while the two men were still undergoing interrogation, something very unusual happened. The Syrian government sent a message to the outside world through the United Nations to the effect that two Syrian shepherds were missing. Was it possible they had strayed across the border into Israel? For the Syrians to make this kind of appeal was unprecedented. When he heard what had happened, my unit commander went to the head of Military Intelligence with a proposal. 'Let's shoot the bastards, and dump their bodies over on the Syrian side,' he suggested. 'That's the kind of message the Syrians will understand.' The head of MI vetoed this suggestion, on the grounds that it breached IDF regulations. Instead of being shot, the brothers were tried in closed court. They were sentenced to many years in prison for conspiracy to murder.

The story of the Syrian brothers became famous throughout the intelligence community, and not in Israel alone. It was unusual because there is an unwritten rule in intelligence work: you never assassinate the opposing side's intelligence officers. The Syrians had attempted to breach that rule. That was what had made my unit commander so angry.

We passed the details of the story on to friendly intelligence services such as Britain's MI6. It became a textbook case. Comparing notes in this way helps intelligence agencies to detect operational patterns. You can recognise which country is behind a given operation from its *modus operandi*. The characteristic details make it almost like reading a signature. The farm-boys operation had 'Syria' written all over it.

I had been too self-assured. Yes, my partner and I had been armed, as always, when we met the Syrians at the crossing-point that night. Yes, our usual special forces back-up team had been on standby 200 metres behind us in case the Syrian army tried anything. But I personally had been very casual at the contact point. This was a lesson to me. With hindsight, my guard should never have been that low in those particular circumstances. It had been, despite the unformed suspicion I had felt about them. With the advantage of complete surprise, the brothers could easily have done for us. I hadn't expected them to be anything but friendly. I'd forgotten that they were Syrians, not Israelis, and that I was standing in the middle of no-man's land in the middle of the night. It had nearly cost me my head.

There's just one thing about the story that has always puzzled me. It was a question that I did not hear the interrogator ask.

What happened to the knife?

It was while I was working for MI that I began to understand the Arabs better. A change was slowly taking place in me, which was to have the most profound and far-reaching effects. It wasn't as if I were in love with the Arabs, or even friendly with any of them. But gradually, with time, I was beginning to understand the Arab point of view on the question of Palestine. I began to understand what they wanted, and why they wanted it. I could even see a certain amount of justice in their position. There I was, busily undermining the Arabs on a daily basis in the course of my work. Yet, at the same time, the work was somehow undermining me. I was no longer so certain that every Arab was a demon, a kind of *Untermensch*.

I reflected. During the year I'd spent training for my present line of work, I'd undergone many lectures on Arab history and culture. I had also been made to understand the political viewpoints and ideologies of the various Arab nations; we had discussed in depth the history of the Arab–Israeli conflict in every conceivable context and from all angles. The lecturers had been extremely professional, adding massive depth to my understanding of events, past, present and future. I had also acquired a rich accretion of Arab culture, and it is very rich. But this was only part of why I had begun to change. There was a much more important factor: it was talking.

In the course of trying to recruit Arab agents, I was brought into daily contact with them. I had to talk with them, get to know them inside out: how they thought, how they felt, how they would react under pressure. We talked of many things, but almost always we touched on the most obvious subject of mutual interest: the struggle between our nations. The more I talked to Arab people, the more I understood that the only right way is to live in peace with them.

Like all Israelis, I had been brought up in the Arab-entirely-wrong/Israeli-entirely-right school of history. This is not to say we were indoctrinated, but Zionist history was taught in black and white with no shades of grey. The dislike and distrust imparted by this teaching was compounded by the almost total lack of contact between the two communities.

Now, though, the more time I spent in Arab company, the

more I realised I knew nothing. My early education was worth nothing. It meant nothing, and it bore no relation whatsoever to reality – which was dangerous for Israel. Encountering the Arabs as human beings, I felt my entrenched antipathy to them waning slightly. It was the first stirring of a different kind of consciousness in me, a feeling that things might just be better done through political change, instead of war. Even so, we were always at war with the Arabs in one way or another. It was a paradox. In the meantime, there was work to be done.

CHAPTER
FIFTEEN

───────▶ ◀───────

Bassam Abu-Sharif

When I got back to work, I kept quiet about my change of heart. I wanted to prove, to myself and everyone else, that I was still as capable as before. I reflected on what had been happening in the struggle for Palestine during my enforced inaction – the near success of Syria in the Yom Kippur war in particular. I thought about our own activities, the hijackings I'd been part of, all the lectures and speeches I'd given across the world. We had wrested back the initiative from the Israelis. We had shown them, and the world, our strength. We'd never give in, or give up.

But for our people nothing had changed. They were still in exile, in fact we were the new Jews – in Jordan, in Syria, in Lebanon – or they were inside the occupied territories, under the Israeli boot. And the Israelis stamped down very hard, socially, economically, politically. They set up a vicious machinery of repression in the West Bank and Gaza, which they used to exploit and humiliate the Palestinians under their control, crushing any spark of resistance.

One man's story shows better than anything the vile machinery used by Israel to corrupt and crush our people. It is the story of the butcher.

Abu Hammed Hussain was a butcher who lived in the West Bank village of Qalkaliya. Abu Hammed wasn't very poor, but neither was he very rich. Though he worked hard for long hours, he made little profit from his trade in meat. He was a disappointed man.

Meat, especially mutton, was much cheaper in Jordan than in the occupied territories. If Abu Hammed were free to cross the border, he could buy meat there cheaply, bring it back and sell it at a profit. But this was 1970. For years, Palestinian guerrillas had been attacking Israel through the West Bank. Because of the armed raids, nothing moved across the border except under conditions of the most extreme Israeli security. Above all, nothing Arab moved. Illegal crossings almost invariably met with an Israeli bullet. For Abu Hammed, this overwhelming control of the West Bank border meant one thing only: he would be staying poor.

Two or three times a week an Israeli would drop into Abu Hammed's shop. This man spoke very good Arabic. He was very friendly. The two would have a little chat about this or that, while the butcher was filling the Israeli customer's order. The butcher sometimes complained about the cost of living, the difficulty of feeding and clothing his family . . . Life was very hard for a poor Arab butcher in the occupied territories. 'If only I could cross into Jordan,' he sighed wistfully. 'Then I could go to the Arab markets and buy some cheap meat. That would make me some real money.'

Abu Hammed Hussain had no idea that his genial customer was an officer of Shin-Bet, Israel's internal intelligence service. 'Look,' said the Israeli to Abu Hammed one day, when the butcher had been recounting his woes, 'all you need is a permit.

Once you have that, you will be free to cross. Then your future is assured.'

'That "all" is everything,' sighed Abu Hammed, rolling his dark eyes heavenwards.

The officer was very pensive on his way home. The following week, when he came to buy meat, he waited until he was alone with Abu Hammed. 'About your little problem: perhaps I can help? I know one or two people; maybe they can fix a permit for you.' He gave a thin smile.

Abu Hammed stared at his customer, not sure whether to believe him. Apart from the security considerations, it was almost impossible to import Arab meat. The Israelis looked on it all as infected, by definition. And yet this man seemed very sure of himself. 'What do I have to do?' asked the butcher cautiously.

'Oh, nothing,' replied the officer. 'Don't you worry. But I wonder whether you have a nice cut of meat for the weekend? We have some people coming.'

Abu Hammed was thrilled, the following week, when he was called to the offices of the civil administration. Having filled in a form and been briefly interviewed, he emerged clutching his future in his hand. He had a permit! It allowed him not only to travel into Jordan but to return with slaughtered sheep. The paper burned like gold in his hand. His head was spinning. A wide grin of idiotic happiness split his face. The most amazing thing about the whole deal was that his Israeli friend hadn't asked for anything in return for this immense favour, unless you counted a joint of meat. It was all rather miraculous. Over the next six months, the butcher crossed into Jordan four times, each time clearing a tidy profit. He was a happy man.

One day, though, just before he was due to make his fifth trip, the Israeli man came back into his shop and asked for his usual order of meat. 'By the way, Abu Hammed,' he said as he was leaving, 'I wonder if you could do something for me on your next visit?'

'Anything,' replied the butcher. 'Anything I can do for you at all. What is it you wish?'

'Well, it's a little awkward really,' said the Israeli. 'I need to know certain things . . . about the other side. Nothing serious, you understand, but it would help me.'

'What do you need to know?' asked Abu Hammed.

'I'd like to know a bit about what some of the Palestinians are doing over there,' continued his new friend. 'Just general knowledge, really. Things being what they are, it's difficult for me to find out, you understand.'

The butcher understood. Exactly what he understood, it is hard to say. But he owed a debt of gratitude – he understood that perfectly well. 'Tell me what you wish to know, and I will do my best to find out for you.'

'What I would like to know is the exact location of the PFLP's headquarters in Amman,' continued the officer evenly. 'What street is it in, and what does the outside of the building look like? How many rooms does it have, and what floor are they on? Who is usually there? At what time of day do they come to the office, and at what time do they leave? Maybe you could even get to know one of them? You could say you support the cause . . . Maybe you do?' As he said this, the man laughed, in a dry, cold way that made the butcher feel as if he were falling, like the fall he sometimes had in a dream before waking.

With these questions, the butcher understood something very serious indeed, but he did not feel able to refuse. Apart from anything else, his prospects, his family's living standards, had improved beyond all measure since he'd begun crossing the border. He had bought himself a little van, which had transformed his business. His daughter was going to a good school. Could he walk away from all that? Would it matter if he did this thing? He could always say it was impossible, he told himself. He had tried his best and failed. But, when it came to it, the butcher got the information he'd been asked to obtain much more easily than he'd expected. In Amman,

144

nobody really noticed a Palestinian butcher: he was invisible. He had a perfect cover.

His Israeli friend was very pleased when he delivered his report. It described the whereabouts and interior plan of the PFLP offices in Amman in detail. 'You have done extremely well, Abu Hammed,' said the Israeli. 'This will certainly go well for you. You have a glowing future ahead.' Then, as he picked up his cuts of fresh meat from the counter, he looked up at the Arab: 'There is just one other thing. Do you think you might be able to meet someone high up in the PFLP? Abu Issam, for example?'

The butcher felt enormous fear again. How could he, a lowly butcher, be expected to meet one of the top PFLP leaders in Jordan? He would surely be discovered. But the Israeli reassured him. He also gave the butcher a large sum of money, 'for expenses'. The butcher went to Amman. He managed to meet Abu Issam by saying he had a message from the PFLP man's mother, who lived not too far away from Qalkaliya on the West Bank. The butcher became a regular visitor to Abu Issam's office on his little trips, usually bringing him a present of some kind.

One day, after several more months, the butcher whispered in the ear of Abu Issam that he knew a lot of Israeli people on the other side, officers and soldiers who came into his shop. 'One of these soldiers,' explained the butcher, 'says he is poor; his army pay isn't enough. He is in debt. He offered to sell me some things.'

'What things?' asked the PFLP leader cautiously.

'Arms,' replied the butcher. 'Rifles and ammunition. Of course I am not myself interested in these things – I am only a butcher – but I wondered if you might be?'

A gleam came into Abu Issam's eye. Getting weapons into the occupied territories was the PFLP's biggest problem. The bloody Israelis were always catching his men. He sometimes paid professional smugglers to do it, Europeans, Arabs, Americans, anyone, but they charged a fortune. It cost him more to smuggle a kilo of explosives into the West Bank than it would to smuggle in a kilo of heroin. And even these expensive professionals got themselves caught. It was ridiculous. Only the tiniest trickle of arms and explosives was getting through. Here was this funny little butcher, though, offering to do it for him.

He contacted PFLP headquarters in Beirut to discuss the offer. They smelled a rat. 'So do I,' said Abu Issam. 'It looks like a trap, and an obvious one. But it's got to be worth a try. If it works, we'll save huge amounts in cash, not to mention men. And what is the risk for us? Only at the pick-up point will there be any danger for our men.'

'OK,' said the men in Beirut. 'If you think it's worth a try. But on your head be it, Abu Issam.'

On his next trip to Jordan, Abu Issam gave the butcher a large roll of US dollars with which to pay for the weapons. 'You will deliver the guns to a dead drop I am going to give you details of now,' he said. 'Someone will come and pick them up in due course.'

The operation ran like clockwork. The Shin-Bet man took Abu Issam's dollars, delivering four Israeli army-issue Galil assault rifles, plus ammunition, to the butcher's shop in return. At dead of night, Abu Hammed drove the weapons to the appointed spot, where he left them. Three nights later, two PFLP men crept up in the darkness and spirited the arms away. They were followed by a team of Shin-Bet surveillance officers.

Then came the crunch test. The PFLP command in Beirut gave orders for the rifles to be used in an attack on an Israeli army patrol. If the attack went ahead, it would mean the butcher was credible. If it did not go ahead . . .

The attack went ahead, but none of the IDF patrol's members was hurt. They returned fire so immediately and so vigorously that the PFLP guerrillas, who were also unhurt in the exchange, had no option but to break off their attack and flee. But still, although no Israelis had died, the PFLP leadership was delighted. Abu Issam was especially pleased. He believed that there had been no Israeli ambush, no kind of set-up involving the butcher. It was a feather in his cap.

Only it had been an ambush. The Israelis had supplied the PFLP with weapons, then allowed those weapons to be used in an attack on their own men. They had done this to set a trap for a much bigger fish. They had been lucky; none of their soldiers had been hit.

Following the success of this first operation, the butcher became very friendly with Abu Issam, still head PFLP honcho in Amman. The Shin-Bet officer also came to see Abu Hammed again. By now, he felt he owned the butcher. The butcher was his. He could ask him to do anything, and the butcher must do it. Why not go for the big one? 'Ask Abu Issam whether you can get to meet Wadi Haddad,' he told his agent.

Now he really was asking something. Wadi Haddad was the big prize for the Israelis – the biggest of all. The whole strategy of hijacking was his, and he had put it into brilliant practice. He was killing Israelis; he was showing the world that Israel could be hit; he was putting the Palestinian cause on the map. Above all other beings on earth, 'the Master' had to be stopped – dead.

The Shin-Bet man thought there might just be a chance of doing it. Of course he could see the hanging tree looming before the butcher, but he did not really care if Abu Hammed ended up on it. He was only a bloody Palestinian. 'Go to Abu Issam, and say to him that you want to meet Wadi Haddad,' he told the butcher. 'Say Haddad is your hero. Say you want to shake his hand. But get to meet him. At the moment the bastard is in Beirut.'

The butcher begged and pleaded with the Israeli. He would be killed if he tried this. It was beyond his powers. But the Shin-Bet man was adamant. If Abu Hammed did not go, the local Palestinian cadres might get to hear he had been working for Israel . . . and we all knew what happened to collaborators, didn't we?

147

The butcher went to Jordan, for one last time, and put his request. It was very unlikely Wadi Haddad would see a butcher from Qalkaliya, even one who had so helped the cause.

To the butcher's surprise and horror, Abu Issam got in touch with Wadi Haddad at once. To his even greater horror, Haddad agreed to meet him. 'OK, send him to me,' he told Abu Issam. 'We shall see what he has to say.' Privately, he said one or two other things about the butcher to his colleagues in Beirut.

Abu Issam came back to the butcher. 'Wadi is very happy that you want to meet him; he will welcome you in Beirut. But he would like one small favour in return. He is planning a big operation in Natania [in Israel], and he would like you to be around at the time of the attack. He needs a report on how it went.'

At this, the butcher became almost speechless with fear. It was all he could do to get up and leave Abu Issam's office. He had been invited into the lion's den; to shake hands, in fact, with the lion. He knew at once what the lion would do to him. But if he refused to go, his Shin-Bet Mephistopheles would deliver him up to the knives of the PLO street-gangs.

He was between the world's most dangerous devil and the deepest of deep blue seas. He could feel his guts slide about inside him, and had an urgent need to empty them. The old lion Haddad would see right through him, he knew, and out the other side. But when he told the Shin-Bet officer about Haddad's planned operation in Natania, the officer nearly died of excitement. That was it. The butcher was going to Lebanon, period.

Shin-Bet discussed long and hard the fact that the butcher might be putting his head on the chopping-block. He had become very valuable to them: they did not want to lose him. Not only was Abu Hammed in touch with PFLP members outside the West Bank, but they had also been using him to set up a Palestinian network inside the occupied territories. When this network had attracted a sufficient number of unsuspecting recruits, they would break it at their leisure, and arrest all its members. But they decided, on balance, that the butcher would probably be safe. The officer told him, 'Anyway, if anything happens, we can save you.'

The butcher went to Beirut.

When he arrived at the pre-arranged rendezvous in the city, a car rolled up with four armed men in it. They seized the butcher, put handcuffs on him and took him straight to the PFLP's underground prison in Badawi refugee camp. There they tied the butcher to the wall, and beat him beyond screaming-point. But Abu Hammed had been well trained by his masters. He did not confess, despite the horrible torture. He was tough. Still, the PFLP had to know what he knew. Haddad was certain the butcher was a spy, and that he knew a great deal that was worth knowing. Clearly some other means must be found to break this man.

The head of the PFLP's intelligence service went to the underground prison and was very nice to the butcher. He had him untied from the wall, and washed. He brought him good food, cigarettes; he told the butcher there was no need to worry any more, he would protect him from his tormentors. It was a classic ploy, the 'nice cop' routine employed by police forces and intelligence agencies everywhere. 'After all, you are a Palestinian, one of us,' said the PFLP chief. 'We shall save your life. But what is important is to save the lives of other Palestinians. Tell us what you've been doing, who you are working with, how they are organised. Tell us everything the Israelis know about us. Then we will take care of you and your family.'

At the mention of his family, the butcher collapsed. He had been trained to stand up to violent interrogation, but nobody had taught him how to resist pleasantness, especially when it came on the heels of such extreme unpleasantness. He began crying, and poured out what he knew.

The Israelis had expected their man to be able to withstand torture for four days without giving much away. In fact, within three he had revealed most of what he knew, including the details of his bogus network: names, structure, everything, along with one or two other interesting little titbits. But there was more to come. It takes a very long time to debrief a spy thoroughly, so that you miss nothing. We were looking forward to much more information from this man. There were some invaluable things he could tell us about the way Shin–Bet operated. But, on the fifth night after the butcher's capture, Israel commando-carrying helicopters landed on a hill overlooking Badawi camp and attacked the PFLP stronghold, with the prison underneath it, head on. There was a vicious fire-fight. The commandos shot their way into the prison, where they killed everybody. Guards, prisoners, even the prison cat. In the cross-fire, the butcher died along with everyone else.

We expected attacks on refugee camps; they were commonplace, the Israelis bombed them all the time. We also realised that the butcher was important to the Israelis. But we had not expected them to launch a specific operation to save a man who was, in the end, a Palestinian. There was blood all around the area where the Israelis had landed, which meant they must have taken casualties. But if they did have dead and wounded, they managed to get them all back on the choppers.

Many on our own side had died. Probably some Israelis had died. Abu Hammed Hussain had died. And all because a humble West Bank butcher had wanted to improve his lot.

CHAPTER
SIXTEEN

Uzi Mahnaimi

A ll spies end on the hanging tree.

In Israel, there are no fewer than three intelligence bodies attempting to recruit Arab agents. Mossad recruits Arab agents outside Israel. Shin-Bet, Israel's internal security service, finds Arab agents inside Israel and the occupied territories. I have described the organisation I worked for. Unlike Mossad and Shin-Bet, Unit 154 does not assassinate; neither is it concerned with Israeli citizens. It is smaller and less important than both Mossad and Shin-Bet. There is intense, and sometimes bitter, rivalry between the three competing intelligence firms. This is almost always counter-productive, but it is endemic.

The operation to recruit the butcher has all the hallmarks of Shin-Bet. It is not very imaginative; in fact it is rather crude. There are much more sophisticated techniques, but it does have the merit of being well tried and tested.

All three Israeli intelligence services are always playing the permit game. It gets results. People in the occupied territories will sometimes do anything to bring back a fiancée, or a body for burial, or get a permit to visit a sick relative. There are a hundred and one things they want to do. But whatever it is, if they need to cross the border, Palestinians need a permit. Because of this, they are open to exploitation. They can be manipulated. They can be recruited.

Qalkaliya is a small Palestinian Arab town on the 1948 Jordanian–Israeli ceasefire line. In the first week after the Six-Day War ended, the Israelis began demolishing Qalkaliya because it was right on the border. They wanted a buffer zone, so they simply sent in the bulldozers. Protests by Arabs and Israelis somehow succeeded in saving most of it. The butcher's shop survived with the rest of the town.

Just as it did everywhere else in the occupied territories, Israel put the squeeze on the Palestinian population of Qalkaliya via an overwhelming, crushing, Kafkaesque bureaucracy, the very same bureaucracy I occasionally exploited. They called it the 'civil administration'.

When the butcher applied for his permit to transport mutton, he was immediately caught up in this remorseless, grinding machine. The first thing he had to do was fill in an exhaustively-detailed form. Every corner of your life, as a Palestinian, is invaded and controlled by Israeli-manufactured permits and forms.

The civil administration clerks who make all the decisions about the Arab applications and requests are supposed to be beyond corruption. But the clerks, on $1,000 a month, might be approached by a Palestinian millionaire, with, say, a factory in Nablus, who wants a permit to export to Jordan. Bribery is commonplace. In Arab countries this system, where the powerful help out the less powerful in return for a reciprocal favour, is known as *wasta*. If you are a powerful person, you lubricate business in return for a certain consideration – sometimes a bribe, sometimes a favour in kind. That is the way things work: it is expected.

Until 1967, the Israelis, unversed in the ways of the Middle East bazaar, were relatively naive. These white-kneed virgin clerks came to the West Bank, and suddenly the man who stamped permits found himself being offered very large sums of money. At first refusing, or uncomprehending, the Israelis gradually got used to the idea of *wasta*, and found it to be excellent. The clerk was suddenly the sheik – he had enormous power over the lives of a whole population.

But he also had a problem. There is another eye that insists on seeing the application forms: the eye of Israeli intelligence. Once the wealthy Palestinian businessman had handed an envelope with $2,000 in it to a clerk, that businessman would not be available for further recruitment. That could be regrettable. So intelligence was always anxious to exploit a weak point in an applicant before the clerks could get their hooks into him.

Every morning the intelligence officers read through the latest batch of Arab application forms. Using computers to cross-check on the petitioners, their families and any other connections, they search for a weakness, a personal angle in the applicant they can exploit. They might notice, for example, that the nephew of a known PFLP activist wants to bring his eighteen-year-old fiancée from Amman to live with him in Qalkaliya. This is a very strong motivating factor. An intelligence agent will contact the nephew and ask for a little favour in return for a permit to bring home his beautiful young wife-to-be.

When he sighted the butcher's permit application form, the duty Shin-Bet officer would not have become very excited. This was a low-level matter. How could this small fry, this little meat-pusher Abu Hammed Hussain, be of any use? Then the Shin-Bet man got to thinking. The fact that he was a butcher could be useful: for example, who bought meat from him? Any Palestinian leaders? Supposing the butcher were to be granted his permit, he could go to Amman. He might perhaps even be persuaded to visit the offices of some of those terrorist bastards over there and gather a few useful details. It was worth a shot. Nothing much else was brewing. Why not?

The first meeting takes place in the offices of the civil

administration. The intelligence man asks one of the regular clerks to call the butcher in, as if for a routine interview. This is for the sake of appearances and to maintain basic security. When the butcher arrives, though, he is informed straight away that intelligence wants to see him, and sent directly along the corridor to meet the Shin-Bet officer. The officer is very genial. He engages the butcher in small talk, mostly gossip about the town. The butcher is astonished: this Israeli knows everything! He is like a magician. He knows which woman is sleeping with someone other than her husband. He knows about all the business deals in town in minute detail. He knows the life story of the butcher's maternal grandmother. He knows about his neighbours' preferred sexual positions, and how much they owe to the bank. He knows everything.

The butcher is amused, and impressed. They have a nice chat. Although Abu Hammed doesn't know it, this display of exhaustive knowledge is part of the intelligence officer's routine. It is intended to show the target that the man across the desk from him knows everything, anyway, so he should beware of attempting to hide anything – anything – from him.

All the time the intelligence man is assessing the butcher, as a character and as a prospect. Very few Palestinians will collaborate. They will, of course, be murdered by their own side if they are discovered working for Israel, but there are exceptions. The officer decides the butcher is at once weak enough and strong enough to be of use, in return for his little permit. He asks Abu Hammed to come to a meeting on the Israeli side, in a safe house.

This safe house has to be in Israel proper. Anywhere in Abu Hammed's own locality is very dangerous for him. It is normal for a Palestinian to go to civil administration headquarters; it is not normal for a Palestinian to go anywhere else, out of the routine, without a very good reason. There are always eyes watching.

At this second meeting the Shin-Bet officer wants to see whether the butcher really is willing to co-operate, or simply agreeing because he is frightened . . . What is his real state of mind? If the butcher agrees to come into Israel at all, it is a very strong signal that he has overcome his fear of being kidnapped, tortured or whatever else he has imagined in his nightmares that the fearsome Israeli intelligence will do to him.

At the safe house the Shin-Bet man gets down to business. 'Abu Hammed, you are a good butcher, like your father before you. You deserve to make more money. You can make a fortune importing mutton from Jordan. We can help you. You have your fortune in your hands, now, it is before you. Take it.' In short, he fills the butcher's mind with romantic nonsense. The butcher will not believe this heady talk, but it will help him to overcome his disgust with himself about helping the Jews. And it works. The butcher loses sight of the hanging tree.

'When would you like to go to Jordan?' asks the officer. 'Next week? Yes? OK, go then. I will get you the necessary permit.' The permit. Both men know the permit is a very easily revocable permit. But the butcher will get his permit. 'Don't do anything in Amman,' continues the Shin–Bet man. 'Just listen; open your ears, make an appointment for a couple of weeks' time with anyone interesting you meet.' At this stage, he does not specify exactly what he means by 'interesting'.

Before he leaves this first meeting, the butcher receives two things. First, he is given the fullest possible cover stories to explain why he had to go into Israel. These are to make him feel personally secure. Then the Shin–Bet man gives him a small amount of money, 'for expenses', he says casually. If the butcher is clever, he refuses the cash. 'I don't need the money. I can get a taxi, no problem.' He understands what it will mean if he accepts the 50-shekel taxi fare. The intelligence officer, though, has to get Abu Hammed to take the money, because it is the next step in plunging him even deeper into the shit. Ninety-nine times out of a hundred, the officer succeeds in getting the target to accept the money.

Once the butcher has taken the money, the Shin–Bet officer says, 'By the way, just to keep the boss happy, would you mind signing this little invoice? Otherwise, he might think I'm fiddling.' Since the butcher has taken the money anyway, he signs, using his real name, not the cover name thought up for him by Shin–Bet. The officer puts the receipt in his pocket and buttons it carefully away. The butcher, if he is clever, understands at this point that he has been recruited. Shin–Bet has proof of his duplicity. There is no turning back.

Abu Hammed goes home. Everyone wants to know where he has been, why has he been, what has he been doing? In most Arab families everyone, down to second cousins, knows exactly what you're doing all the time. In the West, people tend to live as private, even isolated, individuals. Arabs live in one another's pockets. It is not necessary to ask for help in an Arab family. Everyone already knows you need it, and is looking for ways to give it.

The butcher tells his family he has been to Tel Aviv to buy a spare part for his van. It was the only place, he explains, that he could get it. This seems to satisfy them.

The following week he sets out on his trip to Jordan. He has almost managed to forget about the intelligence officer. When he comes back, though, he is called to a second meeting in a safe house. He goes. This is a very important meeting, because the butcher has to decide whether to start lying straight away or put off lying until later. One thing is for certain: he will lie.

Shin–Bet knows the butcher has a relative distantly connected to someone in the PFLP – maybe his cousin is married to the head of the PFLP office in Amman. If the butcher were going to Amman, he would normally get in touch with every family member. It is very impolite, as an Arab, to leave anyone out on a family visit. The case officer tells the butcher, 'Sit and ask this lady, "How are you? How's your husband? I hope to see him one day."' The butcher does what he's told. 'Yes, no problem,' replies his cousin. 'We are having a big family lunch in a month's time, why don't you come?'

Abu Hammed goes to the lunch. No one is surprised to see

him because he is family, even if very distant family. Now it depends how good or bad the butcher is at spying.

The butcher is not bad. He has his story ready, he has not forgotten it. He tells the PFLP man that many Israeli soldiers come to buy meat in his shop, and that one of those soldiers has whispered that he would like to sell some weapons, some Galil rifles, because he is horribly in debt. The PFLP man is interested – very interested. He excuses himself from the table and goes for an urgent meeting with his superiors. They, too, are interested.

When he gets this news, the Shin–Bet man feels the thrill of the chase. Now things are really warming up. He has some very intense discussions with the head of Shin–Bet about whether or not to give the butcher the assault rifles. The Shin–Bet chief decides to go ahead: they will give Abu Hammed a few rifles and some ammunition. It will establish his credibility. But, now, the agency takes severe and strenuous measures to track the butcher's every movement. They cannot afford to lose the weapons.

Classically, in the arrangement to pick up the guns, a PFLP contact man in the West Bank will approach the butcher and give him a password: 'I am Abu Ali. I have come to collect the special meat order we talked about for the wedding.' He tells the butcher to leave the weapons at a certain 'safe' drop. The Israelis now put on a truly massive surveillance team to watch the weapons. After two or three days, or a week, the watchers see two men pick up the rifles. They photograph the men, follow them back to the PFLP safe house. Here, they join the other members of the terrorist cell. By watching and listening, by observing patterns of activity, the surveillance team concludes that the cell is planning to attack an Israeli patrol.

At this point the head of Shin-Bet has an urgent meeting with the Commanding Officer, Israeli Forces West Bank. Should they go the whole way, take the risk, and allow the terrorist attack to proceed? The Shin-Bet chief finds himself in a position where Israeli soldiers can die as a result of his underling's little adventure. He is sweating. Does this agent, this butcher, have the long-term potential to be worth even one dead or injured Israeli soldier? Still, there are some factors in favour of taking the risk. Shin-Bet thinks it knows where the PFLP ambush will take place, because it has been watching the Arab group members observe Israeli army patrol routes, stop-times, change-over routines and so on. They favour a certain junction to the south of Qalkaliya. When Shin-Bet and the army have reached a decision, they refer it to the Defence Minister for a final yea or nay. It is that serious.

The Defence Minister decides to let the PFLP attack a patrol. But the Israeli army changes all its patrols in the Qalkaliya area. The usual conscripts are replaced by regular Special Forces volunteers who know exactly what they are getting into. They are more than alert: they are super-twitchy, sitting with their safety-catches off, ready to shoot at the first sign of trouble. The attack comes in. The Special Forces boys put down so much fire so quickly that the attackers cut and run. No one is hurt. The Israelis get away with it.

Now the butcher is a fully-fledged double-agent. This situation is very difficult for him, because he has to lie to both sides. Somehow, he can never tell either party the entire truth. It is very likely that the butcher will have a breakdown and simply give up at this point, the strain on him is so great. But now the PFLP chief in Amman has confidence in the butcher: the attack on the patrol was followed through, if unsuccessfully. And the Shin-Bet people know the chief has confidence. The butcher has become a very important man for both sides, far too important to be left in peace. Every month, in the meantime, the butcher gets a sum of money from Israeli government coffers. Sometimes they are rather large amounts, to encourage him to keep on going.

The big question now for Shin-Bet is how to make the best use of their butcher. If you are running an intelligence operation, one of the most important things is to know when to stop. What are the limitations of your agent? What are your own? What, realistically, can you get that agent to achieve? Every agent has a finite span of useful life.

The better you are as an intelligence officer, the longer your operation will work for you. There is always the temptation to try for more and more information from the source, once it is on stream. If you are an over-ambitious controller, your agent will inevitably be blown. This is one of the main reasons why very few agents end up living in discreet retirement. Push too far, and it will end up in the mire.

The man who runs the butcher understands the capacity of the butcher better than anyone, probably including the subject himself. He has to make a decision about what to do next. He could just go to his chief and say, 'He's reached the end of his rope. Let's round up that PFLP group he led us to, and finish with him', or he can push for a new operation to go forward. He decides to go forward. The temptation is very great. He has a plan that will, if it works, result in a stunning intelligence coup, a personal triumph. His career will be advanced: perhaps he will be a hero. Anyway, he has convinced his chief by now that the butcher is capable of greater things.

The Shin-Bet officer's plan is to use the butcher to get to Wadi Haddad, the PFLP mastermind, the man behind all the hijackings and the killings of Israeli soldiers and civilians. Of course, the great plan fails. Of course the officer should have realised Haddad was unlikely to swallow a cover story like the butcher's. He should have known the Master would swallow the butcher instead. But he parted company with reality because his ambition, and the prize, were so great. And it doesn't really matter: the butcher was only a Palestinian. It had to be worth a try.

Then something else happens. The IDF raids Badawi refugee camp, which they know harbours a large nest of active PFLP guerrillas. It is very unlikely this has anything to do with the butcher. It has been planned for a long time. Israelis put their lives on the line only for other Israelis; it is just a punitive strike. But the butcher has been imprisoned inside the camp. In the cross-fire, he gets shot.

The Shin-Bet officer does his best to take care of the butcher's family. The man has been tortured by the PFLP and shot by the Israelis. There is a procedure. A committee decides on the level of compensation: sometimes a lump sum, sometimes a monthly pension. The Shin-Bet man pushes for as much compensation as possible.

Sometimes, after all, agent and controller become friends.

CHAPTER
SEVENTEEN

Bassam Abu-Sharif

I went to the 1974 Palestine National Council meeting in Algiers a changed man, but that didn't mean everybody else had seen the bright light of peace dawning in the sky. Ever since the '67 War, the PLO had been a prisoner of its own rhetoric. There had always been a very big bandwagon rolling, with slogans such as 'Negotiation is surrender' painted on its sides. Nobody was allowed to get off this ideological juggernaut – on pain of death. But where was the organisation headed? Wasn't it rolling aimlessly, without purpose? Were we really going to get anywhere nearer to a Palestinian state by making a virtue of intransigence? It must at least be worth trying to step outside the closed circle of bellicose rhetoric and violent action for a second. We might find a different landscape there to walk in.

It was nice to dream, but the 1974 meeting was packed with the usual hawks squawking 'War, war.' Then, quite suddenly, I made a very important discovery: that maybe Arafat was not as much of a hawk as he was pretending to be.

I'd noticed Arafat sending out odd little signals earlier. In private, with an American delegation, he would say, 'Perhaps we shall be able to meet Resolution 242 (Land for Peace) in the near future . . .' or, 'The PLO *does* wish to renounce violence . . .' At first I'd thought he was playing politics with these platitudes. Now I saw these little messages for what they were: Arafat pushing ever so gently at the door of peace. It was too dangerous for him to say anything clearly, in a single packet, to come right out with it: 'The PLO wants peace. We want to negotiate with Israel.' So he had to tiptoe carefully around the idea, but I knew he was interested in it. The discovery gave me great hope.

I had great hopes, too, for the 'Ten point programme' I'd helped draw up for the meeting. The main thing I wanted to get some action going on was the 'Two State' solution: the idea of a separate Palestinian authority in the West Bank and Gaza Strip, in accordance with UN Resolution 242. If we could get this accepted it would be a big step in overcoming the 'no compromise' merchants. To help sugar the pill, I presented it as an interim step only: total victory over Israel would inevitably follow, once we had the Trojan horse of Resolution 242 inside the gates.

This modest proposal came in for some very harsh criticism. But it wasn't rejected unanimously, which was a slight encouragement. Then, at the October 1974 Arab Summit in Rabat, the Arab nations, for the first time, recognised the PLO as the 'sole, legitimate representative' of the Palestinian people. This gave us the theoretical right to manage our own struggle without constant interference from the Arab states. Arafat had always had to juggle these states, playing one off against the other to survive. But jugglers have to stand still. Now, just maybe, he could take a step or two forward along a different path.

In November of that year, Arafat addressed the UN General Assembly. 'I come, bearing an olive branch and a freedom-fighter's gun. Do not let the olive branch fall from my hand.' At least he had mentioned the olive branch. In the meantime, the war in Lebanon came close to finishing me off.

Karma, our first child, was born on 5 April 1975. I took Amal and the baby girl up into the hills to the Khoury home, where they could rest and recover in peace and quiet. Like the proud father I was, I stayed there with them. One week later, on 13 April, a Christian Phalange militia group murdered twenty-seven Palestinians on a bus in a suburb of Beirut. Immediately PLO groups went on the rampage against the Christians in general, and the Phalange in particular. Muslim militia groups were soon drawn into the fight. Beirut spiralled headlong down into ever greater violence. Phalangist gunmen set up a road-block on the Beirut ring road, pulled all Palestinians out of their cars as they drew up and cut their throats with butchers' knives. When they found out what was happening, Palestinian militiamen put up road-blocks on the other side of the city and started massacring Christians. It was medieval. With obscenities like this taking place, the city, and soon the whole country, fell apart. It was hell let loose.

We wanted to get back into West Beirut with the baby, to live in our own home, but we were up in a Christian-controlled area. Getting caught by the wrong militia would be a very bad idea for me. We reached the city eventually, but I knew the time was coming soon when I would have to move on again.

Throughout 1975 and on into the new year, the civil war in Lebanon raged uncontrollably. Beirut was unliveable, and yet we lived there. We even managed a certain amount of social life. Early in 1976 an unexpected visitor knocked at our door; it was Carlos. He looked terrible; I had never seen him looking so devastated. I drew him gently inside. We had become very friendly over the years, he came often to see Amal and me. Always the gentleman, he invariably brought flowers for her, as he did for all his female friends. He would stay to dinner and we would talk, long into the night. This time, though, he did not have the usual bouquet in his hand.

For a few seconds Carlos stared distractedly at the infant

Karma trying to pull her little body upright with the help of a chair-back, then he led me urgently to one side. He was still visibly distressed. 'I have been dismissed,' he began. 'Haddad has sacked me. I am no longer with you – I'm out of the PFLP.'

Just before Christmas, Carlos had led an extraordinary mission, fronting the six-strong team that stormed the OPEC meeting in Vienna. They had succeeded in taking several dozen oil ministers and their officials hostage, including the mighty Sheik Yamani of Saudi Arabia. Haddad had given Carlos a list of demands, to be met in return for the release of the hostages. His orders were that if the authorities refused to meet these demands, Carlos should begin shooting the oil ministers, one by one, until they were met. But Carlos had hesitated. He had not shot any of the hostages. He had failed to carry out instructions.

Instead, the Austrian government had given Carlos an aircraft, on which he had flown all his prisoners to Algiers. Here, the Algerian Foreign Minister had persuaded Carlos to release the hostages in return for safe passage out of the country for himself and his team. Carlos also received a very large amount of money.

None of the financial and political objectives of this immensely complex operation had been met. Haddad considered the mission a complete failure. Carlos had missed a fabulous opportunity.

The Master was very angry. He thought his protégé had developed a star complex, and told him, 'Stars are very bad at following instructions. You have not followed my instructions. There is no room for stars in my operational teams. You can go.' And that was the end: Carlos went.

He told me he was going to strike out on his own, set up his own direct action group, maybe in South America where there were plenty of fascists who needed sorting out, but I knew it would never work. It takes a mastermind to run that kind of operation and the man before me was no mastermind, he was an executioner. And for once he had failed to execute.

In 1977 Egypt's president, Anwar Sadat, opened up a chink in what Yitzhak Rabin called the 'wall of hate surrounding Israel'. When Sadat signed the Camp David peace accords with Israel in September of the following year, the whole Arab world rose to condemn him. The PLO leadership was particularly vitriolic. But for me, the accord was a sign of real hope. Why pretend we could defeat Israel by force of arms? If that wasn't possible, why not face reality and deal?

During these years I was still editing *Al-Hadaf* as if everything were normal. But I was living a lie and, as time went on, that lie became clearer not just to myself, but to my colleagues. I might still be the official voice of the PFLP but I wasn't saying what any of its members wanted to hear. It was war with Israel I was supposed to be preaching, but I couldn't do it. Either I ducked the issue or I hinted at the desirability of peaceful negotiation. Habash and the all the rest were furious. They called me 'appeaser'. And, just like Carlos, I was suddenly sacked. They dismissed me from *Al-Hadaf* and put me out to grass, in charge of external PFLP offices world-wide. This was internal exile – Siberia – what it meant in reality was that they no longer trusted me. It was a full stop. It was also, for me, a turning-point.

I was a marked man – a pariah in my own camp. This was very unpleasant, and I tried several times to resign. But you don't simply walk away from a group like that, you have to think about your own and your family's safety. And then, every time I offered to resign, Habash would come and talk me out of it. Though he knew now that my heart was no longer in the same place as his own, still he didn't like the idea of it going elsewhere. He always managed to make me feel that staying with the organisation was a personal favour to him.

But I knew I had to get out. The question was, how?

Uzi Mahnaimi

Trouble was brewing. Ever since the ceasefire between Israel and the PLO came into effect in the summer of 1981, Ariel Sharon had been waiting for an excuse to break it. The Israeli Defence Minister repeatedly called the truce a big mistake. He warned that the PLO was using the peace to re-equip for war: re-arming, re-organising, transforming its military wing into a more formidable foe. Sharon was trying to whip up his own crusade to drive all Palestinians from the shores of neighbouring Lebanon.

The Israeli cabinet had turned down Sharon's plan for a full-scale invasion of Lebanon, but he was determined to press ahead with it regardless. He pretended to be obeying the government line, which was for the IDF to create a 40-kilometre buffer-zone in southern Lebanon. But his hidden agenda was to reach Beirut and re-draw the map of the Middle East; a map with no Palestinians in it.

To forward his covert invasion plans, Sharon beefed up the Mossad presence in Jounieh, the main coastal stronghold of the Lebanese Maronite Christian community. Jounieh is a pleasant seaside town about 20 kilometres north of Beirut. The Mossad team formed very strong links with the Phalangists, the extreme right-wing Maronite group, building on a relationship that dated back to at least 1976.

During the run-up to the invasion, Israeli navy fast patrol boats ferried senior Phalange military commanders by night to Haifa, in Israel. Here the Christian officers were briefed on the latest Israeli plans for the invasion of Lebanon, while the more junior Phalangist ranks underwent military training. On the way back to Jounieh, the Israeli ships ferried consignments of arms and ammunition to the Maronites.

The Christian forces were a very important element of

Sharon's masterplan. Once his own forces reached Beirut, he wanted them to open a fourth front, squeezing the PLO from the west of the city while the Israeli troops poured up from the south. (In the event, this never happened: Fatah threatened to flatten Christian East Beirut if the Maronites joined the attack.)

When Sharon had achieved his objective and kicked the PLO out of Lebanon altogether, the plan was that Israel would then sign a peace agreement with the Maronites and set up a new government under their leader, Bashir Gemayel. Sharon intended, in short, to create a new order in the Middle East, with the Palestinians nowhere in the picture. He was playing Napoleon. But in Lebanon he would meet his Waterloo.

Bassam Abu-Sharif

I was in my office next to the PFLP Politburo offices near the airport when the Israeli fighter-bombers struck. It was 5 June, the day after Shlomo Argov, the Israeli ambassador in London, was badly wounded in an assassination attempt. Their target was the Beirut sports stadium and, apart from retaliation for Argov, they were hitting it for a very good reason: underneath the playing-field we had stored ton upon ton of weaponry and ammunition.

The Israelis obviously knew about this arsenal; so much for our security. The building I was sitting in shook as the shock-waves from the explosions whacked into its foundations. They bomb Beirut whenever they need a bit of extra target practice, but I could tell it was starting. I knew in my heart this was the real thing: the invasion was beginning.

I had known, in fact, that the Israelis planned to invade Lebanon as much as six months previously, thanks to the boy. It was on a Friday afternoon, Friday 8 January 1982, to be precise. My secretary called me up that day on the intercom:

'There's a young Lebanese man here who wants to see you urgently. He says it is very important, he can talk only to you.' At the time I was still head of the PFLP's external directorate – still in Siberia, but any PFLP interests or personnel outside Lebanon, Syria, Jordan or Palestine came under my control.

I asked one of my bodyguards to step into the office, and to remain in the room. After the parcel-bomb, I never took any chances. 'Send him in,' I said.

Even from where I was sitting, ten feet away behind a desk, I could see the boy was very nervous. The pieces of white paper fluttering wildly in his hands betrayed him. 'I want to see you alone,' said the visitor. 'It must be alone.'

'Sit down,' I said, as calmly as possible, in an effort to relax him. He sat down, his eyes darting everywhere. He was shaking so much that I was afraid he might fall right off his chair. One thing was for certain: this was no professional killer. I dismissed Abu Ali, got up, and moved my chair next to my visitor's. He had placed the pieces of paper he'd been clutching face down on my desk.

'This is top secret,' he hissed at me, pointing at them with a trembling forefinger. 'You are the only one I will tell. This is the map for the Israeli invasion of Lebanon, which will happen in June . . .' He turned the first sheet of paper over, and I glimpsed a map of Lebanon with menacing bright-red arrows sweeping across it.

I stared at him. My thoughts were racing to catch up with what he had said. 'Who are you?' I asked the boy. 'Where are you from?'

'I am Sa'al,' he replied. 'That is all I can tell you. Take this information; it is serious; it is correct. Look at it.'

I studied the map. It was marked 'Top Secret', in Hebrew, and had every sign of being a genuine Israeli military document. It gave concise forward details of Israeli military dispositions, the start-lines for a June invasion of Lebanon, including the projected IDF invasion routes. The major sea, air and armoured thrusts were explained more fully on separate sheets. If this were the real thing, and it certainly looked like it, the boy, or somebody he knew, had to have been in on a preliminary briefing. Was it the real thing?

'Why did you bring this to me?' I asked.

'Because you are the easiest to see,' he answered. 'If I tried to . . . if I took it to Abu Jihad, or George Habash, I would never get in to see them. And somebody must know. This is serious. The Israelis are coming for you. You must all be prepared for them.' Bemused, I looked at the three sheets of paper in front of me, a time-bomb ticking on my desk, then back at him. 'You don't believe me?' he demanded, his voice rising. 'I will tell you.' He began briefing me about the invasion strategy and tactics the Israelis would be using, referring occasionally to the papers laid out in front of us.

Straight off, the boy had struck me as genuine. As he elaborated on the documents before us, I became certain. He knew it all, in detail and in sum. He knew too much to have made it up. He told me exactly when, how and where the Israelis would invade. Sa'al was too eager, in an innocent way, to be an Israeli plant. The excitement bubbled up in me. Talk about an intelligence coup – this was dynamite! Armed with this information, we could prepare a very warm welcome for our Israeli summer visitors. We just might make them wish they had never come on holiday.

First, I had to get all the PLO leadership on my side: make them understand I had something deadly important in my hands. What better person to start with than my own boss, George Habash? I took him the map and explained how I had come by it. He glanced at it. 'I don't think the Israelis will invade,' he said, dismissively. 'Why would they do this? Who is this "Sa'al"? You never met him before the other day, did you? You don't know him?'

'No,' I replied, as patiently as I could, 'but I am sure he is on the level.' I tapped the war map. 'He's telling us the truth. This stuff is dynamite, George – it's the real thing.'

'No, Bassam,' said Habash wearily, 'I do not think so. I do

169

not think even that bastard Sharon would dare try to take over the whole of Lebanon.'

Next I tried Abu Jihad. As leader of the PLO's military wing and Arafat's second-in-command, his opinion was critical. 'Yes,' he said phlegmatically when he had studied the documents, 'that is quite likely. Quite likely.'

'Well, what shall we do about it?' I asked. 'What preparations can we make to throw them back?'

'I will think about this,' said Abu Jihad pensively. 'We shall see what can be done.' He photocopied the main map, but he took no further action.

The next day one of the PLO's fortnightly meetings was scheduled. These Saturday meetings were used to thrash out common policy aims, maintain and encourage co-operation between the diverse factions and so on. Stubbornly, I presented my information again, this time to the whole leadership, backing it up as well as I could by repeating the boy's briefing.

No sooner had I finished speaking than Abu Ali Mustafa, the PFLP Deputy Secretary General, got to his feet. His opinion was instant, and crushing. 'This is bullshit,' he said. 'There isn't going to be any invasion.'

I stared back at him in disbelief. How could he say that, so immediately, and with such confidence? I looked at the others. Most of them refused to meet my gaze. Then I realised what was happening: they thought I was trying to redeem myself, to make up for my previous political incorrectness. They thought I had dreamed the whole thing up. It was like some kind of bizarre nightmare. None of them believed me. Finally, and furiously, I found my tongue. 'But suppose it is true?'

Yasser Arafat came to my aid. 'The *kamasha* will certainly take place,' he coolly told the assembled PLO. 'We should not ignore this information.' The literal meaning of this word is 'biceps', but Arafat meant the three-pronged Israeli invasion strategy as indicated on the map. A wave of relief washed through me. Arafat, at least, was persuaded. And if he believed me, the rest of them would have to listen.

I was wrong. Even with the weight of the Chairman behind me, the people refused to listen. The Israelis would not be invading the whole of Lebanon, in June, July, next year or at any other time, they agreed. The IDF might invade the south, to set up a buffer-zone, that was obvious, and limited Israeli strikes against our positions in the region would continue, but there would be nothing more. They went even further. They said Arafat and I were exaggerating, conspiring to create fear. They accused us of talking up an invasion in order to blackmail them into making even more compromises with our enemies. In short, they said we were inventing a fiction to win a more moderate PLO line.

Only one constructive decision came out of that meeting, as far as I was concerned: that in spite of our bad relations with them, we should pass on the invasion plans to the Syrians. On the one hand they were saying it was all an invention, and on the other that we should make sure the Syrians had access to it.

Over the course of the next few months, right up to the very eve of the invasion, I kept up a relentless campaign to convince the PLO that the Israeli threat was real – and imminent. I reminded them that we had knowledge of the entire invasion plan and that we could use it to great effect. I kept insisting we had better get on with our own military preparations. Nobody took a blind bit of notice. It was if they didn't want to confront the reality.

At the beginning of May, on an official visit to Aden, I made a long speech on local television repeating my fears. I predicted that the invasion would take place in fifteen days time after my broadcast. 'Sharon will shortly be at the gates of Beirut. I call upon all Arabs to prepare to help the beleaguered Palestinians.' On 22 May, I gave a similar press conference in Kuwait. The invasion was imminent, I stated. All Arab states must come to our aid with money, arms and military force.

When I got back to Beirut at the end of May, it was my turn for an all-night duty. As a matter of routine, members of the Politburo took it in turn to run PFLP headquarters overnight, in case of emergencies. Sitting in the silent offices, I thought I'd pass the time by looking through the organisation's future business schedule. It was always a good idea to read through the agenda before a Politburo meeting; forewarned is forearmed.

A meeting was scheduled for 7 June. Casually I began leafing through the Politburo file. I came at once upon a letter written on yellow notepaper by Abu Ali Mustafa; attached to it were newspaper clippings of my TV interview in Aden and of my speech in Kuwait. The letter demanded my expulsion from the Politburo, and my removal from membership of the PLO Central Committee. I looked at it for a while, turning it over in my hands, quite stunned by its vehemence and malice. I was to be unpersoned in true Stalinist style – stripped of all office, shut out of the PFLP. It brought home just how much some of these people hated me.

Mustafa's memo ranted that I was a propagator of Arafat's hidden agenda, raising scares about a fictitious invasion in order to appease Israel. It said I was against the Politburo's official line of no compromise with Israel, and that I was, in short, 'a capitulationist, a seeker of compromise, and a traitor'. Instant dismissal, opined my colleague, was too good for me.

Usually Politburo members add their comments to the file while they are reading it, before passing it on. I added no comment to this letter, but I waited.

Abu Ali Mustafa was so sure there would be no invasion that he left Beirut for a vacation in Czechoslovakia, intending, he said, to return for the Politburo meeting on 7 June. The fuse was burning right up to the powder-keg, and nobody was taking any notice.

On 3 June, I chaired a meeting of the PFLP's External Committee. I gave them my own analysis of what would be happening over the next few days – an Israeli invasion – which of course contradicted the opinion of the PFLP Politburo. 'Because of this,' I told them, 'you have twenty-four hours to get back to your own countries before the airport closes.

When you get there, you will begin enacting the programme of support and aid to the Palestinian fighters that I have set out for you.' This was a package requiring the PFLP offices in all foreign countries to raise financial aid, medicine, emergency supplies and all other useful material, sending it immediately to Lebanon. All twenty-four of the PFLP's top overseas officials duly packed their bags and left.

Next day, Israeli air strikes began raining in on the sports stadium, strike after strike in a continuous wave. The building I was in started quaking at the knees. The 'impossible' was happening.

I had prepared three or four apartments for the impossible, for use as alternative headquarters. We cleared all the documents out of the PFLP offices, moving them and all the office machinery to the first of these hideouts. I'd already arranged with the Beirut Post Office to switch my international phone lines to the alternative numbers.

Even with the very focused, very intensive Israeli air-strikes now coming in on the city, my colleagues still thought I was mad to take even these elementary precautions. 'What's the matter with you?' they kept asking. 'Why are you doing all this?' I could only repeat, as I had done so often over the preceding months, my invariable formula: 'The invasion is imminent.' Even in the face of what was clearly a pre-invasion softening-up bombardment, they refused to entertain the reality. 'You are too stubborn,' they told me. 'Why do you stick so closely to your opinion?' 'It is not a matter of opinion,' I shot back at them. 'It is a matter of fact. The invasion is taking place. Now.'

Yasser Arafat was in Saudi Arabia on 5 June, at the funeral of King Khalid. Abu Ali Mustafa was still on vacation in Czechoslovakia. When he decided to come back, he could no longer get into Lebanon, as every entry point was blocked. He stayed in Syria, remaining there for the entire duration of the Israeli siege.

Many families of Palestinians not originally from Lebanon began evacuating the city. I suggested to my wife that she do the same. 'I will remain with you,' was her only answer. One month later, it had become so dangerous in West Beirut that even she was obliged to move the children into East Beirut. It was arguable whether they were really any safer there.

CHAPTER
EIGHTEEN

Uzi Mahnaimi

D olphins played around our landing-craft, the sun shone, it was a perfect summer day, the sea was millpond calm. The 'invasion' had begun and it was surreal, like going on a pleasure-cruise. I was lucky enough to be directed out on to the upper deck of our assault ship, *Bathsheeba*. In the sunshine, leaning back against the hatch of my APC, enjoying the view, I felt a lot like a tourist. It was only the webbing chafing around my waist, the flak-jacket weighing heavily on my shoulders, the M-16 hot in my hands, that reminded me we were going to war.

Already from far out at sea we could see the black pillars of smoke towering skyward where our F4 and F16 fighter-bombers had begun pounding the Lebanese oil refineries and other targets. Even this looked like something on a distant film-set, detached from reality.

The Awali is a small river in reality, but large in Middle East terms. We approached the sandy beach very, very slowly, our screws barely turning in the water. Behind the town of Sidon soared the beautiful mountains of Lebanon. We had been joking, up on deck, that nothing serious was going to happen, that it would just be a quick trip to the seaside and back in a couple of days. At that moment the first shell whistled over from one of the PLO positions in the town, flinging a pillar of spray high above our heads on *Bathsheeba*'s port side. This wasn't quite so funny. That shell was followed by a steady stream of others, none of which, mercifully, hit anything.

Bathsheeba's bow-ramp splashed down, and we surged ashore in our Second World War vintage landing-craft. Whether by accident or design, it was the same date as the 1944 D-Day landings, 6 June, only thirty-eight years later. A pair of Cobra helicopter gunships rode shotgun for us on either flank, hovering there like massive predatory insects, rotors thundering, their long nose-cannon questing restlessly for prey. We ran forward tensed for fire in small groups, dropping and covering one another, then up and running again. But apart from the odd shell from the interior there was nothing. No resistance. Despite the fact that we were splashing ashore in broad daylight, at two o'clock in the afternoon of a burning blue day, there was nothing. The Palestinians were obviously unprepared for us. Maybe they hadn't imagined the Israeli Defence Forces would dare come ashore so deep inside Lebanon, no more than 30 kilometres from Beirut. Maybe they just hadn't heard about the invasion yet? Then we came up from the beach on to the main road, and what we saw there stopped us in our tracks.

It was a feast-day for the flies. They buzzed among the bodies in their thousands, black and swarming, rising and settling in thick clumps as the breeze prevailed. There was an overwhelming smell of burning rubber in the air; throat-catching, thick, nauseating. There were a great many dead. When you kill people by the car-load, the numbers mount up quickly. They lay among the wreckage of their vehicles, the young and the old, the crippled and the fit, men, women and children together, never knowing what had hit them. The wrecked saloons and jeeps contained entire families, coming back along the coast-road to Sidon from a shopping-trip in Beirut or a picnic at a favourite beach. Many of the corpses were charred beyond recognition, arched and burned black by a brewed-up petrol-tank. By the roadside where we waded out of the shallows, a local man was sitting with his hands over his guts, trying to push them back inside his ruptured stomach. Beside him what had once been a woman lay carbonised.

Vehicles stretched back along the road in a crazy jumble, at every angle to it for as far as the eye could see, smouldering still in the afternoon heat; some pointed wildly to the sky or had overturned. Elsewhere a car had stopped short where it was hit, sitting quietly as if stalled, undamaged, as if its occupants were just sleeping.

During the night our paratroopers had helicoptered in to secure the beach-head. They had established their perimeter, set up their weapons, and waited. In the pitch dark, unable to see what was coming at them, they'd poured round after round into anything that moved. They knew from intelligence reports that the PLO was sending troops urgently to reinforce the Sidon area. What they didn't know, in the darkness, was whether the people coming at them were guerrilla fighters or civilians. The paratroops had been given clear orders to block these PLO reinforcements at all costs. By the light of day, we could see that this straightforward military objective had resulted in a large number of dead civilians and PLO fighters.

I felt a strange coldness, a distance again, as if all this was being described to me by someone, as if I weren't quite experiencing it at first hand. I could tell from their faces, and their total silence, that the rest of my brigade was similarly taken aback by what we had stumbled on to. Expecting to meet stiff resistance, we were standing instead among so much human litter. Chaos and gruesome death at two o'clock on a bright summer day.

I began asking myself some serious questions. What was the precise military advantage of killing all these civilian people around us? And what in the name of God were we really doing here, so far inside Lebanon? It was clear, now we had actually landed, that something much more than the creation of a 40 kilometre buffer-zone was going forward, as we had been led to believe. But what? And why had we not been told the real objective, outright? I was by no means the only person asking this kind of question. The only trouble was that no one was around who could give us any answers.

Shocked still, we began forming up into an armoured column: Merkava and Centurion tanks, M-113 armoured personnel carriers, the odd half-track, going through the motions automatically, like men in a dream.

The invasion was three-pronged: one force thrusting straight up the Lebanese coast to Beirut, a second punching into the centre of the country, through Beaufort Castle, the third striking deep into eastern Lebanon and the Bekaa Valley. My unit, part of the 96th Airborne Division, was in the van of the coastal force. Our orders were simple: sweep north up from our beach-head, clearing all resistance in our path, then take Beirut. Not everyone accepted them. At the final briefing, a young paratroop lieutenant had stood up and demanded to know why all the arrows on the maps pointed to Beirut if we were supposed to be taking only the south of the country. What was the real objective? He did not get a satisfactory answer.

Having landed and formed up into our armoured column, our first task was to join up with a second unit of paratroopers waiting about 10 kilometres north of us. We drove along that road, through the unending stream of burned-out cars and burned-to-death people. The horror of what lay in our path was made more horrible still by the easy-going, pleasure-loving Lebanese civilisation that formed a backdrop to the dead: attractive-looking French restaurants fronting the beach, souvenir shops, promenades, swimming-pools, gracious villas behind, their gardens pretty with palms and flowers. The contrast was so shocking that I forgot all about the fact that we were rumbling through a hostile area in a thin-skinned, very vulnerable APC.

In an hour or so we came up on the other paratroop company. Sleepless since they landed in the night, they looked utterly exhausted. These were the guys who had done all the shooting.

Bassam Abu-Sharif

Now began a completely different way of life for me, a life of hide and seek, of hit and run. As one of our PLO Operations Rooms was hit, we would move to another. Yasser Arafat, who had made it back into Beirut, and the entire PLO Command, with bodyguards, would have to vacate a compromised or bomb-damaged centre at a moment's notice. Our task, in the face of this, was to collate all the information coming in on the progress of the Israeli forces, their location and strength, and to co-ordinate our resistance to them. The Israeli bombardment, by sea, air and land, went on almost continuously: it rained bombs and rockets from the aircraft, projectiles from their ships, shells from their tanks and their self-propelled guns.

If you went underground, there was a risk that the building would be bombed flat on top of you. When you went up into an apartment block, there was a good chance that one of the Israeli naval guns might land a shell on it. If you lived on the street, in your car, as I sometimes did, an Israeli assault team might hit you. It was a certain kind of hell. And yet, paradoxically, it was a time of great freedom for me: I could live as I liked. I was entirely free for the first time I could remember, free of the PLO bureaucracy. I could act as I wished. I had made the decision, the decision we all have to make in times of great fear, to outface it or to run. My decision was to stay. Having taken it, I had to conquer my fear, the terror that would otherwise cripple me. The only way I could do this was through fatalism: I had to reach inside and persuade myself that I was truly prepared for death. 'If God wants to kill me, he will kill me. That's it.' I repeated this formula like a mantra. It was a way of finding strength to carry on.

That I did not die at once during the invasion is entirely due to Yasser Arafat. His reputation for scenting out trouble is legendary, and entirely justified. He has sixth sense, and some measure of a seventh.

We were at a leadership meeting on the third day after the Israelis had attacked. The usual precautions were being taken to safeguard the leadership: PLO commanders were ferried to a 'blind' rendezvous, using inconspicuous transport; they were then taken one by one to the actual meeting-place. Only our security people knew in advance where this would be: we in the leadership did not.

The entire top echelon of the PLO was at this council of war. Arafat opened the proceedings with a speech summarising the position to date. He was at the lectern, in the middle of this address, when he suddenly fell silent. His face changed, taking on a slightly waxen hue. He looked mesmerised, his eyes even beadier, staring ahead of him. Then, suddenly, he opened his mouth: 'Everybody out!' he yelled. 'Everybody out!' There was an embarrassed pause. Had the man gone mad? Someone said, 'But, Abu Amar, we have not even started the meeting . . .' 'Everybody out!' shouted Arafat. 'Get out of the building – now!' He ran straight for the door, stopping only to grab my hand and drag me along with him. I was as startled as we all were, but I could sense his fear, and my feet moved like quicksilver. Pell-mell down the stairs we went, bursting out into the street. Arafat got into his car. '*Imshi!*' he shouted to the driver as we scrambled in. 'Quick! Let's go!' We took off at break-neck speed along the street and down into the underground car-park of the Piccadilly Centre. On the fourth floor down we screeched to a halt. 'Wait,' said Arafat, staring at me. 'Wait.'

Seven minutes later the bomb hit. The building where we had been meeting was flattened, reduced to smoking rubble by one thousand pounds of high-explosive.

'Abu Amar,' I said, seized by a kind of superstitious awe of the man sitting next to me, 'it is impossible. How did you know?' He smiled at me. 'How?' I repeated. 'How could you know?' Arafat still kept silent, gazing at me like the Sphinx. 'Come on,' I persisted, 'you've got to tell me. What do you mean, smiling like that? Tell me how you knew.'

'When I went into that room,' he replied slowly, 'I looked up and saw some people on the balcony watching us. That area we were in has a large number of foreigners in it. It suddenly occurred to me: any one of them could phone the Hotel Alexander, where Sharon is bunkered, and tell him that the PLO was meeting right next door.'

'Is that the real reason?' I asked.

He hesitated. 'I don't know. It is an instinct. I have had it for years, without being able to explain it. An inner voice just told me that I must leave right away. So that's what I did.' He took my hand, shaking it warmly for a minute, and smiled again. 'And we are safe, my friend. We are safe. We live to fight another day.'

Uzi Mahnaimi

Arafat was luckier than he knew. He escaped so many times, by a hair's breadth, from so many attempts to kill him.

Once we were into Beirut, the order came down: 'Get Arafat.' We had dozens of Arab agents in West Beirut during the siege. They were our eyes and ears. Each agent had a simple walkie-talkie radio and one of our intelligence maps. On these maps the city was divided into very small grid-squares. This meant it was usually possible for an agent to designate a target very precisely, even down to a specific building, if he saw something interesting happening in or around it. Something interesting like the PLO General Command holding a meeting, for example. Then we could send in an air-strike, lay down some artillery fire or call up snipers.

In the last few days of the siege one of our Arab agents spotted Arafat sitting in a car outside a nondescript building in the west of the city. He was obviously waiting for something. It was a golden opportunity. We had never, ever, caught the PLO leader out in the open before. We had a sniper close by, equipped with a head-set and a throat mike. When he heard who the target was, the sniper started sprinting towards him. He was at the location in three minutes. Arafat was still there. Trying desperately to bring his breathing under control, the marksman settled into position and took careful aim. His rifle came steady. A head wrapped in a black-and-white chequered *kaffiyeh* jumped into his scope. Lining his sights up on the centre of the cotton material, he took up the first pressure on his trigger. Speaking softly into his mike, the sniper reported: 'I have Arafat in my sights.' But a voice crackled urgently in his headset: 'No! Don't shoot. Repeat, do *not* shoot. Disengage.' Startled, the marksman took his finger off the trigger, slithered backwards, rolled over on his rooftop and stared for a long time at the blue sky. He found himself shaking with the unused adrenaline. Why had they done that? Why hadn't he been allowed to shoot? What better chance would they ever have?

The PLO leader had agreed to get out of Beirut under US supervision. At that precise second, at the moment of his nemesis, it had become politically undesirable to kill him.

Arafat was lucky, all right.

Bassam Abu-Sharif

T he Israelis were using vacuum bombs. We had no other word to describe this terror weapon. In a flash, it could suck the guts out of an entire building. We thought that, unlike a conventional bomb, this device contained a fuel-air mixture in the place of high explosive. It was a refinement on napalm, and just as obscene. Instead of exploding on impact, the bomb had a very short time-delayed fuse. It penetrated the outer shell of a target building, sometimes falling through several floors, sometimes ripping right through it altogether to the basement. Once it had come to rest, it went off. The explosive aerosol mixture expanded instantly to fill every corner of the available space. Then it ignited, creating a massive blast, but the exploding vapour also gulped all the air from the building. This created a huge vacuum. More air rushed in to fill the void. The combination of initial blast and return pressure-wave destroyed almost any building's internal structure completely. It is exactly as if you saturated every surface in your house with petrol, left it for a short time, then set a match to it. Only these bombs were a thousand times worse.

The apartment block the Israelis hit this time was very near Beirut's Green Line, which divides the city into Christian and Muslim sectors. It housed families expelled from a refugee camp in East Beirut by the Phalangists. About 480 families were living there, mostly Christian as it happened, mostly women, children and old men.

There was almost no sound as the bomb went off; it was muffled by the building's outer walls. Instead, there was a sound like the shaking of a gigantic matchbox, an eerie trickling as the apartment block collapsed from within, floor by floor, one floor on top of the other. Everybody inside that block was killed, except for one man who by some miracle was thrown clear of a balcony he had been standing on. All of this man's eight children, and his wife, were killed.

He lost his mind.

CHAPTER
NINETEEN

Uzi Mahnaimi

Although I'd been in the first wave of the coastal assault, fresh orders came for me at dawn on the second day. I was to join another unit right at the sharp end of the coastal invasion group. More spear-point than spearhead. Worse still, the outfit I was joining was below even normal platoon strength. We were to be a tiny assault force, comprising no more than twenty-five men: fifteen from No. 50 Parachute Regiment, with another ten men of the Golani Brigade. The Golani Commanding Officer, Lt-Col. Spigel, was in personal charge of this miniature army.

Leaving the cosy comfort of the division's temporary headquarters, aromatic with the smell of coffee, we began moving northward. We were spread out in skirmish order, advancing on foot. Better to walk it than fry in an APC when the opposition got busy with its anti-tank rockets. It was eerily calm for a while. We were on the beach, at the water's edge, the broad blue of the Mediterranean sparkling to our left, the coast road about a hundred metres to our right. The road was too dangerous for us to use: easily within range of Palestinian small-arms fire from the buildings behind it. Our armoured support was rumbling cautiously forward along it, though: three Merkava main battle-tanks and a tracked 20mm Gatling gun.

We were just coming into the resort area around Khalde, a place of hotels and motels, of little quays harbouring sleek, expensive-looking speedboats, of tennis-courts, tourist shops, casinos and pleasure-gardens. Although some of them showed war damage, it was a place built for swimming-trunks, not flak-jackets. The infrastructure of the Lebanese leisure industry: this was where the real fight would begin.

PLO militiamen had taken up positions in some of these waterfront buildings. Hour upon hour of bombardment from the sea had failed to dislodge them. Now it was our turn.

Hard contact came on us suddenly: the throaty roar of a heavy machine-gun shattering the still morning air. Shit, they were firing at us! At me! Gouts of sand kicked up in a line stitching arrow-straight towards where I was standing, frozen for a moment to the spot. The bullets came so close that they sprayed sand over my right boot. It happened before I had time to think, let alone react. Then I began running.

In a heavily built-up area of the kind we were going into, the tank can be worse than useless to an infantry squad. Among buildings, tanks have to be protected from ambush. The only way to clear occupied buildings in a city is the hard way: by hand, one by one.

Suddenly I looked down and saw a dead Israeli soldier, one of my troop, just lying there next to me with his eyes open, staring up. I hadn't even noticed him getting hit. Modern high-velocity weapons do truly horrible things to flesh and bone. Real death is sordid. When I saw the smashed and bloodied results of his bullet-wounds, I became terrified. I knew that at any second, the next second or the one after it, I could be lying dead like that. Part of my mind started screaming quietly to itself: 'Get wounded! Get a wound so you can go home!'

Age is a very important factor in the way soldiers view war. When they are nineteen or twenty, most young men believe themselves god-like, invulnerable. They think that nothing will ever happen to them – until it does. In the battle for the Golan Heights ten years previously, I had been almost completely unworried, completely unthinking. Now, married with a family, at the age of thirty, that younger self was long gone, replaced by a different person: one who was deadly scared, one who kept thinking, 'What will happen to my family if I'm killed?' The only way I could cope with it all was just to think, 'Right, what's the worst that can happen to me? Death. OK, expect death. If you expect death, all the time, you'll get through.'

By nightfall we had reached Khalde, just south of the airport. We were now within a few kilometres of Beirut city centre. It was here that we encountered our first real resistance. We had advanced at a fantastic pace, exceeding even Sharon's expectations. Too far for comfort. Our lines were so extended we'd get no help if we hit trouble. Exhausted, we dug in to what cover we could find among the rubble of a half-smashed apartment block. The Palestinians were very close to us, not more than fifty metres away; so near I could hear them talking. Then the bombardment started. The PLO had brought up their Katyusha batteries. They let rip with these multiple-barrelled rocket-launchers, raining 140mm projectiles down on our temporary bunkers. In a way we were lucky they were using Katyushas: they're notoriously inaccurate. Most of the rockets whined over our heads and punched into the sea a few metres behind us. Had they been using something a little more accurate . . .

There was another company of Israeli paratroops about one kilometre to the east of us, near Kafar Sil, part of No. 35 Parachute Regiment. They were in deep shit. They had run slap into a much larger force of Syrian army commandos, well entrenched and well organised. Our paras were stuck on a ledge of rock, under merciless Syrian fire. They were taking casualty after casualty. They wanted to retreat, but they couldn't find a safe way down from the ledge. Over our radios we could hear their panic mounting as their position became

186

increasingly desperate. They were pleading with Headquarters, 'Please come, please save us. Send reinforcements. We must have reinforcements immediately!'

In fiction, war is the stuff of heroism. What was happening next door to us was anything but heroic. 'Please come! Please save us,' the platoon commanders wailed over their field radios.

There were no reinforcements. We ourselves were pinned right down; there was nothing we could do. Along with the Katyushas, shells fired at us from the Uzai refugee camp along the beach were smashing down around our own position. No other back-up was available. The Syrians, in overwhelming numbers, were slaughtering our colleagues and we could only listen. The terror in those voices was unbearable, unforgettable. We knew it could so easily be us.

That night two more of my platoon died of shrapnel wounds. Several more were wounded. The paratroopers lost almost half their number dead and wounded. The shattered survivors straggled over to us as the light came, the Syrians for some reason drawing back.

Now that we were surrounded by our own dead and wounded, I couldn't get the image of the Arab dead on the coast road out of my mind. Nine years previously, in the war of attrition with Syrian aggression, youth and an unswerving conviction that I was fighting for the right cause had carried me blindly forward. I saw Israel in those days as a tiny country beset by fiends of Arabia. Now, it seemed to me, we were ourselves the aggressor. My grandfather believed it was enough to defend your own country from attack. Self-defence is a necessary and sufficient task for any nation. But waging a punitive war, a war of aggression, in a country whose inhabitants were mostly blameless was something else. Like many others in the invasion force, even among the élite troops, I was losing faith fast in what we were doing. Not knowing what our objective was, I had no sense of purpose, moral or military. Would this operation achieve 'Peace for Galilee'? It seemed extremely unlikely. Our actions were more likely to provoke increased resistance in southern Lebanon from groups that had previously been against the PLO, like Amal. Stirring up Shi'ite hostility did not strike me as a particularly good idea.

With daybreak, we began moving on our own primary target: Beirut airport. Then came news of a ceasefire. This made us extremely happy, since we had been without sleep for two nights running. We were just settling down to get some kip when our gunners, ignoring the ceasefire agreement, opened up on the PLO emplacements. The first salvo of 155mm Israeli shells fell among our own lines. This was definitely not fun. We were very lucky not to take any further casualties before we radioed them to adjust their range. Naturally enough the Syrian army and the PLO, with our shells screaming down on them, started answering back in kind. End of ceasefire.

We began our advance, on the road now, spread out on foot among the armour, M-16s at the ready. One of the three tanks with our unit was about 200 metres behind me. Then, up ahead, I saw a black object wavering through the air towards me. It was flying just above the surface of the road, wobbling slightly up and down, making straight for my stomach. Squat, stubby, and exceedingly ugly, there was something horribly familiar about it. Then I heard the noise, that unforgetttable flat drone like a miniature V-2 rocket. And I realised: it was my old friend the 'Sagger' missile. At once I was transported back to the Golan Heights. It was another fucking Sagger, with my name on it!

The correct procedure when you see a wire-guided missile like this coming at you is to lay down intensive fire on the operator, if you can spot him. He is controlling the missile's flight at the other end of the command wire. If you can make him frightened enough, you can sometimes put him off his aim. I forgot all about this and stood mesmerised, watching the rocket as it trundled past. The AT-3 anti-tank missile flies at 150 metres per second. To my bleary eyes, in the clear light of that morning, it seemed to be moving in slow motion. It was not coming for me, I saw, it was homing on the Centurion at my back. I spun round to shout, but it was already too late. The tank's commander was semi-visible, crouched behind his twin 7.62mm machine guns. He didn't seem to have noticed the missile snaking towards him. As the Sagger neared its target, its invisible controller corrected his aim a touch. Swooping up at the last instant, the missile hit the battle tank's turret smack on.

The Sagger has a 2.7 kilogram [6.5 lb] warhead containing a shaped charge, I remembered. This moulds itself against the hull of a tank on contact, forming a superheated jet of armour-piercing liquid. The hot liquid squirts straight through the tank's armour, blowing off sizeable chunks of the tank's inner skin. The AT-3 will penetrate 40cm [15.7 in.] of plate steel. The old Centurion's hull was no match for it. The warhead went in through its steel shell as if it were so much soft dough. The blast blew the tank commander straight out of his hatch, right up into the air to a height of about five metres, like a doll. He was lucky. Exploding in the confined space of the tank, the detached fragments of flying metal killed two of his crew members outright and wounded the third. Thrown right back over the top of his tank, the tank captain landed about ten metres down the road. We ran to him. By some miracle he was still alive, actually staggering to his feet as we arrived. Like his only surviving crewman, he was in extreme shock. We called for a casualty evacuation chopper, patched them up, and left them there on the road. We were carrying no passengers.

Arriving at a junction, we crested a small hill to make a quick reconnaissance. The sight of the airport, quivering below us in the middle distance, brought us all up short. It was a real shock seeing those runways, the scene of so many hijackings, so close to us. We were literally on top of them. We were in deep trouble now, right in the heart of a hostile Lebanon. I felt extremely vulnerable, surrounded, isolated. We were so far in.

Someone had taken a prisoner. 'Talk to him, Uzi,' said the battalion commander. 'Find out if he knows what we will be facing up ahead.' I looked at the man. Then something else caught my eye. Just behind his head, a car was careering down the road towards us at breakneck speed. The thought, 'suicide bomber', flashed into my brain. I dropped to one knee and brought up my M-16. The car was bouncing madly in the pot-holes, close now, coming straight at us. I squeezed the trigger, aiming at the sun winking off the vehicle's windshield. I have no idea whether I hit anything – by now everyone was firing at it – but somebody did. The car started swerving crazily from side to side, veering diagonally away from us. As it flashed by, I saw that one of the men inside had a piece of red cloth tied around his head. Suicide bomber. The vehicle bucketed wildly off the road, lurching behind a nearby building. There was a rending crash as it hit something immovable.

We got up. 'OK,' I told our prisoner. 'You go and see what happened.' Without a word or a backward glance, the man trotted off in the direction of the smash.

'Come on, Uzi,' said the battalion commander. 'What are you doing? He's not going to come back, is he?'

'Well, we'll see,' I replied. After about five minutes, the prisoner did come back. Even I was surprised to see him again. 'What did you see in that car?' I asked him.

'One dead man, and one seriously wounded.'

'How seriously?'

'All his guts are hanging out.'

'Did you help him?'

'No,' said the prisoner. 'He's a bloody Palestinian.'

Our captive was a Lebanese. So much for Arab solidarity.

With greater confidence in him now, we sent our prisoner off to scout ahead. Why risk one of our own, after all? This cynical ploy turned out to be a big mistake. Sent to find out about the enemy, he must have run straight into them. Instead of reporting back to us, he told them we were coming. Snipers began sliding into nearby buildings, pouring a steady stream of fire at us. We returned their fire as best we could, but we were again badly pinned down. We needed a radical solution. As it happened, there was one to hand: the Vulcan.

The Vulcan is a six-barrelled 20mm Gatling gun mounted in a powered turret on the roof of a modified APC. Originally designed for and fitted on USAF fighters, it was known in Vietnam as 'Puff the Magic Dragon'. The Israeli army uses the gun to dig itself out of the very deep tactical holes it sometimes encounters in urban warfare; the kind of hole we were in right now.

Although the Vulcan's rate of fire is cut from 3,000 to 1,000 rounds per minute for its infantry support role, this still means that it fires around two dozen armour-piercing 20mm shells per second. We were about to find out how utterly devastating it could be.

It was clear that most of the people sniping at us were on the fourth floor of a building about 350 metres away. We called up the Vulcan on the radio. It trundled into view, squatting down menacingly on its tracks as the gunner locked its suspension to make it a more stable firing platform. We pointed out the target building. The Vulcan's servomotors whined as the cannon tracked and elevated. Bullets pinged off its armoured chassis, whanging away into the sky around us.

There was a second's silence, then came a sound like all the Furies of Hell let loose together. It was over in five or six seconds, no more. As the dust cleared, I could see that the Vulcan's fat shells had sawn neatly through the entire concrete structure supporting the fourth floor: the rest of the building had collapsed on top of it.

Nobody was firing at us any more.

CHAPTER TWENTY

Uzi Mahnaimi

E very soldier's dream in the heat of battle is to stop fighting, catch some sleep, get outside a decent meal – and wash. My own dream was all that and something extra: to find a working telephone line and call home. Dream on.

Night was falling. The area in front of us was dotted with luxurious villas. This was obviously the place to be if you were Lebanese and rich. Among these very desirable residences we noticed one house in particular, right on the water's edge, stone-built, with the look of a place that would withstand shot and shell. I suggested to the battalion commander, 'Let's get inside that place for the night, instead of sitting here like stuffed ducks waiting to be shot.'

'OK,' he agreed. 'Let's do that.'

We pulled up at the front entrance. I knocked. A Druze man, recognisable by his black trousers and white *kaffiyeh*, answered the door. He had the poised, well-muscled air of the professional bodyguard. 'What do you want?' he demanded, eyeing me suspiciously.

'There are about twenty of us,' I replied. 'We are Israeli soldiers. We would like to stay here overnight.'

He stared at me, then beyond me, trying to make out my compatriots in the gloom. 'Just one minute,' he said, disappearing back inside.

A few moments later a spectacularly beautiful woman appeared in the doorway. She addressed me in French, assuming I knew no Arabic. 'It's OK,' I said to her in her own tongue. 'We mean no harm. May I ask who you are, madame?'

'I am the wife of the Emir Majid Arselan,' she replied haughtily.

I reflected. This particular gentleman, I remembered, had been the Lebanese Defence Minister until not so very long ago, and came from a noble Druze family. He was very old; she was young and beautiful. It was ever thus. 'How do you do?' I continued, rather belatedly. 'This is rather awkward, but I have a platoon of very tired soldiers with me. May we stay in your house until morning?'

This conversation was carried on in an extremely polite tone on both sides, especially when you consider that it took place under a continual hail of Katyusha rockets. She knew I was determined to stay there. I knew she was determined to prevent me. 'We do have a chalet, Swiss-style, in the grounds. It is a small house made of wood, but you are welcome to use it,' she told me.

'I think not, madame,' I replied. 'It is a very kind offer, but we shall certainly be more comfortable here . . .' I could sense the platoon at my back becoming more and more impatient as this exchange continued. The intensity of the Katyusha barrage had increased until a rocket was landing around our ears about once every three seconds.

Recognising that she had no choice, the woman let us into her home, ushering us through into the main reception room. The Druze bodyguard, clearly instructed to do so, took up a strategic position between ourselves and the rest of the house.

193

'There are women here,' our hostess began explaining, 'so you won't mind if . . .' Her words tailed off.

I turned to see what she was staring at. Far from having any evil designs on her female companions, my platoon of hairy-arsed paratroopers had shed their packs, crashed out wherever they could and fallen asleep as one man. Within seconds the only sound in the room was the gentle snoring from a sea of comatose bodies. A warm smell of old zebra had filled the room. Only we three officers were still awake. There was very little chance of rape and pillage taking place that night.

I wanted very much to have a word with the woman's husband, but he was asleep, too. Instead, one of her sons came to talk. He was a handsome youth of about nineteen, dressed in expensive designer clothes. 'My name is Talal,' he announced. Then, 'Did you see a BMW outside?' he asked anxiously.

'Yes,' I replied gravely. 'I saw it.'

'Would you mind going outside to see if it is still OK?' he asked.

All this time, the bombardment was continuing, ferociously, unendingly, the rockets showering down around the house. I considered this question. It combined a quite stupendous degree of arrogance with an obsessive materialism surprising even in a country jam-packed full of obsessive materialists. This boy would clearly go far.

'No, thank you,' I replied. 'But if you would care to step outside yourself?'

In fact I did look outside in a little while to assess the situation in general, and to check that the two sentries we had posted were still awake. The BMW, a 5-series, Talal's pride and joy, had taken a direct hit from a Katyusha. It looked as though a giant had thumped it very hard indeed with a massive hammer. The wreckage was smoking gently. The young man looked up at me as I came back in, biting back the question that was on his lips. 'If I were you, Talal,' I told him, 'I'd order a new BMW.'

I asked for, and was shown to, a bathroom, in what I

suspected were the servants' quarters. Stripping off my dirty uniform, I set the water going, stepping under it naked except for my M-16, which I took with me into the shower. If you ever feel like a difficult physical challenge, try soaping yourself down with one hand while keeping an automatic rifle at the ready with the other. Despite this absurdity, it was a huge relief to wash the grime away.

Leaving the women inside unravaged, but ourselves refreshed, we set off from our temporary shelter bright and early the next morning. We had an airport to take.

Bassam Abu-Sharif

P alestine liberation movement fighters were trained in guerrilla warfare and in the tactics of the 'people's war'. This meant we were entirely unsuited to the type of battle we would have to fight against the Israeli forces in Lebanon. We did not possess an air force, warships or armour, as the Israelis did in abundance. The balance of conventional force was entirely in their favour.

As for the Syrians, despite the fact we had delivered a complete set of Israel's invasion plans, including a detailed map, well in advance of the event, they had done virtually nothing about it. Maybe, like my own leaders, they just hadn't wanted to believe it. Right up to the last moment, the Syrians were assuring us that Israel would do nothing more than 'cleanse' 40 kilometres of south Lebanon of hostile activity, then stop, consolidate, and create a permanent buffer-zone. The Syrians did nothing to oppose the Israelis at first – they just stood back and watched. It was only when the IDF actually attacked the Syrian army, in the region around Bhamdon between Beirut and Damascus, that they started to fight back. But Syrian opposition lasted only four days, before they gave up and signed a ceasefire.

195

When the invasion started, Habash and Arafat held a meeting in the basement of a safe house. The three rooms were so full of PLO officers that they had to talk under the stairs to get any kind of privacy. Abu Jihad was there, Abu Musa, Colonel Abu Ahmed Fu'ar, the PFLP's military commander, and I. Some of the other leaders were sleeping, worn out by the fighting and the incessant noise of the bombardment. But the most important person in the room, because of his military knowledge, was General Said Sayel: PLO Chief of Staff of the Supreme Council for Military Affairs, the military commander of Fatah – and a graduate of West Point. All the various factions of the PLO had agreed to fight as one, under Sayel's leadership. He was the man. He would know what to do.

Arafat and Habash pulled up a couple of chairs, huddling together under the steps to discuss the available options. They agreed the PLO had to make a stand, even if it was its last stand. Beirut was an Arab capital city. At any cost, we had to stop the Israelis from taking it. There had been enough humiliations. At the end of their meeting, Habash stood, gripping Arafat's hand in his own, with all the strength he could muster, despite the semi-paralysis of his by now stroke-damaged body. He wanted to show the PLO leader his determination and his solidarity.

General Sayel called us all round a very large map of Lebanon spread out across a table in the middle of the largest room. He explained his general plan of resistance, which consisted of three defensive lines running south to north through Lebanon. The first ran roughly east–west across the country from Tyre in the south, the second from Sidon. Beirut was the third and last line of defence. Our forces were disposed accordingly. When he had finished explaining his plan, Abu Ahmed Fu'ar, who was in overall command of the second line of defence around Sidon, rushed away to take charge of it.

He was not at his post for very long. The Israelis were attacking in massive numbers, and with massive armoured strength. Following a brief but vicious battle around Ain-an-Hilweh refugee camp, Abu Ahmed quickly withdrew his badly mauled forces to the Bekaa Valley. His experience, of tactical retreat in the face of overwhelming Israeli numbers and equipment, was to be typical. The intensity of the Israeli air, sea, rocket and artillery barrage was much greater than even we had anticipated. Sharon was in a real hurry.

The Israelis were attacking in three main columns: along the coast, through the centre of Lebanon, and in the east, up the Bekaa. These three forces interacted in an attempt to leapfrog Palestinian forces in their path, hoping to cut them off and kill them. The biggest surprise for us was the huge armoured force they'd landed at Sidon, Uzi's force. This simply bypassed our first defensive line, and most of our second.

In short, the defence plan didn't work. They were too many, too well armoured, and already behind most of our lines. Almost at once we lost command and control of our forces outside Beirut. The Israeli advance cut our communications to ribbons. Local commanders had to shift as best they could just to survive. Each refugee camp had its own basic fall-back defence plan, which it tried to carry out. These camps were where some of the worst fighting took place. The young refugees, armed with Kalashnikovs and not much else, were the bravest Palestinian fighters of us all. The Israelis killed hundreds of them.

When it came down to the siege of Beirut itself, we had a slightly better chance. We knew the city backwards, we had prepared bunkers, interconnecting tunnels, underground store-rooms and hideouts, we could hit, and move, and hit again.

When it became clear the Israelis would reach Beirut, General Sayel set up an ingenious system of fortification. It was ingenious because Beirut is an open city. His complex network of fire-traps, minefields, explosive booby-traps, barricades and troop dispositions narrowed the options for the enemy. He made it very hard for them to attack without taking heavy casualties. The city's buildings were our best barricades; shell or bomb them as they might, the Israelis still couldn't drive through the great piles of rubble. Any open streets in between the ruins could be mined.

Units of the Syrian Beirut brigade had been left behind in the city, stranded and forgotten when their other forces withdrew. They had to resist the IDF along with the rest of us, but we were not sure how much use they were going to be. For the most part they were young conscripts, ragamuffin infantry. But there was one regular Syrian tank brigade under a very good Syrian colonel. This excellent force agreed to become part of the interlocking defensive plan. They were the only modern armour we had.

The IDF columns, seemingly invincible, had been smashing through our positions, apparently unstoppable. Then, quite suddenly, at 'the battle of the stadium', things went badly wrong for them.

Sayel had set up this open space as a classic fire-trap.

We were all in the PLO Operations Room, waiting for news of where the main enemy thrust on Beirut was coming from. Suddenly the atmosphere came alive. We got a call over the radio from one of our forward observers that the Israelis were grouping a large force of armour and infantry behind the Beirut racecourse. At once the general gave orders for all available artillery, all anti-tank rocket-launchers, everything we could muster, to be brought to bear. As it happened, there was a PLO anti-tank brigade to hand. He ordered them to take up firing positions on the western side of the racecourse, at the double.

A few minutes later the Israeli naval and artillery barrage lifted. It had been going for seventeen hours non-stop. 'They are moving,' we heard the observer say. He kept a running commentary going as events unfolded: 'A Merkava battle-tank is breaking through the wall on the eastern side of the race-course, followed by another; then many, many tanks, with many infantry, coming behind them . . .'

When they break through the other wall, I thought, the Israelis will be in West Beirut. Where we are. They see the racecourse as a weak point: a point of entry to the city. Let's hope they are wrong about that.

Sayel was on the radio to all posts: 'Hold your fire,' he urged them. 'Keep silence. Hold your fire. Let them come.' The forward observer was spelling out the numbers, 'Twelve tanks ... fourteen tanks ... infantry behind, maybe two hundred.' 'Let them come,' repeated Sayel. 'Silence. Let them come on. Hold your fire.' Then our man reported, 'There are around 400 soldiers in the middle of the racecourse now ... The lead tank is approaching the western wall. They will try to break through it in a few seconds.'

'Fire!' Sayel barked out. Every gun, every rocket, opened up as one, pouring fire on the Israeli force. Stranded in the middle of the racecourse, with nowhere to take cover, the Merkavas started taking hits from our rocket-propelled grenades. Some of them caught fire and began exploding. Israeli reinforcements tried to come up through the withering fire. The IDF men fought on for hours in this hell, very bravely, but their avenue into West Beirut had turned into a deadly trap. They were not going to make it. Their attack turned into a retreat, then into a rout. The Israelis admitted to seventeen killed, with dozens wounded. In reality they must have lost many more. For a little while, at least, we had checked their advance.

On 4 July the Israelis issued a 'peace' proposal. It called on all PLO members to surrender their weapons and get out of Lebanon. We rejected it out of hand. We were not going to have our noses rubbed in it: better to go down fighting. The US government in the form of its special envoy, Philip Habib, began working flat-out for a peace settlement. The Israelis intensified their shelling of West Beirut.

Habib brokered an agreement: Israel would allow Arafat to leave the city with his fighters, and their small-arms. Now, since we were supposed to be in a ceasefire, the Israelis couldn't carry forward the fight; instead, they imposed a blockade on the entire PLO-occupied section of West Beirut. We were cut off inside this area. No food, fuel, electricity or even water was reaching us. The small matter of 500,000 or so entirely innocent Lebanese citizens who were also affected by this blockade did nothing to deter them. The UN passed a resolution the very next day calling on Israel to restore all these services to West Beirut. They ignored it.

With his usual panache, Arafat presented the withdrawal of PLO forces from Beirut on 30 August as a 'victory'. And, in relative terms, it was a victory. With a poorly-trained guerrilla army, we had prevented Sharon's mighty IDF from entering Beirut. They did come into West Beirut, eventually, but it was in direct breach of the signed peace agreement, and only as we were departing. And now they were in Beirut, what were the Israelis going to do with it? Beirut has a history of swallowing foreign armies and spitting out the remains. I did not think the IDF was going to be an exception. And the Palestinian struggle against Israel wouldn't stop because of what had happened here in Beirut. This was something the Israeli government, and their American allies, could never seem to understand. The Palestinian people had suffered a basic injustice. We were never going to give up until we got justice, no matter what. Even if Arafat were killed, someone else would take over. Inside or outside Palestine, wherever we could fight, that is where we would fight. It was very simple, really. In our position, the Israeli people – or the Americans, for that matter – would be doing the same.

The peace agreement stipulated that the multilateral peace-keeping forces, American, Italian, French, would enter Beirut before our departure, which they did; that they would protect our departure, which they did. But it also guaranteed the safety of the Palestinians in the Beirut refugee camps. This the foreign troops did not do. Instead, on the morning of 17 September, the Israelis, who were now in complete control of Beirut, allowed scores of so-called 'Christian' militiamen into Sabra and Shatila refugee camps. These Christian killers went through the camps methodically, butchering the defenceless women, children and old men taking shelter there. They had plenty of time to do their bloody work as there were few able-bodied men left in the camps to resist them. Hundreds, perhaps thousands, of Palestinian civilians died in the massacres.

When we left Beirut many people wrote us off – especially people like Israel's right-wing Likud party. Instead, Arafat pulled off a miraculous salvation of the PLO and, into the bargain, US President Reagan put forward a 'Land for Peace' plan – a giant step towards what we wanted. The plan called for full Palestinian autonomy on the West Bank. We accepted it at once. The Israelis rejected it out of hand.

Sharon's plans to liquidate the PLO, both physically and as a viable political force, had been defeated. The PLO's survival in any form was a clear victory. We had made the IDF pay a very high cost for its Lebanese adventure – more than 650 Israelis had died in Lebanon – and our determined resistance to the invasion made a political settlement more, and not less, likely. What many forgot, as they always forget, was one very simple fact: the PLO was never a camp, never a village, never a military force: it was an idea. Ideas, especially ideas of justice, are the stongest things in life. Ideas are much harder to kill than people.

Still, Arafat's withdrawal from Beirut caused a massive split in the ranks of the PLO. Some refused to see it as anything other than the most abject defeat. A group led by the PLO leaders Abu Saleh and Abu Musa denounced Arafat's conduct of the war as incompetent, excoriated him as undemocratic, and demanded reform. When Arafat ignored them, they decided to form a counter-revolutionary force. The rebels turned to the Syrians. And the Syrians, as always, jumped at the chance of annihilating the PLO. When the true Syrian intentions towards the PLO became obvious yet again for what they were – to annex the Palestinian cause – the rebels lost all support. Had they stayed and worked for root and branch reform within the PLO, they might just have succeeded in forcing it.

Chapter
Twenty-One

—————➤ ◂—————

Uzi Mahnaimi

A riel Sharon, I finally realised, had totally misled the people of Israel about the true nature of the invasion I was part of. This infuriated me. I was quite happy to do something about the fact that the PLO were shelling my mother-in-law's town of Nahariyah just south of the Lebanese border. What we were actually engaged in, though, was not the creation of any security zone in southern Lebanon; it was a form of 'ethnic cleansing'. Sharon wanted to drive all Palestinians, including the civilians, out of Lebanon. This was not what I had signed up for. Killing Arab civilians, forcing them from their homes, this was not the honourable way to make Israel strong, the way of Shalom, my grandfather. My father had found this out to his cost in 1948. I would not be part of another mass expulsion, then live to regret it.

The Israeli invasion of Lebanon was a crunch point, a crucial moment in the Israeli–Arab conflict. Attempting the final solution of war, it impelled the region towards peace. It showed that the PLO was never going to vanish in a puff of

Israeli gunsmoke, however many guns we used. There could be no more Israeli invasions; there had to be some other way. But my experiences in Lebanon weren't entirely worthless; they had gelled the half-baked, half-formed feelings I'd had in the past. I was determined now to leave the army and, this time, it would be for good.

Bassam Abu-Sharif

After we were pushed out of Lebanon there were few people left in the world who wanted to know the PLO groups. The Syrians were the exception, they couldn't wait to invite us in, so the PFLP went to Damascus. But the moment we set foot on their soil, and even before then, I knew: the Syrians were out to destroy us. They wanted to finish Arafat and take control of the whole struggle for Palestine. President Assad had always seen Damascus as the beating heart of the Arab world; Palestine was the major issue for Arabs – therefore, he reasoned, it was Syria's job to control the struggle for Palestine. It was a warped way of looking at things, and it gave rise to some pretty warped Syrian behaviour.

I knew well the fate of puppet groups, whether Syrian, Iraqi or any other kind, so I was really worried. The puppet-master turned the screw, slowly, slowly, until the puppet's joints finally flew apart and the body was gone. I was seriously worried for the future. At every meeting of the Central Committee of the PFLP Politburo in our Damascus exile, I railed at them about this danger. 'We should keep our policy towards Syria under constant review,' I told them. 'We have to be prepared for the worst.'

The real intentions of the Syrian government became clear very quickly. In 1983, less than a year after they had invited him in, Syrian intelligence officers gave Arafat four hours to pack up and get out of Syria. The Chairman sadly called the various PLO faction leaders to his office, and told them he was about to be expelled. Habash and Hawatmeh decided they would support Arafat. All they meant by this was that they would go with him in the car to the airport.

When we got there, a Tunisian plane was standing ready on the runway. The captain came hurrying down the steps to Arafat and said politely that his aircraft was at the PLO Chairman's disposal, as if it wasn't all a matter of coercion. A Syrian officer escorted Arafat up the steps; at the last second, he turned and looked sadly back at us. Then he was gone, into exile yet again.

What amazed and shocked me was that nobody spoke up on his behalf. There was only silence. 'What?' I demanded at the next meeting. 'We're just going to stand by, are we, while the PLO leader is thrown out in this way?' I went up to Habash and Hawatmeh. 'Listen,' I said. 'Going to the airport was a brave thing, but we must do much more than that. If we accept what is happening to Arafat now, if we say and do nothing, the next step will be that a simple Syrian soldier can come and take you, me, any of us to prison. You should have gone with him; we should all have gone with him. The issue here is not Yasser Arafat; the issue is Palestine. Whatever else he might be, Arafat is a figurehead, the symbol of the Palestinian struggle. He is not a common criminal to be kicked about at will. What Assad has done here has only one objective, and it is very deliberate; he intends to humiliate all Palestinians.'

The two remaining leaders scowled back at me while I said my piece, saying nothing. There was nothing they could say. 'We should not stay behind when Arafat is driven out,' I persisted. 'None of us should stay behind.'

The next day, I took my courage in my hands. I could still act as the PFLP's official spokesman. Who would stop me? I issued a public statement in Damascus, condemning Syria's actions and questioning its intentions towards the PLO. I said it was a very regrettable act, for the people of Palestine as for all Arabs, an act that undermined the cause of the people. The minute I had finished speaking, the Syrian Minister of Information rang my office, shouting bitterly down the phone at me about the statement I'd just made. Really, he was objecting to the fact that I'd dared show his government's behaviour up for what it really was: a concerted, calculated attack on the official Palestinian movement. The Syrian government also complained about my statement to George Habash, ordering him to shut me up. I told George what I'd told the Information Minister: yes, the Syrians could tell me to get out of the country and I would leave, but they could not restrict my freedom to speak openly as long as I was there. Still, I thought it would be better to get out of town for a bit. When the Syrians are angry, they don't stop at half-measures. The next day, I left Damascus.

I met Arafat two days later at a peace conference in Prague. There, at a private villa, we had a long talk. 'I am going back into Lebanon,' he told me, 'to Tripoli.' He was refusing to take what had happened in Syria lying down. In fact, by going back into Lebanon, he was going to show them that it was still Yasser Arafat, and not President Assad, who kept the flame of the Palestinian struggle burning.

It was the first time Arafat had shaved in years. Dressed in an elegant European-style business suit, complete with hat and briefcase, his chin was as bare and smooth as a baby's backside. He flew from Tunis to Cyprus under an assumed identity. In Larnaca, he rented a private boat and crossed to a fishing village near the Nahr al-Barred refugee camp in northern Lebanon. He managed all this undetected. It was one in the eye for Mossad, because Cyprus comes under the heading of 'local station' – home turf – for Israel's intelligence services, and the place was infested with them. They should have spotted Arafat, but they didn't. In fact, without his whiskers, nobody would ever have recognised him. Once inside the camp, he changed into his customary battle-dress, complete with trademark *kaffiyeh*.

The Syrians hadn't had the nerve, quite, to kill the PLO Chairman, but they had expected him to get the message: go away and keep quiet. They'd rounded up and imprisoned hundreds of PLO fighters in both Lebanon and Syria in the wake of his expulsion. So when he popped up again in Lebanon a few weeks after they'd kicked him out, like some evil genie sent to haunt them, the Syrians went predictably berserk. Assad treated Lebanon as more or less his own personal property – as a kind of Syrian fiefdom. He could not tolerate any revival of the Palestinian movement in Lebanon. On every front, Arafat was thwarting him.

But, like the Old Guard of the French Army rallying to Napoleon on Elba, Arafat's fighters slipped quietly back to him once they heard he was back in Lebanon. Furious, the Syrian leader sent his Palestinian puppet groups, in particular the so-called 'Palestine Liberation Army', to attack the PLO leader and his men. Regular Syrian army units then joined in the attacks.

In Damascus, I ranted at any members of the Syrian government who would see me. It made no difference. In fact, the ministers I argued with were quite frank with me: 'We want the PLO out of Lebanon – and out of the picture – for good.' Then Israel joined in the Syrian bombardment of Tripoli. Every man's hand was turned against Yasser Arafat; he was like a dog being kicked in a corner. This time, his enemies were determined to go on kicking him until he was finished. They forgot that Arafat had chosen the corner.

Amal travelled up from Beirut to visit the PLO leader, once she heard he was in Tripoli. Like many Arab women, she felt it was her duty to help him any way she could. Shortly afterwards, I got a call. It was Arafat. We chatted for an hour or so about the fix he was in, the fix we were all in, and about the situation in general. To my slight surprise, Arafat rang me the next day, then the day after that. Over the next six weeks we talked on the telephone almost every day. One day when Arafat rang, George Habash was visiting me at home with two or three other PLO Central Committee colleagues. 'Would you like to talk to them?' I asked Arafat, who was still on the line.

'No,' he replied, his voice heavy with sarcasm. 'I wouldn't

want to bother them.' He was bitterly scornful of these PLO 'leaders' for sitting safely in Damascus while he took the hits in Tripoli.

When I put the phone down, Habash said, 'I know what Arafat is thinking. I know what you're thinking. But you must realise – I don't think the Syrians should be shelling the PLO leader in Tripoli any more than you do. But Arafat shouldn't be in Tripoli in the first place. It is futile. He's just provoking the Syrians. What is the point of that?'

'Listen, George,' I countered, 'a lot of people think that. But as usual, a lot of people are wrong. There is every point in Arafat going back into Lebanon: his defiance *is* the point.'

The next day, Arafat asked me what Habash had said. 'He asks what is the point? The point is to keep alive the idea of Palestine. That's what I'm trying to do. That is what you are trying to do. Will the Syrians keep our country alive? Will Habash?'

These phone calls, over the six weeks Arafat and his troops were under continual bombardment, were very important, for me and for him. He knew there was one leading Palestinian figure at least in Damascus who still supported him. He understood that although I was the PFLP spokesman, when I criticised Syria I was speaking not only for my own organisation but for the whole of Palestine. Just as importantly, I was speaking for Yasser Arafat.

Arafat didn't only want to thank me for saying the right thing now and again, or to egg me on to say more: he was using his calls to score political points. As we were talking, I realised he was passing on messages: to the Israelis and the Syrians, certainly, to the CIA, probably. He knew they were all listening in, so he exploited the fact.

What was I getting out of it? I was not really interested in basking in the warm glow of Arafat's fickle affection. But these daily exchanges confirmed the suspicion I'd first had about the PLO Chairman in 1974: he was interested in keeping the peace option going, in putting out feelers, he was keen to explore every possible way out of the blind alley we had all stumbled into. Yes, he was grateful that I was standing up to the Syrians and supporting him. But he knew as well as I did, that sooner rather than later there would have to be some sort of negotiated settlement between the PLO and Israel. It was obvious things couldn't go on as they were much longer. That was the way global politics were taking us.

But how could he achieve a lasting and just peace for the people of Palestine? He could not achieve it on his own. No more could I. He was still the keeper of the flame, the symbol of the Palestinian struggle, a role that had always stopped him speaking openly for peace. But he could send me forward waving the olive branch. He could use me to test opinion. And, in the same way, I could use him. With Arafat's weight at my back, I could open many doors that would otherwise remain closed to me.

And so, without discussing it openly, over this span of weeks we came to a tacit agreement: I would somehow get myself free of the PFLP. And when I'd done this, we would join forces. And we would try to make peace for our people.

It was to be another four years before my chance came to join Arafat. For those long years, missing my family, I was the classic exile, measuring out my hours with rage and rhetoric. What kept me together was my family, Amal, Karma and by now my little boy, Omar, all still in Beirut. I wanted so much to see them, but because of the civil war in Lebanon, the Shi'ites had put a price on my head. Each time I tried to cross the border to snatch a day or two at home, I was risking capture, or worse. I used to slip in secretly, by night, stay for three or four days, never leaving the house, then slip back out again. It was only a question of time before somebody noticed. And one day when I'd made the hair-raising trip from Damascus to Beirut, they did catch up with me.

Very early the next morning, our maid came and knocked

at the bedroom door. She was trembling. 'There is a man called Abu Ali asking to see you,' she said. 'I told him you were not here. But he shoved past me. He's waiting for you in the lounge.'

'OK,' I told her, 'don't worry.' This was trouble. I knew no Abu Ali. Amal sat up in bed staring at me, wide-eyed. 'Who is it?' she mouthed. I shook my head. Reaching over to the bedside chair, I softly slid forward the safety-catch on the .38 Smith & Wesson revolver I always had with me. I noticed little Karma sitting up in her cot watching me anxiously. I smiled at her as reassuringly as I could, motioning her to be quiet. I wished I could reassure myself as easily. Stuffing the gun into the right-hand pocket of my dressing-gown, I walked through into the lounge to meet the intruder, with my finger curled round the trigger.

The visitor was standing in the centre of the room facing me as I entered. He was wearing paramilitary-style combat fatigues, with an automatic pistol in an open-topped holster at his side. His hand was resting on the butt of the gun. 'Who are you?' I asked him.

'I am Abu Ali,' he replied. I looked blankly at him. 'You don't know Abu Ali?' he asked, raising his eyebrows as though I should.

'No,' I said. 'I don't know Abu Ali.'

'I am chief of security for the Shi'ite movement in Beirut,' he said.

'Are you?' I replied. 'What do you want?'

'Nabih Berri, who is head of the Shi'ite movement, would like to see you,' he told me. 'Now.'

'Well,' I replied, 'Nabih Berri is an old friend of mine. We have known one another for many years. He has been to my house several times. If he would like to see me he is welcome here at any time.'

'No,' said the man. 'He is waiting for you with a lot of other people who would like to talk to you. Now.'

This cocksure little gofer was beginning to annoy me.

209

'Tell you what,' I said. 'Why don't we ring him and see what he has to say himself?' The man was taken aback by this suggestion, as I'd hoped he would be. He'd been sent out to make a simple arrest, and here was the prisoner wanting to ring his boss. While he thought about it, I flipped through my contacts book by the phone for the Shi'ite leader's Beirut number.

I showed it to Abu Ali. 'All right,' he said, and began dialling. Nabih Berri came on the line immediately. 'Nabih!' I began when I heard his voice. 'How are you?'

'Hello, Bassam,' he replied in a neutral voice. 'We heard you are in town. Everyone would like to see you. The leadership is all here. We don't have much time because we are going to Damascus. Come, please. At once.'

'OK,' I said, and put the phone down. I knew then that I had no choice. The tone in his voice said everything. Nabih, it seemed, was an old friend who had become a new enemy. They were determined to take me, whatever I did.

I got dressed, saying a very special goodbye to Amal and Karma. I knew I might be seeing them for the last time. Then I went out into the street with the head of Shi'ite security. Outside the door, I stopped in surprise: the building was surrounded by Shi'ite jeeps mounted with machine-guns. Each jeep was packed with heavily-armed Shi'ite militiamen. It was a kidnap, pure and simple. 'What's all this?' I asked Abu Ali. 'Are these all for me, or are we about to invade Israel?'

'This is your escort,' he sneered. 'We don't want Bassam Abu-Sharif to move around without a proper escort, do we?' And, with that, the convoy roared into life. It was headed straight for the Shi'ite headquarters in South Beirut.

I did not feel great fear, but I knew this might well be my last battle. I felt almost resigned to what was coming. I only hoped it would be quick. My little .38 revolver was definitely not going to be a match for this 'escort'. Once inside the ramshackle Shi'ite building, I was taken down to the basement and locked into a small, windowless room. Except for two upright wooden

210

chairs, the cell was entirely bare. I began to get a little angry. Amazingly, they still hadn't searched me. I curled my finger round the trigger of the gun again, just for the comfort it gave. Suddenly, the door burst open, and Mustapha Dirani swept into the room. My heart sank. I knew Dirani was Nabih Berri's inquisitor and chief executioner. His arrival on the scene meant only one thing. A dozen or more armed bodyguards spilled into the room behind him. One of them came up to me. 'Take your hands out of your pockets and raise them in the air,' he snapped. He patted me down expertly, snatching my revolver from its hiding-place. I felt very, very vulnerable.

There was just one thing working in my favour, and I might just be able to use it. I knew Dirani, too, from way back. I'd met him first when he was a wet-behind-the-ears Shi'ite messenger-boy. I was trying very hard to remember his nickname. Then it came to me. 'Abu Staif,' I called out heartily, as if he were a long-lost friend. 'How are you?' For a moment he hesitated. It was just enough to give me the edge. 'Abu Staif,' I persisted, with all the warmth in my voice I could muster, 'how are you? Are you well? I hope you haven't forgotten me?' He stared uncertainly at me. His henchmen had fanned out in a loose circle around my chair. Now we were at the crunch. If he didn't respond to me in kind, I was done for.

Then, slowly, hesitantly, he stepped towards me. We embraced stiffly. He stepped back, motioning his thugs from the room. 'What is wrong, Abu Staif?' I asked when they had gone. 'It seems you are displeased?'

'You know what's wrong, Bassam,' replied Dirani. 'You know exactly what's wrong. You are a Palestinian guerrilla. What do you think you are doing in Beirut?'

'I am visiting my family,' I told him. 'Only that.'

'You know what the scum you lead are doing to our people in the south? Raping our women. Killing our villagers. Extorting money from them. You're one of them. We're supposed to be pleased with you?'

'No,' I said, 'I don't expect you to be pleased with me. I can't defend what some *fedayin* are doing. I can only say I don't go along with it.'

'You know the Israelis shell and bomb our villages every day because you people are infesting them?' He stopped. He had worked himself up into a blazing fury. He was breathing hard. 'You know this?'

'I know it very well,' I replied, as calmly and as coolly as I could.

'Then,' spat Dirani, his plump face creased in rage, 'you understand why we have brought you here, don't you?'

'I understand this, too, very well,' I told him. I took him by the arm; my fate was hovering on the edge of his anger. 'Why don't we sit down and talk it through?' I asked. He broke away, angrily shrugging off my hand. But he did sit down.

At the end of an hour, during which we talked right through the situation in Lebanon, Dirani stood up. 'All right, Bassam,' he said. 'You can go this time. But you can tell your colleagues in Damascus they're not wanted here. And make sure you don't come back yourself. This is the last time we shall make an exception.'

'I shall keep what you say at the front of my mind,' I replied gravely.

'By the way,' said Dirani as he was showing me out of the building, 'how did you get into Beirut past our check-points?'

'As a matter of fact,' I smiled at him, 'a Volvo picked me up from Damascus. It was driven by one of your leadership.'

'What?' exclaimed Dirani, who could see I was telling the truth, even if he didn't want to believe it. 'Who was it? Who brought you here?'

'Come,' I replied, 'you cannot expect me to tell you that. But one of your own leaders drove me straight into the city!'

The same enormous convoy took me back home. Already, the whole quarter was in mourning for me. They had assumed the worst. When they caught sight of me getting out of the jeep, the local women began ululating for joy at my release. I went inside, wrapped my arms round Amal and Karma, and

BASSAM'S PHOTOS

Bassam's father, Towfik
Abu-Sharif, in Jerusalem
during the early 1930s.

Towfik Abu-Sharif and friends on
a day out in the mountains.

Mr and Mrs Towfik Abu-Sharif *(right)* at a party, 1955.

The hijacking season. Bassam Abu-Sharif (*with megaphone*)
next to a hijacked PanAm plane at an airfield in the Jordanian desert.

Bassam, again with
megaphone, on the cover
of *Time* magazine,
21 September 1970.

Ilich Ramirez Sanchez appeared one day, out of the blue, at Bassam's office in Beirut. Bassam recruited him, and sent him under the nickname 'Carlos' on the long and bloody march of terrorism.

'They wanted to kill me because they were jealous of the success with women of the handsome Palestinian' - Bassam, in Beirut, a short time before the Mossad assassination attempt.

Full of pride and dignity, Bassam leaves Beirut with a Palestinian *kaffiyeh* and Russian-made Kalashnikov.

Under siege. Fatah commander Abu Jihad, planning the defence of Beirut from the Israeli invaders.

Below: Abu Jihad whispering to 'the Boss'. Later on, an Israeli assassination squad killed him in his villa in Tunis.

Writing home. Bassam and his wife send a cable to his father during the siege of Beirut.

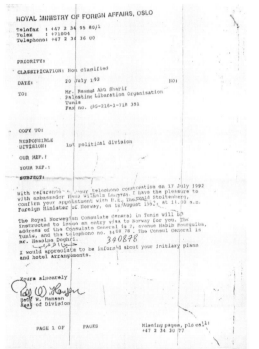

Bassam opens the Norwegian door.
Soon afterwards, Arafat (as always)
was quick to enter the scene
and send his clerks to sign an
agreement with the Israelis.

Below: Bassam's charisma and charm
made world leaders his best friends.
The Boss and others were not always
as happy.

Quick advice for the Boss.

Rome, 1990.

Bassam with his
daughter, Karma.

Bassam with
his father.

The breakthrough with the Americans.

The breakthrough with the British: the first ministerial-level meeting
with William Waldegrave.

The kids with the Boss.

Bassam's wife Amal *(centre)* with George Habash, the head of the Popular Front for the Liberation of Palestine, and his wife.

we just sat there for long minutes of joy, while the relief flooded through us.

I was one of the first, and probably one of the last, people to be kidnapped by the Shi'ites in Beirut and live to tell the tale.

Some years later Dirani himself was kidnapped – by Israeli commandos. He is still in gaol.

I may have escaped the clutches of the Shi'ites, but I was still stuck in the PFLP, marooned in Damascus. During this long time I never stopped criticising the Syrians publicly; I saw no contradiction between accepting a safe haven from them and speaking up when I thought they were acting against the Palestinian interest. The Syrians, though, were getting understandably fed up.

In March 1987 I must have overstepped some sort of invisible line. At the time, *faute de mieux*, I was living in my office, sleeping on the couch. At about 2.30 one morning the telephone rang on the desk above my head. It was a friend of mine, an officer who worked in Syrian intelligence. 'Meet me at the usual place in half an hour', was all he said. The usual place was a restaurant we went to once a week for its extremely good barbecues. But at three o'clock in the morning? I had no car, no bodyguards. What if it were a trap? Eventually I decided to go. Everything was closed. I was very lucky to stop a passing cab. Part of me was sorry that it had turned up. I kept thinking, why am I doing this? It's obviously a trap. Syrian intelligence has finally had enough.

When I reached the restaurant, it was in complete darkness. Then the owner, whom I knew well, stepped out of the shadows: 'Bassam, it's all right,' he whispered. 'Our friend will be here soon; come in.' We waited. And we waited. At last, my friend's big Mercedes cruised to a halt in the sleeping street. We sat and talked over a snack the owner had prepared for us. My friend came straight to the point. 'You have your passport with you?' he asked. 'Of course,' I replied. 'You know the road-blocks . . .' 'Money?' he interrupted. 'Sure,' I said. In my trade, it was wise always to carry a fat roll of notes. 'OK, good,' said the Syrian. 'I have arranged everything else for you. There is a plane leaving Damascus in one hour from now, at five. It is going to Budapest. From there you can go anywhere you like. Be on this plane.'

'Why?' I asked, although the answer was obvious.

'Because, if you are still here tomorrow, I will not answer for your life.'

'What do you mean? Is it so bad?'

'Yes, it's as bad as can be,' he replied hurriedly. 'And I'm telling you this only because you are a friend. That is all I can say. My car is outside. Now go.' I got up, shook his hand warmly, and stepped into the Mercedes. He stayed in the restaurant. Two of his men took me to the airport by a circuitous route, avoiding the usual police checks, and stuck me straight on the plane. I never saw him again, but he undoubtedly saved my life.

I arrived in Budapest feeling slightly bewildered. I had no visa and no luggage. I wandered through into the transit lounge and asked about flights out of Hungary in the next few hours. There was one flight to Algiers. I booked a seat on that. So ended my four-year stay in Damascus. I have never been back. I know what would be waiting for me.

CHAPTER
TWENTY-TWO

Bassam Abu-Sharif

It was a handshake that won me my freedom. You don't simply leave an organisation like the PFLP – you can easily meet with permanent retirement. But if they throw you out . . . I first worked with Arafat in the autumn of 1987. I'd been semi-detached from the PFLP for some time, really, ever since they'd demoted me. Arafat asked me to join the official PLO delegation to the African summit in Addis Ababa. On our way back to Tunis, we stopped in Cairo, where the Egyptian President Hosni Mubarak had invited Arafat for talks. Meeting Mubarak, who had continued and consolidated Sadat's peace deal with Israel, was heresy to the hard-liners in the Arab world. The Syrians, for example, hated him. And we didn't just meet Mubarak: we shook hands with him.

I knew what the reaction would be from the hawks if we supped with the devil Mubarak. But I could hardly stand with my hand behind my back, like a small child in a sulk, when the Egyptian leader was there before me with his own hand outstretched. We shook hands warmly as the videotape rolled.

As soon as the news pictures went out, the PFLP leadership
in Damascus issued a statement branding me a traitor to the
Palestinian cause. The PFLP Politburo called an extraordinary
meeting. A majority demanded my expulsion. They got it. Now,
finally, I'd been formally excommunicated.

I was happy. Here was the opportunity I'd been waiting for:
I was free to join Arafat, as we both wished. And I made sure
I was joining Arafat, not any of the PLO institutions: not Fatah
or any of the other bureaucracies. I would be like a minister
without portfolio at the court of King Arafat. I would act as a
kind of special adviser; I would have the ear of the king but no
official status. I would work to my own agenda. And   would
work for peace.

The last discussion I had with Habash before finally leaving
the PFLP was in Tripoli, Libya, late in 1987. It was a sad
occasion. I was leaving my old mentor, the man who had so
inspired me in the bitter aftermath of the June '67 War. Just as
Habash had sought to steer my opinion in the old days, when I
had been young and green, now I set about trying to convince
him. I tried to persuade him that the PFLP should start acting
in concert with Arafat, officially, openly, and at once: that the
whole PLO, as a unified force, should begin working towards
a negotiated settlement with Israel.

'What are you talking about, Bassam?' he laughed. 'Why
should we do such a crazy thing?'

'Above all,' I told him, 'there is one important thing you have
to take into account.'

'Which is?' He smiled.

'Very soon now the Cold War will end.'

Habash looked at me as if I had gone mad. 'Never,' he
replied, his eyes mocking mine. 'Never, even in twenty-five
years' time.'

'No,' I said. 'The end will come soon.'

'Never,' he said.

'Well,' I persisted, 'we've had INF and STARTs, and SALTs
and SALT IIs. There is a huge will on both sides to reach

agreement on the nuclear front. But that agreement can't be reached unless and until all the world's regional problems are solved: Afghanistan, Nicaragua, South Africa – and above all the world's most troublesome region: the Middle East.'

'Never,' he retorted. 'It will never happen.'

'This will happen,' I said. 'And when it happens, Palestine will be top of the agenda. If Palestine is on the agenda, Arafat is the only game in town. Either the PFLP goes in with Arafat, or it goes out of the game. Negotiations will follow very soon once the US–Soviet thaw has started. A peaceful solution to our struggle is coming.'

'Never,' said Habash. 'Never, never, never. *Ça suffit.*' He paused for a while, staring into my eyes. 'And you, Bassam – how can you go to Arafat, after all we have been through together?

'Well,' I said, with a tinge of regret, 'I must work for the future now; not for the past.'

That same month I published an article in an Arabic weekly, *The Seventh Day.* Without mentioning him by name, it was based on my conversation with Habash. Everyone I knew laughed when they read it. My main point was that the problem of Palestine was the key to peace in the Middle East. So much was obvious. Less obvious was what I had tried to tell Habash: that in the context of defrosting superpower relations, the PLO was not a spent force, as most commentators had been saying. Far from it. The PLO was a force in the ascendant, a force whose star was rising. We held one of the two keys that would open the door to peace in the region. Israel held the other.

It was the Star Wars programme that had persuaded me that the Cold War must end. This grandiose scheme to put up a kind of nuclear umbrella in space was something the Americans had spent billions of dollars on already, and were prepared to spend many billions more setting up. Pushed forward during the Reagan administration, which probably spent more on defence than any government in US history ever has or ever will again, the Star Wars scheme meant only

217

one thing for the Soviets in their arms race with America: checkmate.

Why had Reagan put forward his 'Land for Peace' proposal in 1982? He would not have proposed it without some underlying reason. Why had he chosen that time, when, on the face of it, the plan had so little chance of success? No, the Americans, even then, understood. The old order was changing. Peace must come.

On the day I arrived in Tunis to join Arafat, he asked me into his office on the seafront. 'Abu-Omar,' he began, 'you know I want you to work with me. And you understand why. But what, exactly, do you want to do? Would you like me to create a new department of the PLO with you as its head, or is there some title you would like to have? I am ready to do whatever you want.' He was generous then. I always remember this.

'No,' I told him, 'I shall work simply with you, one to one, as directly as possible.'

The first thing we had to do was formulate our precise strategy and tactics. We could no longer be vague about peace. We had talked around it enough inside the PLO, in meeting after meeting, without really getting anywhere. Nothing was ever made clear: we needed a clear set of principles, and a precise plan of action.

We sat down and began our council of peace. We agreed firstly that the PLO, under Arafat's guidance, must move forward stage-by-stage towards a just and lasting peace. Reagan's plan – that Israel return occupied territory in exchange for the PLO's agreement to UN Resolution 242 – was the basis we would work from. The first step must be recognition of the State of Israel: the PLO refusal to do this remained one of the chief obstacles to a solution. How, though, to manage the massive hostility this would provoke from the PLO hard-liners? Now we must enact the role we'd touched upon during our long-distance telephone calls: I must become Arafat's thought-bubble. That way, I could keep prodding and poking, chipping away at the entrenched resistance of the hawks, by putting forward peace initiatives at PLO meetings, raising the issue at press conferences, soaking up (and taking the blame for) any hostile reaction. We would try it. I would keep sticking my hand in the fire, pushing for a negotiated peace. One day, somebody had to turn off the heat.

Arafat was a tireless worker, but luckily, he was a night-bird like myself. He was usually up at ten in the morning, and would work right through until 4.30 the next morning. I started and finished my work half an hour earlier than him. Sharing his seafront office, we worked cheek by jowl. We had breakfast, lunch and dinner together every day. Occasionally someone would join us in the morning, to finish off a discussion from the night before. Lunch was for general political discussions that would range far and wide, beyond the narrow compass of our own affairs. Arafat and I talked peace, war, politics, information, strategy, tactics, diplomacy, ideas, love and death. But one thing he would never discuss with me was matters of security. Military operations – what he called 'The Circle of Terror' – were taboo. He wanted to keep me out of the circle. I was more useful to him clean than with blood on my hands. I wanted no part of it, anyway. 'It is a vicious circle,' I used to say to him. 'Those who go round in it, go down with it.'

Arafat is a man who thinks of things in stages. Then he thinks about each stage in its particularities. What conditions does this stage need? What is its basis? Who does it need to make it succeed? What is its final objective? He has a very logical and methodical mind.

Like many great political leaders, he resented giving time to sleep. He was driven. He burned. Arafat needed something. And on a very basic level, he needed someone who could keep up with him physically. I could just about keep up, but it took everything I had.

Once, in Baghdad, Arafat went to bed as dawn was breaking over the city. At 6.30 he came out of his bedroom wearing the jogging-suit he favoured in his private time. It seemed he could not sleep. I was still working. 'What the hell are you doing?' he demanded.

'Just finishing up a few things.'

'Believe me,' said Arafat, 'I've seen but two, so far, who are hard workers: me – and you!' From that moment onward he called me 'the Bulldozer'. It was a lot better than some of the things I'd been called.

Uzi Mahnaimi

Having managed finally to shake myself clear of the army in 1984, I wanted a job about as far away from military life as I could get. I had always been a news and information junkie. I had very good contacts with the Israeli military and political establishment, and I spoke fluent Arabic. I'd always enjoyed writing, so I thought: why not try my luck as a journalist?

In 1984 I applied for, and to my surprise got, the job of Middle East correspondent for *Al-Hamishmar*, the left-wing Israeli newspaper. I spent three years cutting my teeth there, two in Israel and one in London. Then in September 1987 I got another big break. I was asked to work as Middle East editor for Israel's largest mass-circulation daily, *Yediouth Ahronot*.

I immediately decided not to do this job in the usual way of Israeli journalists: picking up their copy from the Arab press, recycling the wire services, and so on. No, I was full of fire and zeal. I would develop first-hand contacts of my own in the Arab world, and use them properly. Here was my chance to make a bit of a mark as a journalist on my home ground.

From my years in London I knew Marie Colvin, Middle East correspondent of the *Sunday Times*, who was in touch with many of the leading PLO figures. I asked her to help me get to some of them. She helped me draft letters to Khalil Wazir, better known as Abu Jihad, the PLO deputy leader, and to Arafat. I wanted to interview them both. No other Israeli journalist had ever done so, maybe it was time someone did. I spoke to Abu Jihad on the phone from Cairo; he said he could not talk then, but he would do at some time in the future. I also drew a blank with Arafat. Marie then suggested I contact another source of hers, Bassam Abu-Sharif.

I knew of this man – his face was always on the TV news networks, either with or without the PLO Chairman, he popped up everywhere. I started watching him more closely, and listening carefully to what he said. I could see the sense of Marie's suggestion: Abu-Sharif really did seem to have the ear of Yasser Arafat; he was personal adviser, envoy and media lieutenant all rolled into one: what a source he would make if I could get to him.

There was just one small snag in my plan: talking directly with leading PLO figures was against Israeli law. No Israeli citizen, even a journalist, was permitted to speak directly with any member of any Palestinian organisation deemed 'terrorist', which basically included all of them. And good guys like me, journalists from good old-boy Zionist families, didn't deal with 'terrorists', anyway. Why would they want to? It was out of the question. So I knew I was taking a risk. But somebody had to do something to break the dull mould Israeli journalism had fallen into because no one ever talked directly with the other side. It wasn't a matter of courage. I felt strongly that I had to try to inject some new realism into Israeli coverage of Middle East affairs, if I was going to do the new job properly.

My new paper, *Yediouth Ahronot*, was (and is) a real pillar of the establishment in Israel; 75 per cent of Israelis read it. And it is a very conservative part of the Israeli establishment. All staff journalists referred to all Palestinian leaders automatically and without thought as 'terrorists'. When *Yediouth Ahronot* reported on the Algiers Arab summit, for example, its headline screamed: 'Terrorists meet in Algiers.'

When I had been there a month or two, I started changing all the copy in the paper, replacing the word 'terrorist' in reports with the word 'Palestinian'. This sounds like a very minor change, but at the time in Israel, on such a mainstream paper, it was dynamite. We were saying to our readership that the Arabs were not all demons. I didn't want to change the world: I just wanted to be accurate as a journalist. Many of the people we routinely labelled 'terrorist' were clearly nothing of the kind. And there was no point being Middle East editor if I couldn't make a few small changes around the place, was there?

I phoned Bassam Abu-Sharif: he was very responsive, very open, very ready to talk. On the telephone, at least, we hit it off. As a Middle East journalist I had many sources, but in a very short time, Abu-Sharif became the major source for me on an organisation that it would otherwise have been impossible to get a word out of: the PLO. Without quoting him by name I started putting the stories he was giving me – about current PLO strategy, what Arafat was thinking, and so on – on the pages of the newspaper. This, for many in Israel, was way, way too much. Arabs were all vile; they should not, they informed me, have to read the words of demons over their breakfast coffee. People started criticising me for 'giving a voice to terrorists'. Why, they demanded, was I giving these Arab scum a free platform for their propaganda?

As time went on, I became more and more convinced I should meet Mr Abu-Sharif. I had a feeling there was a lot we had to talk about, and I went to the paper's editor-in-chief, who was also its founding father. He was a tiny old man, rather wizened, with blazing dark eyes who held court behind a desk about the size of a baseball pitch. He was also extremely clever. I explained that I wanted to meet my PLO 'Deep Throat'. He refused permission on the spot. 'Not only is it against the law,' he told me, 'but I don't want too much coverage of the PLO. You put enough of them in as it is; it's become almost nothing but terrorists!' I tried to speak in my turn, but he interrupted. 'Listen, Uzi, this paper has a turnover of millions of dollars. I don't want circulation going into free-fall because you're putting terrorists on the front page. That is my final word.'

'Listen,' I said, finally getting a word in edgeways. 'We are professionals. If we have a source who is Yasser Arafat's adviser, we should use him.' As a journalist, he understood this – he even agreed with me. As a newspaper owner, if he had to, he would throw me straight to the sharks. The next day he sent me a letter formally backing up his warning: it read 'The newspaper would not support [me] in any way if [I] acted outside the strict letter of Israeli law, while dealing with PLO people.' I took this as tacit permission to talk with the 'terrorists' . . .

CHAPTER
TWENTY-THREE

Bassam Abu-Sharif

By the end of 1987, people inside the occupied territories were suffering more hardship than ever. The Israeli administration was grinding Palestinian noses ever harder into the occupied mud. Meanwhile, we were not really making much progress to help them, either inside the PLO or on the diplomatic front. The USA was backing Israel's refusal to talk peace unless the PLO made the big concessions first, regardless of what its protégé did.

Arafat and I had been trying to enact our plan, but we knew the majority of the PLO membership were still miles away from being ready to recognise Israel's right to exist. They were still living in the land of fairy tales, convinced we could destroy the whole state of Israel by force. I felt very frustrated. Peace was a mirage, always receding further into the haze as we tried to reach for it. And while they said they were against peace, people were becoming impatient. There were all kinds of dark mutterings in the Arab world, from Iraq and from Jordan in particular: why, they asked, should the PLO be 'the sole, legitimate representative' of the Palestinian people, if it wasn't achieving anything? We were in a blind alley. But quite suddenly something happened that was to smash down the barriers.

Never come between the grieving and the dead. On 8 December 1987, a truck carrying Palestinian workers was ambushed by Israeli soldiers as it was driving through Gaza. Six Palestinians were killed, two badly injured. The bodies were taken into the local refugee camp, where they were laid out by relatives. Then, during the night, the Israelis stormed the camp, taking the corpses away from their families by force. The bodies were evidence of a cold-blooded Israeli massacre – so they took them. The Israelis also reasoned that removing the bodies meant no mass funerals, and no demonstrations.

The Israelis' story – that the casualties had been involved in a traffic accident – proved to be a bad miscalculation.

It was a single stone that changed the fate of Palestine. The day after the ambush, a Palestinian teenager picked up one of the sharp pieces of flint that lie about all over the Gaza Strip and threw it at an Israeli army patrol. His friends began doing the same; dozens, then hundreds more people joined in. The IDF patrols, firing live ammunition wildly, fell back under the hail of rocks raining down on them. There had always been sporadic demonstrations in the occupied territories, but this was different. The people, as one, had risen. They had had enough. The Stone Revolution had begun.

The resistance, at first local, spread like bushfire right through the West Bank and the Gaza Strip. Barricades of burning tyres appeared on the roads; Palestinian workers went on strike; the PLO flag, forbidden under Israeli rule, sprouted everywhere; and always, always, there were the stones.

The Israeli cabinet met on 29 December to decide how to deal with the mass unrest. Yitzhak Shamir was Prime Minister. Wisely, he suggested withdrawing from all densely populated Palestinian areas, thinking withdrawal, or as he called it, 're-deployment', would reduce the tension. But hard-line Likud members of the cabinet were outraged at the idea. So, too, was the Defence Minister Yitzhak Rabin. Israelis fought fire with fire, they argued, calling for an 'Iron Fist' policy.

At PLO Headquarters in Tunis I was watching the coverage of this particular cabinet meeting very closely; I knew its outcome was of crucial importance to the future of Palestine. Then they came out. The decision was to use massive force. I went straight through into Arafat's office. 'The Israelis have opted for the "Iron Fist" policy,' I told him. 'Here is our opportunity.'

'What opportunity?' asked Arafat.

'Iron Fist means massacres. It means Israeli soldiers killing dozens, maybe hundreds of our people. We can use this to mobilise international opinion. We can get the world to support our rights. We can use all this as a lever to get peace.'

I called in the US network NBC. Arafat gave them an exclusive interview predicting Israeli massacres of children and youths in the West Bank and Gaza Strip. 'Remember this,' I told them when the interview was over. 'It is the first warning of what is going to happen.' Next day we flew to Kuwait for talks with the leadership of Hamas – the fundamentalist group backed by Iran, which was based there at the time – and also with the leaders of Islamic Jihad. Arafat told these leaders that there was a large chunk of Israeli hell coming the way of the people in the occupied territories. He asked them to get their members back inside at once, to help in the resistance. If ever there was an occasion on which we all needed to unite, this was it. And there was no problem about the fundamentalists getting into Israeli-controlled areas: thinking to split the Palestinian movement, Yitzhak Rabin had given Hamas permission to open twenty centres in the West Bank and Gaza Strip. What he had not foreseen was that we might all join in a common cause.

The Israelis were usually intelligent, but they weren't always clever.

The IDF was ordered to put a stop to the revolution by all means necessary. But they could not stop it. The thing was like a massive fire burning out of anyone's control. No sooner did the Israeli army beat down one outbreak than another one flared up somewhere else, and another, each outbreak larger and less controllable. The Israelis shot dead more and more of the stone-throwers, many of them children; it made no difference except to world opinion. As well as shootings, there were mass arrests, curfews, beatings and deportations. And there was torture. A television crew, using a long lens, caught two IDF men in the act, smashing a heavy rock down on the extended arm of a Palestinian boy. Over and over the stone came smashing down, and still the arm would not break. Rabin had growled out the comment, 'Break their bones' – and some soldiers took it literally. It sickened the watching world. When they did catch one of the stone-throwing youngsters, the Israelis would bulldoze his family home, but no matter what they did, they could not put a stop to the unrest. The government of Israel, though it still refused steadfastly to admit it, had a popular revolution on its hands. The people had a word for it: they called it 'intifada'.

For Arafat and myself, the intifada was electrifying. The people were showing us the way. When the first Palestinian boy picked up that first stone, he changed the course of our history. The Israelis, despite their bragging propaganda, could not end the intifada by military means alone. The more Palestinian children the IDF soldiers killed, the more they undermined Israel's international reputation. The world looked on in horror at what the Israelis were doing. The intifada was the Biblical combat, David v. Goliath, but with the roles reversed. Israel came across as the brutal giant. This was no series of disturbances that would die away; the entire world could see that it had devastating political force.

All of us in the PLO were galvanised by this sudden development. I saw that it gave Arafat, in particular, an incredible opportunity. These youths, these dispossessed teenagers and children, these people whose land was being stolen by the ever-swelling Jewish settlements, looked to Arafat for their spiritual leadership. They spray-painted his likeness on the walls of their bullet-pocked homes. They chanted his name in the streets. He was 'Mr Palestine'. Who else was there for them? Their faith gave him a whole new political force.

Sooner rather than later, the Israelis would have to talk peace. If they wouldn't negotiate willingly, the Americans would make them. The US public – and thus its government – would not condone Israel's behaviour in the occupied territories indefinitely. The PLO, I argued, should step in and use the power of the intifada to obtain a just settlement for Palestine. Here was our chance, and we must take it.

Arafat and I held long discussions about how best to proceed. We decided that the PLO must now accept unambiguously UN Security Council Resolution 242: we must renounce all forms of 'terrorism' and recognise the right of Israel to exist within safe and secure boundaries. The PLO bureaucracy was still against this; but it was also running to catch up with events. Now was the moment. In return for their peace, the Israelis would have to return our lands to us – and give us justice. We had to go flat out for peace, and we must do it while the revolution raged.

Uzi Mahnaimi

During the early days of the intifada I got a call from my new source. He was very excited. He told me he had information that Israeli soldiers on the West Bank had buried alive a number of Palestinian villagers. 'Not demonstrators, not stone-throwers,' he told me, 'just ordinary village people. They have been buried alive.' The paper was just about to go to print. I thought quickly. I wasn't really sure whether to trust Abu-Sharif. The more I thought about it, the more fantastic it seemed. Burying people alive? It was impossible, surely, even for soldiers crazed by weeks of stoning and rioting to do such a thing. It must be Arab propaganda. I thanked him and rang off, anxious to meet my deadline.

Next day, I regretted brushing off my caller: his information had been genuine. There were journalists swarming all over the story. Israeli soldiers had taken four Arab men from the village of Salem near Nablus, out into the wilderness, buried them up to their necks in the earth, and left them. They'd remained buried for several hours until being spotted and rescued by passing Bedu. And I had missed a great scoop. I rang Abu-Sharif back, to apologise. From then on, whenever he rang me, I was less suspicious about Bassam's stories.

Bassam began sending me faxes direct into the newsroom, headed: 'Palestine Liberation Organisation – Office of the President.' My colleagues recoiled from them with shock and horror. It was as if he were sending me used toilet-paper through the fax, or toxic waste. More comments started flying my way such as, 'You're being used by Bassam Abu-Sharif. The PLO is taking you for a ride; they're manipulating you.'

'Of course they are trying to manipulate me,' I retorted. 'Of course they're trying to use me as a mouthpiece, but we're lucky to have such a source; no other newspaper in Israel is getting the stories we're getting. Our relationship is not a one-way street.' Luckily the paper's editor-in-chief was now backing me. He could see the news value of what I was doing. It was turning out to be good for the newspaper's circulation figures, not bad. Not only that, the editor of a rival newspaper, concerned at all the attention – and readership – we were getting, had accused me (without mentioning me by name) of 'working for the disinformation department of the PLO'. When a rival starts saying things like this, you know you are doing something right.

The more I persisted in putting forward a balanced point of view, though, the more flak I got. I started receiving hate mail, poison-pen letters, even death-threats. There were vicious phone calls on my answer-phone when I got home at night. Friends I'd worked with in intelligence asked me such questions as, 'You were in military intelligence, your father was a general, so how can you bring yourself even to talk to these terrorists?'

In a way, I could understand the anger. It was as if a British newspaper had suddenly started printing the opinions of an IRA bomber at the height of a bombing campaign, or a US daily gave space to one of Iran's revolutionary leaders at the height of the American embassy hostage crisis. The ordinary everyday flak I could take, but some people were more than angry: they were determined to take action. I was called to a meeting at army headquarters. They told me my services as a reservist major in Unit 154 would no longer be required. Even if Israel went to war again, they didn't want me. I was politically undesirable.

Then, from one of my ex-intelligence friends, I discovered that the dirty-tricks brigade was at work against me: Shin–Bet was tapping my phone. If the Arabs were giving me hot stuff for my newspaper, what, reasoned Shin–Bet, was I giving them?

I wrote the occasional commentary piece following the news pages. In this column, I banged on about how Israel must now negotiate direct with the PLO. To me, the need for negotiation was blindingly obvious; I'd thought as much since the invasion of Lebanon. And, through Bassam, I believed Arafat had genuinely changed his position.

I pumped such opinions out regularly in that comment slot for the five years I worked on the newspaper. Whether it made any difference it is impossible to say. But it was worth trying.

Bassam Abu-Sharif

One night early in 1988, a few months after the intifada had started, Arafat and I were sitting in his villa in Baghdad, discussing our next step. I knew the intifada could not simply remain as it was, a series of more-or-less spontaneous demonstrations. It had to become organised, it had to be continuously engineered. It must take on a true political dimension.

Abu Jihad, Arafat's deputy and the military commander of

Fatah, had been setting up covert teams inside the West Bank and Gaza Strip to consolidate and expand the movement. These teams were motivating people to join the fight, helping them to communicate, organise and develop tactics. By now, Abu Jihad had also set up what he called 'offensive forces': specially trained groups of young men who operated alongside the ordinary demonstrators. Their job was to come in and defend the main body of demonstrators when the IDF troops opened up on them with live ammunition. Though still armed with nothing more than stones, these defence teams were making life even more difficult for the Israelis. But we had to do more than make the IDF uncomfortable. The big danger was that the intifada would run out of political steam. Arafat, particularly, was worried on two counts: that the people would become exhausted, and that the Israelis would resort to even greater force, if that were possible, to crush the uprising. He feared a huge massacre. People were dying in this stalemate. We had to keep up a relentless momentum. We needed some fresh initiatives.

Wrestling with the problem one evening in Tunis, I came up with two ideas that I took straight to the Chairman. The first was strategic: to control the intifada. 'But it is alive, like a wild animal, running mad on the rage of thousands,' responded Arafat. 'How could anyone control such a thing?' Suddenly, the solution came to me: 'It should be like a relay race,' I suggested. Arafat's eyes gleamed at me in the dusk. 'What do you mean?' he asked. 'We should set objectives for the intifada,' I said slowly, feeling my way forward. 'We should have aims that people can feel . . . that they can achieve. When they have achieved one objective, then they move on to the next . . . There is always a fresh target.' It was a simple idea, but Arafat seized on it. 'As the aim of the first relay stage,' he said, 'we shall try for a Security Council debate on the intifada . . .'

And it worked. The people of the Occupied Territories demonstrated for a UN debate – they demanded it. The non-aligned countries succeeded in tabling one, then the people

231

demonstrated to influence the outcome of this debate. Then we set another target for them. In this way, they always had something to demonstrate for. There was always a next step.

There was another benefit: the Palestinian people began to respond in a very direct way to events on the international scene. The intifada became a barometer of world opinion. The people demonstrating on the inside, and those of us working on the outside, were cross-fertilising one another. Something very exciting, and very new, was happening: the PLO and the people of the occupied territories were acting in unison, perhaps for the first time. It snowballed. When they saw how well this relationship was working, the PLO began getting even greater support from the intifada demonstrators. Whenever the PLO appeared to be cornered on the diplomatic front, the people would mobilise to rescue it. When the intifada showed signs of flagging, the PLO came up with a new set of diplomatic objectives.

My second idea was tactical: I suggested that Arafat broadcast a statement calling for simultaneous demonstrations in Gaza and the West Bank, and I asked him to give me authority to issue written instructions to the demonstrators backing up his broadcast. If we could organise it well enough, I reasoned, the Israelis would have to deal with multiple riots in the West Bank and the Gaza Strip at the same time. If we communicated with them directly, I reasoned, the demonstrators would feel even more at one with the PLO leadership; it would make the uprising a coherent movement, one movement of a whole people.

That night, Arafat's message was broadcast from PLO radio stations everywhere: the Yemen, Algeria, Iraq: 'Rise, people of Palestine!' In each city, in each quarter, the activists heard the call. The following day, demonstrations erupted all over the West Bank and Gaza Strip. It was the first case of truly concerted action since the beginning of the intifada. The Israeli security forces, swamped, tried rounding up all the young men and sending them to prison camps in the Negev desert. But the intifada women's committees simply took over, leading the revolution successfully for more than three months. There were more than one million people in the West Bank and Gaza Strip; even Israel couldn't put them all behind bars.

During the months in Baghdad, I set up an intifada information centre in the Rashid Hotel. At the same time I personally issued dozens of hand-written orders to Palestinians inside the occupied territories and to our offices around the world. I also set about getting Arafat on to the world's television screens, identifying him as the leader of the Palestinian struggle and its only leader.

I hadn't reckoned with that most basic of human passions, envy. PLO leaders began complaining bitterly about me. They accused me of 'giving away PLO secrets to an Israeli newspaper', by which they meant the articles Uzi had been publishing. Who had given me authority to do that? they wanted to know. And why was I issuing hundreds of orders on the intifada when I wasn't even a PLO member?

I knew that the real problem was not my new-found authority on the streets of Gaza City or Jericho. It was my closeness to Arafat; this was what they really envied. What, I retorted, were they offering Arafat and the intifada other than small-minded complaints? Abu Mazin, Abu Iyad, Abu Al-Hol, they all wanted my blood. One day, Abu Mazin came to me in a furious rage: 'Why have you turned Yasser Arafat into a belly-dancer?' he shouted, sticking his face into mine.

'If it takes a belly-dancer to keep the intifada going,' I responded, 'Why not?'

Uzi Mahnaimi

A few weeks before the intifada started, in June 1987, I went to a wedding party held by one of Israel's wealthiest and best-known businessmen. There I bumped into Shmoel Goren, the man in overall charge of Israeli administration on the West Bank and Gaza Strip. His correct title was, 'Co-ordinator of Government Activities in the Occupied Territories'. I wanted to do a feature on 'Twenty Years of the Occupation; 1967–1987'. Goren, it struck me, might just be a good man to have a chat with.

'Mr Goren,' I asked him, 'When is the revolution going to start?'

'Revolution? What are you talking about?' he growled.

'It's twenty years since we took control of the territories; when are the Palestinians going to rise up and kick us out?'

Goren laughed, long and loud. 'The situation of the people in the occupied territories has never been as good as it is today.'

It was my turn to laugh at this. But it wasn't really funny – he meant it. His office had published a colourful brochure a few weeks before our meeting called something like, 'The Wonderful World of the West Bank'. According to this imaginative publication, life in the occupied territories was a paradise for the Palestinians; they had never had it so good.

Goren knew I knew the truth: I'd once been part of the machinery of repression myself. I knew exactly how it worked and how well it worked, I knew the depression of the people, the poverty of their conditions, the simmering resentment. And I'd seen signs that they were reaching the end of their rope. So I pressed him again. 'Haven't we ground the Palestinians down to a point where they've got nothing to lose? When do you think they will lose their fear? When will they start rioting?'

'What is all this nonsense?' said Goren. 'You're a typical journalist, living in a dream-world. There will be no rioting in the occupied territories. Not while I'm in charge.'

On 8 December a bus-load of Palestinians from the Gaza Strip on their way to work in Tel Aviv was in a collision with an Israeli-owned car. At least ten of the Palestinians were killed and injured. It was a straightforward accident. As normal, the casualties were all taken to the nearest hospital, but the wildest rumours began flying around in the Palestinian community.

The workers had been murdered, they had been shot by the army, and worse. The families of the dead men came into the hospital and took their bodies away for burial. This very often happened: Palestinians hate the idea of Israeli doctors touching their dead, examining them or, worst of all, carrying out autopsies. But another rumour spread that IDF soldiers had taken the corpses. The next day, mass riots broke out on the Gaza Strip.

Three days later I wrote an article in *Yediouth Ahronot* saying that this rioting was the turning-point: we were witnessing the start of the revolution. The Palestinians had passed their point of no return, I argued, they had lost their fear. Nobody agreed with me. Nobody wanted to agree – the truth was too horrible to contemplate. The uprising caught the whole of Israel by surprise. Israel's authorities were totally unprepared. I thought back to my chat in the summer with Mr Goren. If he were anything to go by, the Israeli civil administration had completely lost touch with what was happening at street level in the territories. Its officials had complacently assumed that Israel's occupation could continue for another twenty years, no problem. But it was Shin-Bet, the internal security service, that had really fallen down on the job. Internal security was supposed to give warning of popular unrest, especially of coming revolution. But although it had put its mark on every individual tree in the Palestinian forest, Shin-Bet had failed to see the wood. They knew Ibrahim, they knew Hamad, they knew what Ahmed's cousin in Amman told him, they had every Palestinian on file, under their control – but they did not see that the masses, in their hundreds of thousands, had had enough.

They soon learned.

CHAPTER
TWENTY-FOUR

— ◆ —

Bassam Abu-Sharif and Uzi Mahnaimi

H igh above the villa, two Israeli Air Force Boeing 707s were tracing long contrails in the night sky. One carried the command and control aircraft for the operation about to take place ten thousand feet below. On board were the IDF Deputy Chief of Staff, Ehud Barak, the Air Force Commander, Aviho Ben–Nun, and the military intelligence chief, Amnon Shahak. The other Boeing was packed to the gills with electronic equipment: radar, communications gear, jamming and monitoring devices.

Two more 707s acting as fuel tankers were standing off nearby. Tunis is a long way from Israel. Above them again, four F-15 fighter-bombers were providing top cover to the whole airborne circus. Back in their underground Tel Aviv command bunker, the Israeli Defence Minister Yitzhak Rabin and the IDF Chief of Staff General Shomron were in direct control of the entire operation. Its objective was to kill Abu Jihad.

The PLO military chief got home from an unscheduled meeting with Farouk Qaddumi, the head of the PLO's Political

Department, just after midnight on 16 April 1988. He went upstairs, greeted his wife, kissed his sleeping son and went into his study.

His driver was already fast asleep in the Mercedes outside, with his window down, snoring. It was a warm evening. A Sayeret Matkal commando team had been waiting in the shadows for the car to turn up. One of them ran forward, woke the driver and put a single round from a silenced .22 Beretta pistol through his head. The driver slumped dead across the front seat.

Two more commandos ran to the villa's main entrance. With the speed of long practice, they laid an explosive charge at the base of its heavy iron doors. The new form of 'silent' plastic explosive they were using made little sound as it blew the doors clean off their hinges. Inside, two of Abu Jihad's bodyguards were standing in the entrance hall, stunned by the explosion. The Israeli commandos shot them both dead.

Rushing up the stairs, the colonel in charge of the assassination team burst into Abu Jihad's study. The PLO military chief was sitting in front of the television in his pyjamas, watching a video compilation of intifada news footage. As he rose to his feet, the colonel brought up his pistol and shot him twice in the chest. Abu Jihad crashed heavily to the floor. The colonel stepped quickly over and put two more bullets into the dying man's head at point-blank range to make sure. Yasser Arafat's right-hand man lay dead.

During the killing and for a few seconds after it, other members of the commando team hurriedly scooped up any PLO documents they could find. As the commandos came back out of the living-room, they bumped into Abu Jihad's wife. She had come downstairs with her young son to see what the noise was. 'Get back in your room,' snapped the colonel in Arabic. 'And keep quiet.'

The commandos could be very pleased with themselves. It had taken them 13 seconds from blowing the main doors to shooting Abu Jihad dead. In practice runs it had taken 22 seconds.

Immediately after the assassination, the PLO launched an investigation into how it could have happened. Familiar as they were with Israeli sledge-hammer tactics, what they discovered staggered even them. The operation to kill Abu Jihad was incredible in its complexity, size and expense. Every element of the IDF had been involved. It must have been the biggest operation anyone had ever mounted anywhere to kill one individual.

This is how the Israelis did it. Their intelligence assessment was that killing Abu Jihad in his house in Tunis was their best option. It was the one place he would always return to, some time or other, to see his family. But they had two big problems. The first: how exactly were they going to murder him? The second: to find out where exactly Abu Jihad was at any given time. Not an easy matter, given that he made it his business to be untraceable.

Half a dozen F-16s could have peppered the villa with 1,000lb bombs, but that would have left a lot to chance. They risked destroying half the city of Tunis and still not getting the man they wanted. The only way they could be absolutely sure of their target was by shooting him at close range. Everything pointed to a commando operation.

It took the Israelis two months to prepare the murder. First they sent a team of Mossad agents to Tunis, which spent two months gathering basic intelligence. Posing as tourists and businessmen, travelling on regular scheduled flights from third countries, they carried out an exhaustive reconnaissance of Abu Jihad's villa and its surroundings. Access roads, points of entry, fence heights and types, windows, doors, locks, defences, the routine employed by the guards; everything was monitored, checked and checked again. They estimated distances, found out what all the neighbours did and when they were at home, and logged the makes, colours and registrations of all the vehicles that came and went.

The team then scouted along the coast until they found a suitable beach where the commandos who would carry out the execution could land. It was an isolated spot east of Tunis, with a gently shelving beach. When they felt happy with what they'd got, the reconnaissance team wrote detailed reports and passed them back to Israel, along with the dozens of photographs they'd taken.

The assassination squad itself was made up of eight Sayeret Matkal commandos. A short time before the attack was scheduled, the colonel who would lead it went to Tunis personally. He, too, travelled on a false passport, arriving on a scheduled flight from Rome. Exceptionally for the leader of a special forces team, he was able to look the target over in daylight – a fantastic bonus for him. He was very impressed by what he saw: Abu Jihad lived in a magnificent beach-front villa with a huge garden, surrounded by similar properties in a superb area of Tunis: Sidi Bousaid. The Israeli colonel returned to Rome the same day, pleased with his trip.

Back in Israel, the commandos rehearsed the killing down to the last detail, over and over again, until they were dreaming it in their sleep. They carried out their practice attacks on a villa in Haifa, an Israeli intelligence safe house. Before making any practice runs, the Israelis waited for 'windows' when the US military spy satellites had gone by. They didn't want anyone watching them.

In training, it took only 22 short seconds from blowing the front door of the villa to shooting dead the dummy target inside. They thought this was good enough. In fact, they thought it was very good.

In Tunis, two women and a man employed by Mossad hired the vehicles that would be used in the attack. The women gave their names as 'Awatif Alam' and 'Ayesha El-Soridi', the man called himself 'George Najib'. Speaking in French, the three presented their Lebanese passports to the car-rental agency one week before the operation. They hired two Volkswagen camper vans and a Peugeot 305 saloon. They said they were going on a driving vacation.

Everything was now ready for the kill, except for one thing.

How could the Israelis be sure their target would be at home when they called? Like every other PLO leader, Abu Jihad was always on the move, never in the same bed two nights running. He knew the Israelis wanted him dead. How could they manipulate him into being at home at a specified time, without alerting him? It was an almost insuperable problem; but the Israelis came up with a very simple solution.

On the morning of the attack, an Israeli police squad in Gaza City swooped. Without any warning, they arrested a man called Faiz Abu Rahma. He was Jihad's cousin. This arrest was a very big deal: Abu Rahma was a well-known lawyer who had a lot of standing in the Palestinian community. Within hours, news of the raid had flashed around the Gaza Strip, provoking demonstrations and outrage.

Just as the Israelis had calculated, Faiz Abu Rahma's daughter was frantic about her father's arrest. What could she do? The answer came to her immediately: ring Abu Jihad, the leader of the intifada, the PLO number two man, and her own uncle. He would know how to deal with the problem.

She dialled the number of Abu Jihad's home in Tunis. All day she rang, but there was never any answer. At last, in the evening, Abu Jihad's wife picked up the receiver. 'He will be back soon,' she said. 'Don't worry. I will tell him what has happened. Ring again later.' This hurried conversation was exactly what the listening Israelis had been hoping for. Now they could be fairly sure Abu Jihad was in Tunis and that he would be home later. It was good enough. Rabin gave the green light for the kill. The four Boeings and their fighter escort took off.

At about midnight, Tunis time, Abu Rahma's daughter rang her uncle's number again. Because there was no direct line between Israel and Tunis, she dialled via the PLO switchboard in Cyprus, which is nicknamed 'Castro'. The PLO operator put her through direct to Abu Jihad's home.

This time the target himself picked up the phone. The Israelis had the final and most important piece of the puzzle in place. Now they knew they had him.

The Sayeret Matkal team were waiting on a civilian cargo ship standing off the Tunisian coast – a nondescript old steamer, one that regularly plied the route between Haifa and Barcelona. (It probably flew under a Greek flag, though this is one detail we never discovered.) The eight killers on board were dressed in black fire-retardant overalls, black balaclavas and French 'Palladium' rubber-soled boots. All were armed with silenced .22 calibre pistols and silenced 9mm Uzi machine-guns. Like the clothing, their ammunition was unmarked and untraceable. Each man was wearing a personal radio with earpiece and microphone that kept him in direct, unbroken contact with the command team overhead and with the command bunker in Tel Aviv. In case anyone was captured or got lost, every member of the squad carried a personal locator-beacon.

Just before the attack went in, Fleet 13 frogmen – the naval equivalent of Sayeret Matkal – landed on the chosen beach to make sure it was clear. The eight killers raced to the shore from the mother ship in high-speed 'Zodiac' rubber boats. The Mossad agents were there to meet them, handing over the keys to the three hired vehicles. The commandos drove along the coast to Abu Jihad's villa. Once they had killed him, they drove back the way they had come, abandoned the rented vehicles on the shore, climbed back into the boats and returned to the mother ship.

The most interesting question, in a way, was not why the Israelis had killed Abu Jihad, but why had they gone to such enormous trouble and cost to kill him just then. In fact, it was an act of desperation. Since they could find no answer to the intifada, they were reverting to their old policy, the same one that had so very nearly finished off Bassam: kill the PLO leadership. But killing Abu Jihad wasn't going to stop the revolution. If anything it would inflame passions further, and create another Palestinian martyr. As a response to the intifada, Abu Jihad's murder was point-less.

Uzi Mahnaimi

Quite a few people in Israel felt that with or without the intifada, Abu Jihad deserved a bullet in his head. For years he had been in charge of all Fatah military operations against Israel. He had been personally responsible for the deaths of many innocent Israeli civilians.

But Israel was trying to fight a new war with old methods. The government did not understand that the intifada had a life that was all its own. Rabin and the others wanted to believe that the uprising was controlled from afar, because this meant they could stop it by killing the people who were supposedly pulling the strings: like Abu Jihad, for example. Only nobody was pulling the strings.

The Israelis were not in the habit of losing. The huge Israeli army stood in front of the intifada, and they felt helpless. They did not know what to do with all these crowds of children throwing stones. So Israel lashed out in the only way it knew.

Abu Jihad had been the underground stream of the intifada, gradually building up his cadres in the occupied territories, always trying to fan the flames. But Bassam Abu-Sharif was the surface current of the intifada – his expert use of the media was making Arafat look good, and he was coming up with great ways for the PLO to get the most out of the intifada. Almost every day he was on American television networks, giving devastating interviews, taking advantage of the shooting incidents, doing Israel's image in the world immense and lasting damage. If Israeli commandos were going to execute anyone to take the steam out of the Stone Revolution, they'd have been better off killing him.

242

Bassam Abu-Sharif

By the end of 1988 the Israeli government had a very big problem on its hands, and very few ideas about how to deal with it. They had tried force, and it hadn't worked. They had killed one of the intifada's early architects, Abu Jihad, to absolutely no purpose. The economic situation in the territories had become ever more terrible, adding more and more fuel to the fire. And the IDF soldiers themselves were the biggest asset we had in keeping the uprising going, shooting dead, on average, one Palestinian demonstrator a day. Every death kept the pot of hatred boiling. This was what their Iron Fist policy actually meant in practice: day after day after day, the Israelis were sticking their bayonets into a hornets' nest.

The intifada gave us a chance to break the log-jam. But to get peace, we were still going to have to work for it; it wasn't going to come simply because the Palestinian people were throwing stones. We had to make the new situation tell on the diplomatic front. We must win hearts and minds in the quiet halls of power. My role now was to chip away at the iceberg – knock on the closed diplomatic doors in the West – and make them open.

The intifada might just be winning the war for us inside the occupied territories, but we still had to win the peace in the outside world.

Even though it had not been officially sanctioned, Arafat agreed I should go all out to project the PLO's new line. I began a diplomatic charm offensive, using all the contacts in the world's media, among foreign governments, in Arab circles, that I'd built up over the years. I had to get across the message that the PLO meant business, that a real change of heart had taken place.

We'd always had some kind of channel to the United States, the major power-broker in the region, but we had very poor or non-existent relations with Western Europe. Most countries refused officially to talk to the PLO. These fences were the first that should be mended. I would begin with the British, who might no longer have a great deal of power, but certainly did still have some influence.

There was a permanent PLO representative in London, but he enjoyed absolutely no official recognition or diplomatic status there. I applied for a visa to enter the United Kingdom. The British ambassador in Tunis, who lived next door to me, saw the application form and invited me round for breakfast.

'What is the purpose of your visit?' he asked.

Jokingly I replied, 'I'd like to go shopping.'

'Come on,' he said smiling. 'Bassam Abu-Sharif doesn't go on shopping trips.'

'Well,' I said, 'if someone in London were willing to have a free and frank exchange of views with me, I'd be very happy to meet him. Your Minister of State at the Foreign & Commonwealth Office, for example, Mr Waldegrave. Would he consider meeting me?'

'What is it exactly you'd want to talk about?'

'The PLO wishes to go in a new direction,' I replied, 'and we need your help. We would like you to help us get peace.'

'Mmmm,' said the ambassador, buttering his toast with extreme care. 'I'll see what I can do.'

A few days later a text drawn up by the British Foreign Office landed on my doormat. 'If, following a possible meeting with a member of the British government,' it read, 'you felt able to make a public statement along the lines of this proposal, then a meeting might very well be possible . . .' So that was perfectly clear. I skimmed through the text. It expressed the gist of the PLO's new programme as I had explained it to the ambassador: the recognition of Israel, the renunciation of terrorism, the stipulation that all states in the region should have safe and secure boundaries, and that Israel return the territory it was occupying to the PLO. I told the ambassador I agreed to it. I flew to London.

During the initial meeting with British Foreign Office officials, we went through two texts: one that the Minister would read to the press, and another I would give myself. My text was a straightforward presentation of the new PLO policy. William Waldegrave's 'would, under certain conditions, evaluate positively the PLO, and henceforth the UK . . . would set up official channels of communication with the PLO . . .' In other words, we'd be allowed back in from the cold if we were very good boys.

After our meeting with Waldegrave, the journalists were waiting for us at the bottom of the Foreign Office steps. When I was sure Waldegrave was watching me, I carefully folded up the text that had been prepared for me and stuck it into my inside pocket. I could see Waldegrave was very taken aback. What was I going to say? Was I going to double-cross him? What could he do about it if I did? When he'd finished reading his own statement, I paraphrased my text from memory. Waldegrave relaxed visibly as he realised I'd just been having a little bit of fun with him. But I'm not sure if he ever forgave me.

It was the first time the PLO had had relations at ministerial level with the UK government. We had opened the British channel.

Following the success of this first meeting, I had talks with the big chief himself, the Foreign Secretary, Douglas Hurd. Middle East peace negotiations were very complicated at that time and very badly stuck. The US Secretary of State, James Baker, was having great difficulty persuading Shamir's government to go on with the process at all. Baker had put forward his five-point programme, but the Israelis kept ducking and dodging the issue.

'It doesn't look too good to me,' said Hurd. 'What is your view?'

'I have no doubt the peace process will go forward,' I replied. 'But it will require even more effort than the United States is able to provide, great as that is. I think the United Kingdom can do much to help the Americans persuade the Israelis to sit at the negotiating table.'

'Mr Abu-Sharif is more optimistic than any of us,' Hurd laughed. When he laughed, all his officials laughed with him.

'Always,' I rejoined. 'I am always optimistic. Peace will come.'

CHAPTER
TWENTY-FIVE

—▶ ◀—

Uzi Mahnaimi

I'd told my editor-in-chief I had to go to London to meet 'sources'. I think he understood exactly what I meant.

Marie Colvin, once again, had set up the meeting. It was to take place in a very good French restaurant, the Rue St Jacques, in Charlotte Street. Marie and I arrived on time, taking up station at the bar in true journalistic style. About twenty minutes later a blocky, grizzled-looking Palestinian with curly dark hair and a humorous, shrapnel-pocked face came through the door. It was Bassam Abu-Sharif. He had with him a personal bodyguard, a man from Nablus and a female Palestinian activist, Karma Nabulsi. I thought that was all his entourage. In fact, Bassam now tells me there were no fewer than four men from the British Foreign Office 'protocol' department also watching over him in that restaurant, too. I was trained to spot types like that. These four must have been very, very good, because I missed them.

I was in a suit and tie. Bassam shook my hand, then he said, 'I thought all Israeli journalists wore battle-dress?' which broke the ice nicely. I was very curious about this man. This was the first PLO leader I'd ever met. He consumed several large Scotches by way of aperitif, then ordered one of the most expensive bottles of wine on the list, about £120 worth of Château Margaux. I exchanged glances with Marie. Was the Murdoch Empire going to foot this bill? Was Yasser Arafat? I very much doubted if I could get it past expenses.

I played the objective journalist, probing to get at the real opinions underneath the charming surface answers. But I quickly found Bassam was genuine – he really did believe in a peaceful solution. I realised he was reading me, too, trying to see through my professional front. He was keen to know how the idea of a peaceful solution was going down in Israel.

The problem for me was that having quit Israeli military intelligence four years previously, I still had knowledge of and access to all kinds of sensitive information. I still knew the names of Israeli intelligence agents operating at the heart of the PLO. I was terrified of revealing any secrets, anything that might be in any way useful to the PLO or get our men into trouble.

In fact, long before meeting Bassam, I'd been called to the office of Ehud Barak, then head of Israeli military intelligence. He'd been a friend of my father's, and was still a family friend. 'Uzi,' he said, 'it's a good job I still hold this position. I think you are a good journalist, and I can see what you are trying to do. But, a word to the wise: don't push too hard, eh? Those people [he meant the PLO] can use you, and you could get yourself into a lot of trouble on our side. You know what Shin-Bet are like: once they target you, they are extremely aggressive, yes?'

He was telling me he knew about my forthcoming meeting with Bassam Abu-Sharif and, as quietly and informally as he could, he was warning me off.

'Yes,' I said, 'I know what they're capable of.' I knew only too well. 'I do my work as a journalist, and I know where the limits are. I'll do my best not to breach them.'

'Right,' he said. 'You do that.'

My newspaper was translated into Arabic and circulated widely on the West Bank and Gaza Strip. It was a very useful test-bed for Arafat's peace agenda – how far could he go, what was the climate of Arab opinion like? And I got the good PLO stories well in advance of my rivals. We were useful to one another. But we felt something more than a thirst for mutual exploitation by the time lunch was over. We might be on opposite sides of the divide – but we had realised something much more important: we were both looking in the same direction.

At the end of the meal we exchanged business-cards. On the back of mine, when I turned it over, was written the single word, in Arabic: 'Peace'.

Bassam Abu-Sharif

A Lebanese friend who lives in London, Eli Khalil, invited me to dinner one evening shortly after my visit to the Foreign Office. At the table was the British politician and novelist, Jeffrey Archer. He was very sharp, very witty. It was clear he knew how to get things done in the UK and might, therefore, be very useful to me. He had been Deputy Chairman of the ruling Conservative Party and was close to Margaret Thatcher.

We got on well over the meal. I explained what I was trying to do in the UK – make the PLO acceptable, and push forward the peace process. He was vehement in agreeing there should be no more violence in the Middle East. But although he was very knowledgeable in general about world affairs, there were gaps in his knowledge of the region.

'What passport do you travel on?' he suddenly asked.

'A diplomatic Yemeni one,' I answered.

He was astonished. 'Why Yemeni?'

'Because we don't have passports any more in Palestine,' I replied. 'Not since the British left in 1948, anyway!'

'Oh? Why don't you have passports?' he persisted.

'Jeffrey,' I said gently, 'it seems that you don't know our history? We don't have a country any more . . .'

Later, one-to-one, we had a long talk about the history of Palestine and my own family's part in it. I could see that he was deeply affected by what I told him. In his mind, it all boiled down to the simple fact that both sides in the conflict should have their rights, and peace should reign. Becoming very enthusiastic about what I was trying to do in London, he promised to help me with my peace offensive, and help he did.

Archer was very critical of the way the PLO had gone about its business in the UK up to that time. We agreed to a second meeting. Sitting over drinks together, he explained how he thought the organisation should structure its activities in Britain: how we should develop and manage our media relations, how to organise our political activity, how to set about building contacts with British politicians, and mobilise public opinion. I was extremely impressed. He was clearly very knowledgeable and able in these fields. After that first meeting, whenever I made one of my very occasional trips to London we would usually get together.

While I was in Britain, the Oxford Union, Oxford University's debating chamber, invited me to give a lecture on peace in the Middle East. When I arrived, I found the place packed to the rafters. It was standing-room only. There were Arab ambassadors, Foreign Office officials, students, journalists, a sprinkling of important townspeople, and yet more students. For forty-five minutes I set out the PLO's new initiative, then invited questions from the floor. 'Only take the most hostile and the most difficult questions,' I told the chairwoman. 'I feel like a bit of knockabout!' I could tell from the atmosphere and heckling while I'd been speaking that there were a fair number of extreme right-wing Zionists in the hall.

Microphones are not allowed in the Oxford Union – you either shout or go unheard. A young female student called a question from the balcony. I couldn't hear a word she was saying. 'The Israelis have helped me go three parts deaf,' I called back to her. 'Would you mind coming down here to put your question?'

The girl came down. Unused to being before the public, she was visibly trembling. But she put her question gamely: 'How can the Israelis make peace with a terrorist like Yasser Arafat?' The hall muttered and murmured at the use of the emotive word. I could feel everyone watching, wondering how I would answer.

'Yasser Arafat,' I proclaimed, 'is a terrorist.' Caught by surprise, the audience fell completely quiet. I waited. The expectant hush continued. Then I raised my voice to the loudest shout I could muster: 'Yasser Arafat is a terrorist,' I bellowed, 'in as much as George Washington was a terrorist . . .!' The rest of what I had to say was drowned out in the huge roar. To this day I am unsure whether it was a roar of approval, or protest.

It seemed to me that if any European leader might be prepared to meet Yasser Arafat, it would be President François Mitterrand of France. Arafat, I was determined, should be seen in Europe, shaking hands with its leaders: it was an important step in ridding him of the 'terrorist' label Israel had tied round his neck. I must get him accepted on the world stage for what he now was, a statesman who was pushing for peace.

A socialist, Mitterrand had perhaps the most open mind on the subject of Palestine. He was on record clearly saying that the Palestinian people must have justice. Not only that, but most of the French President's advisers, as well as many in his social circle, were Jewish. The Israelis were always very quick to cry 'anti-Semitism' if anyone prominent in world affairs sat down with the PLO. But, given Mitterrand's Jewish entourage, even if he did agree to meet Arafat the mud was unlikely to stick.

251

I approached Pierre Joxe, the French Defence Minister, for help. I met Joxe several times, trying to persuade him that a Mitterrand/Arafat meeting would help keep up the momentum of the PLO peace initiative. At length he called a big meeting, with all sort of officials from the various ministries on the Quai d'Orsay, who grilled me about the peace programme. 'How serious was the PLO's new initiative? What was the time-frame?' and so on.

I explained that we'd spent a total of 296 hours in the PLO discussing whether or not to act on the recommendations of that 1988 document, and if so, how. We'd given more than twelve days of our lives to the decision, a lot of it in hot and hard debate. Of course we were serious! The French also questioned me closely about the PLO Charter. How did that fit with our new policy?

'Well,' I replied, 'it is quite simple. The new policy super-sedes the charter.' Joxe was still suspicious. 'Look,' I told him, 'we don't want France to exert pressure on Israel; we don't want France to lose its good relations with Israel; but we would like to see France improving the quality of its relations with the PLO.' That struck home: I could see he liked it.

'Perhaps France could help get Israel and yourselves around the table once again. But why, among all these other ministers,' he asked, looking around the vast oblong table, 'have you chosen me to approach for help in this matter?'

'Well,' I replied, 'you're the only one who has breakfast with the President every morning.'

He laughed. I'd done some homework, and I knew that it was so. 'Leave it with me,' he said. 'I'll see what I can do.'

Mitterrand duly met Arafat, and it was at this meeting that Arafat made his famous statement to the French press. The original PLO Charter, he declared, was *caduque* – redundant. Another fence had been dismantled, but there were plenty more to go.

With the ball now rolling on the diplomatic front, the next big objective was to get the whole PLO to accept peace negotiations with Israel. The intifada meant we could bargain from a position of strength. This opportunity was unlikely to come again soon, if ever. We had to take it while it was there.

Arafat had asked me to take charge of drawing up the daily instructions to the solidarity committees in the West Bank and Gaza Strip. I was also liaising on the diplomatic front and, as always, talking all the time to the international media, keeping the intifada at the front of the news, putting our gloss on it wherever possible.

Then, suddenly, I realised we had no final stage in the relay race. When we reached the finishing line, what was the prize? What did we actually want? Many people had come up with ideas about what the intifada should have as its final goal, but the PLO had no coherent aim. I went to Arafat and explained my train of thought. 'I'd like some time to work on this,' I told him. 'We must have a clear sight of what we are aiming for.'

'Go ahead,' he told me. 'And with God's blessing.'

It took me three weeks, at the end of which I had a three-page document written in English. It was a very straightforward presentation of the policy I had formulated with Arafat since 1987. It had a ten-point summary of our objectives. I told Arafat I'd finished drawing up the 'finishing-line document', but we had to fly straight out to Addis Ababa for the African summit. 'Take a look at this,' I said to him, once we were airborne, handing him a copy. 'OK,' he replied. 'Leave it with me. I'll read it later.' But for whatever reason, the relentless pressure of political engagements, the endless travelling, Arafat never read what I'd written. At last, to escape my relentless nagging, he suggested I show it to a member of the PLO's Executive Committee, a man called Sorani.

When he'd been through what I'd written, Sorani nearly had a heart-attack. 'This is too dangerous for me to respond to straight away,' he stalled. 'Let me study it overnight.' Next morning, he came back to me. 'My son,' he said, 'this document is very sensitive. Very sensitive. You know what it means?'

'Of course,' I replied. 'I wrote it.'

'If you understand what it means, go ahead.'

In the car that was carrying us to meet the Zambian President, Kenneth Kaunda, I told Arafat what Sorani's reaction had been.

'How do you wish to proceed with this?' he asked.

'I think we should publish the document,' I replied, 'but under your name.'

'Yes,' he replied, 'let us publish this. But not under my name, Bassam,' and his eyes twinkled at me. 'Under your name.'

'But you haven't read it . . .' I began.

He cut me off. 'No matter. Publish it.'

I tried the *Washington Post* first, because I knew Jonathan Randall, the paper's Middle East correspondent, very well. 'I would like the article to coincide with the Reagan–Gorbachev Moscow summit on 29 May,' I told him. I knew the superpower leaders would be discussing Palestine at that meeting; that was the day I wanted my ideas to be in the market-place.

Randall was very encouraging. 'Send it to Mr Rosenfeld [the editor],' he said. 'I'm sure you'll get what you want.'

But I didn't: the *Post* spiked my article. The summit ended with it unpublished.

Still, there was always the big one: the Arab summit, which was scheduled for Algiers in June. Why not try to publish then? I compiled a brochure which had a few articles about the peace process in it, then my own bombshell. I called it, 'Prospects for Peace in the Middle East: the Two-State Solution'. That was dull enough to conceal the explosive material inside. Whether it would save me from the PLO gallows was another matter. I handed out copies to the hundreds of journalists and delegates at the summit during the opening session on 5 June.

That evening, at dinner, Yusuf Ibrahim of the *New York Times* sidled up to me. 'Bassam,' he said, 'that article of yours; I've just read it: it's dynamite. Incredible. But I can't touch it. It would burn my fingers!'

'That's up to you,' I replied.

Next day, though, Geraldine Brook, of the *Wall Street*

Journal, published excerpts on the newspaper's front page. Tony Lewis of the *New York Times* and James Dorsey of the *Washington Times* immediately asked for copies, publishing the text in full. The Arab newspapers all published it; and then the roof fell in on me.

Uzi Mahnaimi

I met Bassam a second time in London in 1988, in his St John's Wood flat. Peter David, business editor of *The Economist*, agreed to join us. With him there, I could still claim I'd been attending a press conference if the Israeli authorities got wind of my illegal meeting.

At this meeting, Bassam told me about his peace plan, and I realised at once it was a news story we had to cover. To my surprise, the newspaper's editor agreed. The plan, which became known as the 'Abu-Sharif Document', was in every respect radical. It caused a sensation at the Arab summit; it also lit a touch-paper in the White House. In Israel there was a huge reaction: here, for the first time, was a PLO man, Arafat's mouthpiece, saying that the PLO would be willing to recognise the State of Israel. The general reaction there was one of suspicion and disbelief: exactly the same reactions that were to come from the Arab camp.

It was the Oslo Agreement, almost word-for-word, five years before the event.

Bassam Abu-Sharif

I knew the document would stir up a lot of trouble – it was meant to. I just hadn't expected so much of it to come my way. When they'd stopped boggling at my peace agenda, the

255

PLO Central Council called a special meeting in Baghdad. There was a huge row.

The delegates were furious with me. The ten points I'd put forward, they ranted, were a traitor's charter. Arafat tried his best, but there wasn't much he could do to calm them down. How did I dare publish this abomination? I was a turncoat, a Quisling, a compromiser and an Israeli stooge. Everybody wanted my head, they wanted to peel my skin. They formed an 'interrogation committee', a sort of Star Chamber, to force me to give a full account of my actions. This kangaroo court was supposed to interrogate me on why I'd published the document without prior PLO authority. I dealt with this interrogation committee by ignoring it.

Although most of the PLO bureaucracy issued statements condemning me, many leading Palestinian figures *inside* the occupied territories came out publicly in support of the proposals. It was this support that probably saved me. For the dinosaurs of the PLO, what I'd published was an indefensible capitulation to Israel. For those actually suffering under Israeli rule, it was exactly what they had been asking the PLO to produce for years: a logical, pragmatic, political programme that responded to the needs of the people on the ground, that could carry the intifada forward to concrete success.

All the PLO men who attacked me wanted to know if Arafat was behind what I'd written, or whether I'd been acting alone.

I, too, wanted to know the answer to this question.

CHAPTER
TWENTY-SIX

Bassam Abu-Sharif

L ate in November 1988 the PLO and Israel started making covert, indirect contact. Direct negotiations were still out of the question: neither Arafat nor the Israeli leadership wanted to be seen giving ground. But a meeting between an American Jewish group led by Rita Hauser, a New York lawyer and peace activist, and Khaled al-Hassan, Chairman of the PNC's Foreign Relations Committee, in Stockholm, was to have historic importance.

Hauser had written to me suggesting we meet after reading my document. I'd passed the message on, and Khaled al-Hassan, who was really a kind of PLO foreign minister, agreed to meet Hauser in Stockholm to test the water.

Sten Andersson, the Swedish Minister of Foreign Affairs, had very good contacts with the American State Department, and in particular with George Shultz. Arafat and I also knew Andersson well. At the same time Rita Hauser, as a member of the US Council of Foreign Relations, had good links to Shultz, and well-developed links with the Israelis. It was a complicated circle, but it was complete. There was the possibility of opening the one thing we all needed: a secret, deniable channel between Israel, the PLO and the United States that could succeed where the public talks in Washington were failing.

After some preliminary fencing, this initial meeting came up with a proposal for peace. Yes, the PLO would agree to recognise Israel and its right to exist, and forswear terrorism, in return for a two-state solution to the conflict. Officials of the PLO and an influential Jewish group were talking. The ice was breaking.

Khaled al-Hassan came back to Tunis with the text of the tentative proposal. Although Arafat, when he read it, wanted to make one or two small amendments, he approved the text in general. It was in line with the PNC's policy decisions of 15 November. Sten Andersson had left the door open – and the facilities available – for further talks between ourselves and the Hauser group. We decided on a second meeting; only this time, Arafat would be with us.

I came to a very cold, snowy Stockholm with the PLO leader on 6 December. Several helicopters whisked us off the tarmac to the Haga Palace in a suburb of the city.

After lunch, we got down to business. Several hours of hard talking later, it was agreed that a member of the American Jewish team and I would formulate a final, developed statement of the initial peace proposal. What most of us didn't know was that while I was doing this, Sten Andersson was in direct contact with George Shultz at the State Department in Washington. Shultz sent a secret letter by courier saying that if the PLO were ready to publish the proposal I was even then struggling to draw up, the United States government would recognise the PLO.

When we saw the letter, Chairman Arafat and I were shocked; here was the same Shultz, who had so recently branded Arafat 'an accessory to terrorism', welcoming us into the official fold. There were certain stipulations: as ever, the Americans wanted the PLO to renounce terrorism clearly and unequivocally, and recognise the right of Israel to exist behind safe and secure boundaries. But in return, Shultz agreed that the Palestinian people should be granted their full political rights.

After we'd talked the whole thing over, Arafat told Andersson he agreed to Shultz's proposal, but that he wanted to make a few small amendments. The main one was a clause stating that the PLO Executive Committee would act as the official government of Palestine until such a government was established. And Arafat also wanted all states in the region to enjoy safe and secure boundaries, not only Israel; finally, he wanted a guaranteed right of the Palestinian people to self-determination. To the astonishment of delegates from all sides, the US government accepted these changes.

With this, we all became very excited. It must mean that the US government really was going to recognise the PLO at last. There was the prospect of a new era in which the PLO would play its full part, for the first time, as an equal partner in the region. It was exactly the conclusion I'd been working for.

Arafat stayed up all that night, ringing all round the world, canvassing opinion about what he was doing from other members of the PLO Executive.

The Swedes wanted Arafat to announce this incredible breakthrough at a press conference in Stockholm the following day. This would be followed two or three hours later by a reply from Shultz, announcing formal US recognition of the PLO and the beginning of an official US–PLO dialogue. Arafat, however, wanted to announce the breakthrough to the UN General Assembly.

We flew back to Tunis, where Arafat called an urgent meeting of the PLO Executive Committee, which rubber-stamped the Stockholm deal. I then flew to London with the other members of a small specialist committee, to work on the exact wording of Arafat's Geneva speech. I tried to word it so as to be acceptable to the radical elements of both the Jewish and Palestinian sides – a task I found almost impossible.

When I arrived in Geneva on 12 December, I found Arafat

besieged by hundreds of journalists who had got wind of the impending breakthrough. They were feverish with the special excitement only journalists show when they're on to a really hot news story.

The next day, Arafat stood up and gave his speech. He announced our new peace initiative, and stated publicly the three points the US government had wanted. But this was not the speech I had written: the three major points were carefully buried in widely-spaced chapters of the speech. Arafat wanted to say the words, right enough, but it was hell for him actually doing it. He had been trying to spare himself pain. This lack of clarity caused a big problem. Shultz responded by saying that Arafat had not done what was agreed. Arafat was very angry. He felt he'd done his bit, fair and square, and now the Americans were reneging. Arafat called in Sten Andersson, told him the US was in breach of the agreement, and threatened to resign his post as PLO leader and renounce the peace process unless matters were immediately resolved.

In the Palestinian camp, we were convinced that he had met the US conditions. The form of words had been woolly, but we had heard him say them. Nothing we could do or say, though, would budge the State Department lawyers: we had failed the test.

But there were those of us who did not want to give up. Why not have another stab at it, while the chance was still there? It would probably be the last chance. There followed a night and day of the most intense and concentrated electronic communications between our several parts of the globe.

In my own little hotel room I had two high-ranking officials of the Swedish Ministry of Foreign Affairs – and about half the PLO. We were in direct contact with two senior officials at the State Department. The portable fax machines the Swedes had brought with them were soon glowing red-hot from the sheer volume of words passing through their innards. What exactly was it the Americans objected to? I asked. Arafat had expressed all the necessary points.

I was far from being the only person working to resolve the problem: Arafat's suite, too, was packed out with PLO men and Arab diplomats, not to mention a small constellation of senior Palestinian businessmen. President Mubarak of Egypt and King Hussein of Jordan were on open telephone lines with the Chairman, along with other Arab leaders.

I kept on insisting to the Americans that their conditions had indeed been met, and in full. 'In that case,' they shot back, 'Arafat won't mind repeating clearly tomorrow the points we asked him to make.' The faxes whizzed back and forth. At last we found a form of words that satisfied the Americans. But would Arafat stand and deliver?

Furious still, Arafat went over to the nearby Palais des Nations at about 8.30 on the evening of 14 December. Stepping up into the glare of the television lights, slowly, resentfully and with much encouragement, he repeated what he had said in his speech – only this time the message was clear: the PLO renounced all forms of terrorism, recognised the right of Israel to live behind safe and secure boundaries, and accepted the right of the Palestinian people to self-determination. Now would the Americans be happy?

As if to spike things even at this final second, the US TV networks covering the event were garbling what Arafat had just said. Keeping half an eye on the television in my room, I noticed several serious mistakes in their coverage. They weren't helped by Arafat's uneven English pronunciation. At one point he announced that he had just agreed to give up tourism! 'Thank God for that,' I thought. 'No more airline food.'

I was still in my room, along with a gaggle of PLO Executive Committee members. Gloom and pessimism hung heavy among the cigarette smoke. Given their reaction to Arafat's first speech, no one expected the US negotiators to respond positively. We were all very hang-dog, very sad: so much effort, so little reward. Then the phone rang. I rushed to pick it up. 'I have a call for Mr Abu-Sharif from Washington,' said a voice.

'Yes,' I replied. 'I am Abu-Sharif.' My heart came winging

back up from my boots. It was an American friend of mine, a bigwig in the US State Department.

'Bassam,' he told me gleefully, 'in half an hour Shultz will be on TV, recognising the PLO officially and declaring the start of the official peace dialogue.'

'Are you sure?' I asked him, wanting to believe.

'Yes,' he replied. 'Trust me.'

Arafat was still not back from the conference hall. I turned to the room: 'Let's put the TV on,' I suggested.

'Why?' asked someone.

'Because, in half an hour, George Shultz will be on TV recognising the PLO!' I exclaimed.

'You're dreaming, Bassam,' teased my colleague. 'Forget about it, it's over.'

'No, I'm not dreaming,' I insisted. 'Shultz will be on television soon. Let's get some drinks together to celebrate.'

'We'll have a drink,' he said morosely, 'but we won't be celebrating any marvellous breakthroughs.' We poured ourselves generous measures. Half an hour later, Shultz came on to announce that the US recognised, and would engage in formal talks with, the PLO.

I had to keep pinching myself to make sure it was really happening.

CHAPTER
TWENTY-SEVEN

Uzi Mahnaimi

Arafat the peacemaker, Arafat the winner of the Nobel Peace Prize? Well, Arafat had been dragged to the peace table by the force of world events and a certain aide of his called Bassam Abu-Sharif. But I know Arafat has the blood of one innocent man, at least, on his hands.

While I was living in London in 1987, working for my old newspaper, *Al-Hamishmar*, I developed my own little routine. Every day I drove my daughters Maya and Tamar from our flat in Exhibition Road, just off Hyde Park, to their school in Sloane Avenue. After dropping them off, I was in the habit of crossing back over the Brompton Road for breakfast in a little French brasserie nearby.

One morning, sitting reading through my small pile of daily newspapers, I noticed a stranger at the table next to mine. I was used to being the only person in this café who read three languages; with this guy, I had serious competition. He was reading through a stack of journals, in English, French – and Arabic. Immediately I wanted to know: who was he?

I started talking to him. He told me his name was Naji al–Ali. He worked as a cartoonist for the Kuwaiti newspaper *Al–Qabas*. His office was just across the road from where we were sitting, in a sleepy little corner of London known as Ives Street. *Al–Qabas* was one of the newspapers I had in front of me at that moment; it had just about the biggest circulation in the Arab world. I realised I knew its cartoons – this man's cartoons – very well. They were very distinctive, very political, and very cutting. They'd given me more than one belly-laugh over the years. I was very glad to meet the person who drew them.

After that we met most days, exchanging a little light gossip about the Middle East. A Palestinian himself, with all kinds of inside contacts, he was a mine of information about the PLO. He was talkative, friendly, and as any cartoonist must, he had a great sense of humour. I liked the man. His cartoons were very influential in the Middle East, and I could see why.

Two or three months after I first met Naji al–Ali, at about 3.30 on the afternoon of 22 July, I drove across town as usual to pick my daughters up from school. But turning into Sloane Avenue, I ran into a solid wall of police vehicles; wailing sirens announced the arrival of even more. There were policemen everywhere, swarming all around the entrance to Ives Street, which was sealed off with police tape. I didn't stop to find out what had happened, but I feared the worst.

Not long after I got home, the London *Evening Standard* dropped on the doormat. A banner headline across its front page said that the well-known Palestinian cartoonist Naji al-Ali, the man I had been drinking coffee with that morning, had been shot in the face.

The newspaper report was sketchy. It said that a swarthy-looking man had been seen running up to Naji al–Ali. The unknown assailant had pulled a pistol from his pocket, fired once, and run away. The attack had taken place just outside the offices of *Al–Qabas*. The bullet had gone in through the cartoonist's cheek, and lodged in his brain. He was not dead, but he was on the critical list in intensive care.

Two weeks after he had been shot, Naji al–Ali died in hospital.

It was not such a very rare occurrence for an Arab to be shot down on the streets of London, but why, I wondered, had anybody wanted to kill this man? As far as I'd been able to tell, he was a harmless cartoonist. It made no sense. In fact the more I thought about it, the less sense it made.

I started making a few gentle enquiries among my intelligence friends, both in London and back in Israel. What I found out shocked even me: this had been no random killing or business grudge: my contacts said Yasser Arafat had ordered the murder.

I knew from reading *Al–Qabas* that Naji al–Ali had attacked Arafat regularly in his cartoons. He'd objected to Arafat's dictatorial methods, his corruption, and so on. Arafat ran the PLO like a medieval kingdom. The drawings were in the great tradition of the political lampoon, satirising the PLO leader's dafter deeds and words. They were very biting, very effective. A good political cartoon can be much more devastating for a politician than an article, but it is still never anything more than an amusing sketch. Then I remembered that one of the cartoons about Arafat, earlier that year, had been more personal in nature.

In those days Arafat had a lover, an Egyptian journalist called Rashida Mahran. Naji al–Ali discovered this secret. Not only did his strip make public this supposedly secret liaison, it mocked Arafat for helping his girlfriend with her career.

To Naji al–Ali, poking fun at the high and mighty was his job, but Yasser Arafat had other ideas. For him, it was one attack too many. He thought Naji al–Ali had humiliated his girlfriend, and made a laughing-stock of him. He decided to have the last laugh. He instructed his Force 17 network in London to kill the cartoonist. How do I know this? Because the London Mossad station was in on the killing up to their unwise necks.

'Force 17' was Fatah's covert élite strike force. It was named after the telephone extension in Arafat's Beirut headquarters which he rang when he wanted his henchmen. Its main task was to hit Israeli targets; it had been responsible for carrying out many atrocities in Israel, mostly against civilians. But its other function was to do Arafat's dirty work, in secret, leaving his own hands apparently clean.

Shortly after the attack on Naji al–Ali, a Mossad agent named Ismail Sowan met his controllers in Tel Aviv's Sheraton Hotel. Sowan was a Palestinian, born in Jerusalem, who had been living in Britain for some years. He was in Israel to show his new English wife, Carmel Greensmith, the city of his birth. Mossad had asked Sowan to penetrate the Force 17 network in London. To Mossad's great delight, their plant succeeded not only in penetrating Force 17, but he became a friend of the organisation's London commander, a man who used the name 'Abu Mustafa'. In Sowan, Mossad had a wonderful double-agent. Mossad knew exactly what the Force 17 chief in London was planning to do almost before he'd planned it himself.

During the Tel Aviv meeting with his Mossad control, Sowan told them that just before he'd left London for Israel, a Force 17 man lugging two heavy suitcases had knocked on his front door. 'He said that Force 17 urgently needed to dump the suitcases somewhere,' explained Sowan. 'He asked me to look after them for a while. When I wanted to know what was in the bags, he just smiled, and told me not to worry. "He who asks no questions is told no lies", was all he would say. When he'd gone, I looked inside the bags. They were full of arms and explosives: enough Semtex to blow up the Tower of London, AK–47s, pistols, detonators, the works. And Carmel – my wife – knows this stuff is in the house. She says if I don't get rid of it, she's leaving me. And we just got married. What the hell can I do? You've got to help me.'

The two Mossad men held a brief discussion in Hebrew. 'Don't worry, Ismail,' they told him. 'Just sit tight when you get back to London. A man from the Israeli embassy will come round and take care of the problem. He'll introduce himself to you as "David".' Much relieved, Sowan caught the plane back to England.

But when he arrived at Heathrow airport, armed Special Branch officers were lying in wait. They handcuffed him, hustled him into custody and charged him with the murder of Naji al–Ali. When the policemen asked if he had anything to say, Sowan protested loudly that he was a Mossad agent, and that far from killing the cartoonist himself, he had tried to prevent the murder by warning Mossad about it well in advance. When their Palestinian captive shouted that he was working for Mossad, his interrogators laughed out loud.

The day after they'd arrested Sowan, Scotland Yard made a triumphant announcement to the world's press: it had solved the murder of Naji al–Ali. The British police lost no time in exposing the whole network, displaying publicly one of the largest hauls of arms and explosives ever found in London: the contents of the suitcases in Sowan's and Carmel Greensmith's flat.

For a few days, I thought like many others that Scotland Yard had done another piece of the brilliant detective work for which it was famous. Then I heard from a friend that all was very far from what it seemed. The British police, my friend told me, in fact knew almost nothing about the murder of Naji al–Ali, not even the true identity of his killer. They had the wrong man behind bars. It was Mossad's London station, continued my friend, that had alerted the British to the arrival of the 'guilty' man, Ismail Sowan, on a flight from Tel Aviv. But my contact wouldn't tell me anything more. By now, though, I had to know the truth of what had happened. 'There's no logic to this pattern of events,' I thought. I smelled a very big Israeli rat.

A few days later I heard from another contact that a second Palestinian, a man called Bashar Samara, had been arrested at Dover immigration as he tried to enter Britain from France. Like Ismail Sowan, Bashar Samara was on the list of Force 17 members wanted for the killing of Naji al–Ali: the list that Mossad had so helpfully passed to the British authorities. In a carbon-copy of the Sowan arrest, armed Special Branch officers grabbed this new suspect and took him away for questioning.

Under interrogation, Samara kept asking the police why he was being held. 'I told my Mossad controllers weeks ago that Force 17 was going to kill Naji al-Ali,' he protested. 'How can I be to blame if the Israelis allowed the killing to go ahead? I was working for Mossad – that is why I was in Force 17. I'm a Mossad agent, the agent of a government friendly to yours, not a killer. Why are you holding me for something I tried to prevent happening?'

Now the British had a second man in custody claiming to be a Mossad agent. Like their first 'killer', Samara seemed to know a great deal about the workings of the Israeli intelligence agency. The two stories checked out in every detail against one another. Gradually the British, in their turn, began to realise there was something very fishy going on. One side or the other was engaged in a very elaborate deception, and they didn't much like being on the end of it.

Determined to get to the bottom of the mystery, the Special Branch interrogators went back to Samara in his isolation cell and had another go at him: 'You say you told Mossad everything. You say you told them in advance that Naji al-Ali was going to be killed. Who exactly did you tell?'

'I told Albert, in the Israeli Embassy,' replied the bewildered Palestinian. 'I always worked directly with him.'

'Right, then,' said the police. 'Let's go and see if we can find this "Albert", shall we?'

For the next few days, an innocent-looking delivery van was parked near the Israeli embassy in Kensington. Inside, always in a position where he could see who came and went, were Bashar Samara, and his Special Branch minders. Finally, late one afternoon, Samara let out a stifled yell of triumph. 'It's him!' he said, pointing excitedly through the one-way glass in the van's rear windows. 'There he is! It's Albert!'

One of the British surveillance team recognised 'Albert' immediately. Albert was officially a face on the Israeli diplomatic

268

list, but the watcher knew he was in fact the London Mossad controller.

Now the British had the last piece of a bizarre jigsaw in their hands, they had only to compose the whole picture. Within a matter of hours, they had worked it all out. What they discovered shocked them to the core. The Israelis had practised a complicated deceit on them. The two Palestinians they had in custody had been telling the truth, the whole truth, and nothing but the truth. They really were Mossad agents; they'd both penetrated the Force 17 network in London; and both had given Mossad plenty of prior warning that Force 17 intended killing Naji al-Ali.

Mossad had allowed the killing to go ahead on the streets of the British capital knowing full well what was going to happen, and when. They had lied to their allies, and they were still lying. They had cynically manipulated their British colleagues, taking them for fools in order to embarrass Arafat. Worse still, the real killers had escaped scot-free. On the very same day Naji al-Ali was shot, no fewer than fourteen Force 17 men, including their leader, 'Abu Mustafa', had flown out of Britain. They did not buy return tickets.

The British were furious when the full extent of Mossad's duplicity became clear. Of all the world's intelligence agencies, Mossad was the one with which British intelligence had the closest links. So close were (and are) they that Britain's foreign intelligence service, MI6, has a full-time liaison officer in Tel Aviv. The Israelis, wittily, call him 'Shylock'.

The British decided they would have to teach Mossad a lesson – one it would never forget. This 'Albert' at the Israeli embassy – they'd have his head on a plate, for a start. The security services requested permission from their political masters to arrest 'Albert' and bring him in for questioning about his role in Naji al-Ali's murder. But the Israeli was covered by his diplomatic immunity. The arrest would be unprecedented, even though 'diplomats' are not supposed to be accessories before the fact to murder in cold blood on the streets of

London. The decision was referred up and up through the pyramid of power until it reached the very top of the British government. The British had been insulted.

As Prime Minister, Margaret Thatcher had always taken an interest in the intelligence services, and she was not one to shirk from tough decisions. The answer came back quickly: 'Bring him in.'

At two the next morning, two Range Rovers and a Jaguar slid to a stop in a quiet Hampstead street. It was still no more than a few hours since Samara had positively identified 'Albert' outside the Israeli embassy. The British policemen were certain of getting their man. They'd show at least one of these Mossad bastards the interior of a high-security prison cell. Silently, they got out and surrounded 'Albert's' home. One of them had a freshly signed arrest-warrant.

'Albert's' wife answered the insistent ringing of her doorbell blearily. It was the second time in the space of an hour that her sleep had been very rudely interrupted. The policemen burst past her when she opened the door. In a few seconds they had searched right through the flat: no Albert. They confronted the bemused woman. 'Where is your husband?' they demanded.

'My husband?' she said, astonished that the British police were invading her diplomat husband's home. 'Oh, some people from the embassy came round about half an hour ago. They said he had to go to Israel urgently. He'll be at the airport by now. You might just catch him if you're quick.'

The bird had flown the coop. The Israelis, it seemed, had a mole in the security services, or inside the British government. Someone had tipped them off about the impending arrest. A small party of Mossad men from the Israeli embassy had driven round to 'Albert's' address at breakneck speed, grabbed him, bundled their man into a car, stuffed some money and a passport into his pockets, and driven him directly to Heathrow. There, they'd put him on to the first flight out of the country.

Even that wasn't quite the end of the story. Margaret Thatcher was absolutely enraged. Early that morning, the phone lines from Downing Street started burning. She told Mossad to pack its bags immediately and get out of the United Kingdom for good.

To this day, 'The Institution' has not been allowed back into Britain. That is, not officially . . .

Ismail Sowan, thrown to the wolves by Mossad, was released from Britain's Full Sutton prison in December 1994, having spent seven years in gaol for something he never did. The British authorities deported him to Jordan where, as he pointed out just before his release, he is certain to receive a very warm welcome from the men waiting there to greet him . . .

As for Arafat, using violence to forward the aims of your 'liberation struggle' is one thing. Having a man shot down in cold blood because of personal pique is something else again.

CHAPTER
TWENTY-EIGHT

Bassam Abu-Sharif

Just before the momentous events in Geneva, I happened to be passing through London. I told Jeffrey Archer that Yasser Arafat would be speaking to the United Nations Assembly, and what he was going to say. Like so many other people in the world, not least the US and UK governments, Archer wanted Arafat to make a clear, concise and direct statement of the PLO's readiness to recognise Israel, renounce violence, and show a willingness to talk peace. I was able to give Jeffrey some good news. Arafat would be making such a statement in Geneva on 13 December.

Excited by this information, Archer at once picked up the telephone and called Mrs Thatcher. She, too, was very interested. She asked whether it might be possible for her to have a look at Arafat's text, before he read it out. 'Of course,' I replied. 'That will not be a problem.' But I spoke too soon. The next day I went back to Tunis and told Arafat that Mrs Thatcher had asked for a sneak preview of his speech to the UN. He readily agreed, but there was a technical hitch: the people responsible for sending it flew out to Geneva that evening, to make a few last-minute arrangements, and simply forgot about it. No sooner had Arafat made his speech than I had a phone call from Jeffrey Archer. I'd made him look to his political mistress like someone who could promise but not deliver. He was hopping mad, and there wasn't much I could say to placate him.

So much depends upon personalities. When George Bush entered the White House in 1989, he appointed James Baker Secretary of State for Foreign Affairs: an inspired choice.

I began to study Baker, as I had studied all previous US Foreign Secretaries. I always tried to find out everything I could about these key players, from what they liked to eat, their education, family background and formative experiences, to what it meant when they winked in a certain way. Don't just know your enemy – know your friends.

The more I knew, the easier it would be to assess how to approach them. Kissinger, for example, lived and died confrontation, in both his personal and political life. If Kissinger had remained in office a thousand years there would never have been a peace settlement. He saw black, and he saw white, nothing else. Naturally the Arab side was always black. Baker, though, was a man of rare touch and understanding, a man of calibre, the kind it takes to come to grips with the myriad complexities and currents of the Middle East.

Baker was very straight about the basics: he believed genuinely in the 'Land for Peace' initiative, and he was clear about what the word 'Peace' actually meant. Peace meant economic co-operation and development between all sides to make life better for all, and to make the peace agreement durable. Unfortunately, while Baker was in office so were the biggest Israeli hawks: Shamir and Sharon.

Whenever Baker came up with a proposal, the Israeli government would find a way of wriggling out of it. Israeli society being what it is, the bulk of the people always support the decisions of the party in power, no matter how extreme that government is or how muddle-headed its decisions. Not a very good recipe for progress, really.

Still, Baker never gave up. He always tried to reduce a given peace proposal down to its minimal formulation, so as to leave the Israelis with a minimal opportunity of saying no. They rejected everything: no matter what the US came up with, nothing would do.

Eventually, though, Baker prevailed. Shamir agreed to a peace conference in Madrid with the US and the PLO on 30 October 1991. Baker, co-chairing these talks with his Soviet counterpart, was again very practical and pragmatic. He said the first stage would include Israeli–Palestinian negotiations, with the non-PLO negotiators agreed individually by Israel in advance. The second stage would involve direct Israeli–PLO talks. True to form, Shamir did his best to mess up the arrangements by objecting to anyone and everyone in the Palestinian delegation, but in the end the Israelis were brought to the peace table.

No firm agreement was reached at Madrid but the negotiating framework that was agreed was another breakthrough in the long war for peace. Madrid made it almost impossible for either side to turn back. And Madrid helped Israel's Labour Party to scrape a win in the general election later that year – bringing a rational Israeli government to power for the first time in many years.

Uzi Mahnaimi

I'd failed to get to Arafat through Bassam Abu-Sharif. Getting that exclusive interview, though, was my dream, as it was the dream of every interested journalist. I realised the normal channels wouldn't let me reach the PLO leader, but there might just be another route: a man called Jibril Rajoub. Rajoub, nicknamed 'Abu Rami', was a colonel in Force 17, who had spent seventeen years in an Israeli gaol for terrorist murders. He was released in 1985 as part of a joint PLO/Israeli prisoner exchange. I knew this man was very close to Arafat; if I could persuade Rajoub to see me, his master might just agree.

But how to get to Rajoub? I was the last person he would speak to. But then I got a lucky break. I had an Arab friend in Jerusalem, Dr Ahmed Tibi, who was a well-known Palestinian activist. Tibi knew how badly I wanted to talk to Arafat. One day he came to me and said, 'Uzi, I've fixed it for you. You can go to Tunis. Jibril Rajoub will wait for you at the airport.'

No Israeli journalist had ever gone to Tunis before. This was the lion's den, the very heartland of the PLO. If Rajoub wasn't there to meet me at the airport, if he double-crossed me or something went wrong, it meant certain capture for me. The Tunisians would take one look at my Israeli passport and that would be it: straight to the PLO dungeons.

I flew to Paris first. It was October 1991, just a few days before the Madrid summit. For me, if the interview came off, it would be a once-in-a-lifetime journalistic high. If the great arch-demon really did speak to me, I'd put his words straight on to the pages of the newspaper. That should make the Israeli public sit up and take notice . . .

The PLO chief in Paris had been told about my arrival. His job was to make sure I could board the plane to Tunis. If I didn't get his personal sanction for the trip, there was no way any airline would let me on a flight. With an Israeli passport, I couldn't exactly apply for a visa to Tunis. To smooth my path, he got me on to a Tunis Air flight. They let me on the aircraft, but then something extremely worrying occurred to me. I was on an Arab airline: in an emergency, the plane might be forced to land somewhere like Libya, and I'd have a job explaining what I was doing to Colonel Gaddafi's secret police. I felt incredibly conspicuous and Jewish-looking. But everyone around me was chattering in Arabic, they assumed I was an Arab, they spoke to me in Arabic. I played my part, but the Israeli passport in my pocket was burning.

We arrived at Tunis' Carthage airport just as dusk was falling. I got on the shuttle-bus to the terminal. Now was the critical moment: if Rajoub wasn't at the barrier, I was done for. I got off the bus and started walking towards immigration control. I could see no one. Usually immigration queues move with agonising slowness. This queue was moving forward at absolutely terrifying speed.

Then I saw a tall, athletic-looking man with a heavy moustache and piercing eyes approaching the control-point. I knew him at once for a Palestinian: I'd had plenty of practice spotting them. Rajoub was on time, where someone like Bassam Abu-Sharif was never, ever on time. When you are a gunman, as he was, you can't afford to be late. He seemed to recognise me, maybe from PLO photographs. He came straight up and said, 'Hello Uzi, how are you? Give me your passport.' I handed it over with some relief, obscuring the words, 'State of Israel' with my thumb. A contingent of uniformed Tunisian security men escorted us past customs. Outside was Rajoub's huge black Mercedes. 'Abu Rami,' I began [this was Rajoub's nickname], 'could you please take me to the Hilton?' He laughed out loud in his deep, booming voice, 'Uzi, a hotel is much too dangerous for you. I have special instructions from Mr Arafat. We have made special arrangements for you. Come.' I went. But being totally in the hands of this man was terrifying.

When we got in the car, he pulled a Kalashnikov rifle out from under the seat, and laid it across his knees. He swung the car out into the early evening rush-hour without any regard for road conditions, and began driving at an insane speed through the dense traffic, one hand on the gun, one on the wheel. 'Abu Rami,' I asked him, 'what is the gun for?' He looked at me with profound contempt: 'Haven't you heard about Abu Nidal's people? They've just killed two of my good friends.

276

It is very dangerous for us here in Tunis now.' He meant Abu Iyad, Arafat's right-hand man, and Abu Al–Hol, Head of Fatah Security and Operations, who had been shot in their Tunis villas, allegedly by Abu Nidal's men, about ten months previously.

We pulled up at the PLO's official guest-house, a three-storey villa. There were heavily armed PLO guards everywhere. This was really bizarre now. Here I was, an Israeli and an ex-intelligence major, at the heart of the enemy's camp. It was a very, very strange feeling. My intelligence training having taken over temporarily, I couldn't stop myself recording everything: the disposition, armament and numbers of the guards, any weak points in the compound, the layout of the various offices. This complex had been a number one target of ours for years. Now here I was strolling through it.

Inside, Tunisian servants brought us mint tea. 'OK, Uzi,' said Rajoub. 'Now you are here, and here you will stay as our hostage until we can trade you for some of our fighters in your stinking Israeli gaols.' I thought this was a very funny joke. And, of course, he *was* joking. But I had the strongest feeling that if Rajoub had his way, he really would hold me to ransom – at least, the bits of me that were left after interrogation.

The next day, at eleven in the morning, Rajoub came to take me to PLO Headquarters in Yagurata Street. 'Now you will meet Arafat,' he said flatly, as if it were the most natural thing in the world. When we reached the building, the PLO bodyguards became very agitated. They sensed the enemy. On the first floor, as we rounded the staircase, I saw Arafat walking towards me. He was bald – completely bald – the top of his head shining slightly in the light. He was without his trademark olive-green battle-dress and there was no pistol on his hip. I was so surprised at the way he looked that I almost didn't recognise him, but it was definitely Arafat. I greeted him in Arabic. We embraced in the traditional Arab manner, holding arms and touching cheeks on both sides.

'I've heard a lot about you,' he said. 'I read what you write in

277

your newspaper.' He was genial. 'Come this way,' he continued, 'and we will talk.' He led me through into his private office. Here, surrounded by a small army of his bodyguards and acolytes, I recorded my precious interview. To my surprise, when we'd finished talking, he invited me for lunch. 'The other guest will be the Russian *chargé d'affaires* here in Tunis,' he said.

Over lunch, I told Arafat that Ilana, my wife, was from Nahariyah in northern Israel. 'This is a place you like to shell,' I said. 'Ilana's street was hit twice by your Russian-supplied 130mm cannon.' Arafat laughed merrily, his beady eyes twinkling; the Russian diplomat laughed even more loudly. 'Yes,' agreed Arafat, 'and I am only sorry that the Iraqis, or the Russians' – he looked archly at his companion – 'didn't supply the long-range missiles we asked them for. Then we could have hit Haifa!'

'Well, Mr Arafat,' I said, 'your mighty cannon has been captured. It stands now at the entrance to Nahariyah, facing north – towards your positions in southern Lebanon.' Arafat thought this was another very good joke.

The next day Rajoub came to see me again, clutching a beautifully-wrapped little box in his enormous hands. Across his hijacker's face was written a very untypical hesitation. 'This is a present from Chairman Arafat,' he muttered uncertainly. 'It is for your wife.' I looked at him in amazement. Now it was my turn to hesitate. It was one thing to interview Arafat; it was quite another to take presents from him, a man who was after all an implacable enemy of Israel and up to his elbows in Israeli blood. But I took the box, tearing aside the wrapping. Inside, nestling in tissue paper, was a marvellous amber necklace, together with a little note in the PLO Chairman's hand, which read, 'To Ilana, with my sincere apologies . . .' I later discovered from Rajoub that this poetic gesture had cost the Palestinian revolution $800 US.

The next day I was invited to meet Arafat again, over breakfast. At the table were all his operational staff, including the Force 17 commanders. They stared at me, and straight through me. They couldn't believe that a one-time major in Israeli military intelligence could be sitting at breakfast with them, even a major who had hung up his sheriff's star. But since Arafat wanted me there, and probably found it amusing to have me there with them, there was very little they could do about it.

I stared back at my breakfast companions. These were the men who planned and ordered all the attacks on Israel. Turning to Arafat, I asked, 'On the night of 7 June 1982, during the siege of Beirut, I was with a unit under heavy bombardment by your Katyusha rockets. We were at the Khalde junction, right next to Beirut airport. I heard your fighters talking in Arabic no more than ten metres in front of me. We lost some good men that night. Can you tell me who those men were?'

Arafat was spooning honey, his favourite food, on to a freshly-baked roll. He looked like a very large bee. He smiled lazily at me. 'Uzi,' he replied, 'I was the one launching the Katyushas, and this gentleman,' he indicated the grimmest-looking of the thugs across the table from us, 'was the man you could hear talking. You lost a few men. He lost fifty of his fighters to your shells that night.'

Tunis was a personal and professional triumph for me, the peak of my career as a journalist to date. The headline for my article, quoting him, read, 'With me, you will get peace in two weeks.' On the eve of the Madrid summit, the interview was a real coup, the culmination of four years of coverage of the Middle East.

It was also my last story for *Yediouth Ahronot*. Why? Partly because I realised I could probably only go downhill as a journalist from that point; and partly because, in the end, journalism, though it can be a wonderful job, is also, in the end, a rather pathetic occupation. Very few journalists end up old and rich, like their counterparts in the established professions. I didn't want to end up scrabbling at the door of the newsroom for a job in my old age, as I'd seen so many do. On my thirty-ninth birthday I handed my resignation to the editor.

Bassam Abu-Sharif

The Swedish channel was closed to us when Sweden's social democratic government lost the general election in late September 1991. Sten Andersson, sadly, was out of office. The official Arab–Israeli talks, as ever, were fruitless. Then, later on the following year, I had another thought: the Swedish channel had worked really well for a while, so why not try using another Scandinavian country that had the same advantage of complete neutrality: Norway?

Excited by the idea, I telephoned Norway's Foreign Minister Thorvald Stoltenberg, whom I had met several times before. At once he invited me to Oslo. 'Go,' said Arafat when I informed him of the invitation. 'And may God go with you.' It was as easy as that.

I arrived in Oslo on 17 August 1992. The PLO's ambassador to Sweden, Dr Eugene Makhlouf, came with me. We talked long and hard in the Foreign Ministry, both with the Minister and with the State Secretary, Jan Egeland. Stoltenberg had a meeting coming up with Rabin, in Berlin. If he could convince Rabin of the opportunity, we agreed, there was a real chance to open a new channel – Norway – between the PLO and Israel. What could Stoltenberg say to Rabin at this meeting to ensure it did open?

I made a list of possible topics for their discussion. The first was headed: 'Measures for reducing tension.' Underneath I wrote: 'Prisoner releases; halting new settlements; greater freedom for Palestinians in the occupied territories', and so on. There were some things the new Israeli President could do that would mean little to him, but very much to people in the occupied territories: for example, Palestinians were not allowed to plant trees. Why not rescind this kind of petty restriction?

The second major item on my list began: 'Time is short. Labour must not hesitate to use its victory for peace.' We all knew that Rabin would hesitate, because of the right-wing lobby inside his own government. 'There is a contradiction between Rabin and his Foreign Minister, Shimon Peres.' I remarked. 'They are long-time rivals for power. Peres wants to go fast, Rabin is more cautious. Prevail upon Rabin. Tell him he has to deal now, while his party has its tenuous grip on power. Tell him we are with him, in the PLO, and that we are serious. And one other thing – tell him that if he does this, he will go down in history as the man who made the peace.'

My third topic, 'Direct PLO-Israeli negotiations', went on, 'We in the PLO are determined on peace to the extent that we are ready to negotiate directly with the Israelis. We understand the difficulties Prime Minister Rabin has inside Israel; we understand that things must be done gradually; we understand his majority is very slim. But the conditions have never been so favourable. Let us take the prize while it still awaits. Let us begin direct contacts, but in secret.' The Minister was very enthusiastic about this idea. 'I will put this to him,' he promised.

Stoltenberg duly met Rabin, deftly using his personal relationship with the Prime Minister to convince him of the need for speed. Still Rabin hesitated. His majority was very small. Could he survive direct contacts with the PLO? He would have to legalise them first.

'Be patient,' Stoltenberg told me in a telephone call to my office in Tunis directly after this meeting. 'He is not against the idea, but he needs time to think about it.'

As always, I wrote Arafat a full report about what I'd done and said in Norway. I explained about my meeting with Stoltenberg and about his subsequent conversation with Rabin. I concluded by saying that there was a very good chance the new avenue could lead to direct negotiations, in Norway, between ourselves and the Israelis.

I was not part of the PLO delegation when the secret talks began a few months later. For one thing, I was not an official member of the PLO. When it came right down to it, I was nothing more than Arafat's freelance advisor. In the past this had given me freedom of action, now it meant I was excluded from the game. By then, it was a game many other people had taken a hand in, who did much more than I did to make the peace. But at least I had done my bit as one of the initial icebreakers.

Like the Israeli government, the PLO had to be very careful about losing support within its own ranks. None of the PLO's full-time official leadership would accept Bassam Abu-Sharif, a man they had always seen as an upstart and an interloper, leading the Palestinian team. Arafat needed someone who was not only a member of the PLO Executive Committee, but also a member of the Central Committee of Fatah, his political core group. He needed a man who would add weight to his own drive for peace on both these committees.

There weren't many candidates who fitted the bill. Farouk Qaddumi, PLO Minster of Foreign Affaris, who qualified otherwise, was a rejectionist, utterly opposed to any peace talks. So Abu Mazin, a founder member of Fatah with Arafat, was finally chosen. I had done some of the preliminary bulldozer work, clearing rubble and rocks from the path. Now it was time for me to step aside.

Abu Mazin and the other PLO negotiators in Oslo were in direct daily contact with Yasser Arafat in Tunis, but Arafat kept the progress of the meetings to himself. Even I was in the dark about what exactly was happening. All I knew was that it was happening.

The only problem with this was that in my own efforts to keep the peace ball rolling, I was inadvertently, in some of my briefings to the press, commenting on issues being thrashed out at the Oslo table. The Israelis threatened to withdraw from the talks unless I stopped giving away all the details of the secret deals. But I was in the dark about the details!

In May 1993 I gave an interview to the French political daily, *Libération*, in which I talked about 'The Gaza–Jericho solution as a first step towards peace.' This caused the most enormous fuss. The Israelis accused me of deliberately leaking sensitive information. But it was obvious that Gaza–Jericho should be a first step: it was the easiest step for both sides to take. Jericho was the ideal linking point between Gaza and the occupied West Bank: it had the least number of Jewish settlements, the smallest contingent of Israeli soldiers and a relatively small Palestinian population.

Many of those who knew about the Oslo channel were sceptical about the possibility of a breakthrough. I was sure it would come. In the PLO, I was known as 'the eternal optimist'. But it was time. The peace beavers, myself and all the others, had been gnawing away to the point where the log-jam had to give.

As soon as the final draft of the secretly negotiated agreement was reached, Arafat brought it before the PLO Executive Committee for full discussion. The news about it started to leak. Little bushfires of argument sprang up. Once word of what was happening became official, the internal battles raged for days. Many of the Executive Committee opposed the Oslo agreement, root and branch. But, to his eternal credit, Arafat, stretching his political skills to the limit, won a majority in the end.

The long war for peace, it seemed, was over; but very soon we realised we were still only at the beginning.

Uzi Mahnaimi

Bassam asked me recently if I knew why Mossad had tried to kill him all those years ago. I had no idea. I, too, wanted to know who'd given the order. It seemed like a strange decision to have taken, in retrospect.

The head of Mossad between 1968 and 1974, the very worst years of the terror war between Israel and the Palestinians, was a man called General Zvi Zamir. By making a few enquiries, I found out that he was responsible for sending the letter-bomb to Bassam. I rang Zamir and said I wanted to meet him because I was writing this book. To my surprise, he agreed to see me at once. 'I have seen some of your journalism,' he said, 'and your father was a friend of mine. Come.'

We met in his small office in Tel Aviv, in the government-run Israeli Petroleum Institute. Zvi is now the Managing Director of this organisation. He is in his late sixties, not a tall man, with a sharp beak of a nose set in a tough-looking face. Before joining Mossad he was a general in the IDF.

I explained briefly what I was trying to do, and asked him why he had ordered the execution of Bassam Abu-Sharif. 'I don't think Israel can ever admit to engaging in terrorism,' he told me.

The use of this expression brought me up short. 'Did you mean to use the word "terrorism" then?' I asked.

'Yes,' he replied, 'it was terrorism, what we did in those days. I'm not very proud of it, either as a human being or as a Jew. Part of me, even, regrets it. But you must understand that we had no choice back then. We were suffering under a wave of terrorism at the hands of the Palestinians, especially the PFLP. We didn't know what to do about Haddad's new ways of waging the war: bombing, hijacking, all the rest of it. Neither the Americans nor anyone else were helping us to counter this threat. We had to find our own way of dealing with it. So we fought fire with fire.'

'Yes,' I said, 'I understand that. But Bassam was a media spokesman, deputy editor of the PFLP magazine. Why go all out to kill him instead of the man in charge, Wadi Haddad? Is it really true, as I've been told, that you targeted Bassam because he was the easiest to get to?'

'No, no, no, no, no,' retorted Zamir. 'Bassam Abu-Sharif was much more dangerous than you seem to think. He was a fanatic.

He wasn't some kind of meek-minded little press officer. He worked directly with Wadi Haddad. He didn't merely preach terror, he practised it. He was one of the biggest and most dangerous hawks we faced. Bassam Abu-Sharif is not an angel, Uzi, as he is trying to appear in your book. He deserved what he got. It was a tough war, and though we have peace now, I have no reason to go and shake this man's hand.'

Bassam Abu-Sharif

W hen Yasser Arafat shook hands with Prime Minister Rabin on the White House lawn in October 1993, it was the culmination of everything I had worked towards for so many years. Only one thing disappointed me: that I was not there on that piece of finely-mown turf to see it happen. Arafat needed someone in Washington who could make the most of this opportunity to present him as a man of peace. I knew how to do this. I was used to working the US media to our best advantage, I knew how the complex political system in Washington worked. Arafat's appearance at all in Washington was a triumph for him; but much more could have been made of it.

'Land for peace' was a fantastic US formula. But 'peace' should not mean only 'the end of war'. At the same time it must mean the beginning of a search for common interests, the development of joint economic, social and political programmes.

Israel could never fully become a part of the Middle East unless and until it made peace with the Palestinians. Palestine is Israel's bridge into the region. It is through a self-governing Palestinian state, which includes the whole of the West Bank, that Israelis will eventually drive to shop in the Souq al-Hamadiyyeh, the magical ancient central market in Damascus.

CHAPTER
TWENTY-NINE

— ➤ ◄ —

Uzi Mahnaimi

O
n the wall of his office, President Assad of Syria has only one picture. It is a large photograph showing the Horns of Hattin, the site of Salah-al-Din's last big battle against the Christian Crusaders. Saladin's victory here on 4 July 1187 began the final annihilation of the Christians in the Holy Land. It paved the way for the Muslim reconquest of Jerusalem and all Christian-occupied territories.

Assad's attachment to this photograph is significant for Israel. He views modern Israelis in exactly the same way as his predecessors viewed the Crusaders, the Turks, the British and every other occupying force in the history of Palestine – as a very big nuisance, but as a temporary nuisance. What if Assad does make a nice little pact with Israel in return for the Golan Heights? His son, or his grandson's son, will kick the Zionists out.

Assad believes the Arabs only have to wait, to outlast and see the back of the state of Israel. And Arabs excel at waiting.

286

My grandfather Shalom came to Palestine with a dream. To a great extent, that dream has been realised. The Zionists have fought for, and won, their state. But Shalom did not come to Palestine with war in his heart. He wanted to build a normal country, where he could live as a normal person, to build a 'nation among nations', as David Ben–Gurion put it. Instead, we have built ourselves another ghetto. We have lived in the midst of 100 million Arabs, and we have communicated with them principally by means of the bullet and the bomb.

This was not the stuff of the Zionist dream. Shalom had to fight, my father had to fight, I have had to fight – that is all we have known, and it is just about all we do know: how to win wars. The peace, for the new generation of Israelis, may be much harder.

For as long as we were at war, Israelis could draw upon their immense stocks of courage, ability and military strength. But peace gives the Israelis only one choice: they must integrate into the region. Few of them are willing to do so. Most people in Israel know nothing about Arab people, and care less. They have no Arab friends. Their gaze is west, not east: they look to Europe and the United States. They are different by religion, by culture and by nature. They think themselves superior in every way to the Arabs.

Even if Israelis wanted to integrate, the Arab world, over the past few years, has been hit by the hurricane of Islamic fundamentalism. If Jordan, Egypt, Syria, go the way of Iran, Israel will not be allowed to integrate. It will remain a pariah state for the Arabs, a regional ghetto.

Some people think the milk and honey will finally flow for Israel: the vision of my grandfather will be realised, the Promised Land will come, the future will be a rosy love story between the Israelis and the Arabs.

I personally think the chances of Israel surviving very far into the twenty-first century are no better than fifty-fifty.

Bassam Abu-Sharif

The Oslo agreement was an historic step, but it was only the first step, not the last. The challenge for Arafat, the challenge for Palestine, the challenge for Israel, is 'What next?' Building a state from scratch is not the same thing as running a political party in exile. Palestine is not the PLO. Arafat has to adopt new methods for the new job, or perish in the shambles.

What all Palestinians must aim for is to start where others have ended; not end where others have started. If they do not, Palestine will never survive as it is now, sucking on the economic teat of Israel. Fundamentalism feeds on poverty. Palestine must become a modern, high-tech state which delivers a reasonable standard of living to the whole of its citizenry, and fast.

As for Israel, it has built its bridge into the Middle East. It has no option but to cross it. The peace will be secured. It will be hard, it will even be bloody at times, but the region will live in peace. Some Israelis, the Likud and the more extreme settlers, say they cannot do this. No matter. As common interests develop, as the business contacts between Israel and Arab countries expand, an economic community will inevitably flourish, which naturally includes Israel, Palestine, and all the other Arab states as equal – and politically stable – partners.

Those who cling to violence and extremism will become of less and less importance. The peace train is rolling, its tracks are firm, and the advocates of violence sit grimly in the last wagon. Eventually, the faulty coupling will break and they will roll gently backwards into obscurity. That's what I believe.

But then, I always was an optimist.

288

INDEX

289